Anthropology and the Riddle of the Sphinx

Anthropology and the Riddle of the Sphinx seeks to relate the problems of maturation and ageing to the life course as a whole. As it is treated here, the riddle posed by the sphinx asks 'What is it that changes as we age?' and is concerned with the enigmas of this total process. Ultimately, the ways in which we experience these problems stem from our view of ageing and the contradictions of society itself.

The essays in this volume consider aspects of this problem with reference to a variety of cultures. The young, the mature, and the elderly have distinctive identities, but they form a continuum whose profile is culturally constructed.

Anthropology and the Riddle of the Sphinx is intended as a contribution to the growing literature on ageing, deliberately broadening the topic in the search for a wider understanding. This volume aims to stimulate interest in neglected aspects of the ageing process within social anthropology and to present an anthropological point of view to others who have an interest in problems associated with the life course. It will be of particular value to the students of social anthropology and medical sociology.

ASA Monographs 28

Anthropology and the Riddle of the Sphinx
Paradoxes of change in the life course

Edited by Paul Spencer

London and New York

First published 1990
by Routledge
11 New Fetter Lane, London EC4P 4EE

Simultaneously published in the USA and Canada
by Routledge
a division of Routledge, Chapman and Hall, Inc.
29 West 35th Street, New York, NY 10001

Cover illustration: My wife and my mother-in-law by W.E. Hill, 1915.

Typeset by NWL Editorial Services, Somerset

Printed and bound in Great Britain by
Mackays of Chatham PLC, Chatham, Kent

British Library Cataloguing in Publication Data
Anthropology and the riddle of the Sphinx: paradoxes of change in the
  life course – (ASA monograph; 28)

  1. Adults. Ageing. Social aspects
  I. Spencer, Paul, *1932–*   II. Series
  305.2'6

Library of Congress Cataloging in Publication Data
Anthropology and the riddle of the Sphinx: paradoxes of change in the life
  course / edited by Paul Spencer
    p.   cm. – (ASA monographs; 28)
  Includes bibliographical references.
  1. Ethnology–Congresses. 2. Aging–Congresses.
  3. Adolescence–Congresses. I. Spencer, Paul, 1932– . II Series:
  A.S.A. monographs; 28.
  GN485.A57 1990   89–70234
  305.8–dc20   CIP

ISBN 0–415–04089–2

To the memory of John Blacking

Contents

Contents

Contributors

Ray Abrahams is University Lecturer and Fellow of Churchill College, Cambridge.

John Blacking was Professor of Social Anthropology, The Queen's University of Belfast.

Elisabeth Croll is Research Fellow in Chinese Sociology and Anthropology, School of Oriental and African Studies, University of London.

Tamara Dragadze is Research Fellow for the project on rural families under Gorbachev: comparative study in Georgia and Azerbaijan, School of Oriental and African Studies, University of London.

Iain Edgar is Senior Lecturer in Social Work Studies, Newcastle upon Tyne Polytechnic.

Haim Hazan is Associate Professor of Social Anthropology, Tel Aviv University.

Ladislav Holy is Professor of Social Anthropology, University of St Andrews.

Richard Jenkins is Senior Lecturer in Sociology, University College, Swansea.

Leonard Mars is Lecturer in Social Anthropology, University College, Swansea.

Iona Mayer is a member of the Centre for Cross Cultural Research on Women, Queen Elizabeth House, Oxford.

Philip Mayer is Emeritus Professor of Anthropology, University of Durham.

Judith Okely is Lecturer in Social Anthropology, University of Essex.

Paul Spencer is Reader in African Anthropology, School of Oriental and African Studies, University of London.

Stuart Thompson is Lecturer in Chinese Anthropology, School of Oriental and African Studies, University of London.

Paul Yates is Lecturer in Education, University of Sussex.

Preface

The topic selected for the 1988 Conference of the Association of Social Anthropologists was 'The Social Construction of Youth, Maturation and Ageing'. This title was deliberately broad, seeking to view the subject of ageing in its widest sense, fostering a holistic approach to the life course. It was a topic that revealed its own array of anomalies to be teased out: the problems of youth, the elusive concept of adulthood, the dilemmas of marginality in old age, the existential experience of ageing, the entanglement of ageing with history, and above all the cultural and gender constructions that shape the life course. A feature that added to the general rapport within the discussions was that the whole range of the topic is frequently implicit in social anthropology. But more than this, it can be argued that much of the groundwork in the sociology of ageing that has developed over the past twenty years or so in America has made liberal use of anthropological sources, and it has become a recurrent topic in American anthropology for nearly a decade. One single conference could only touch on a few selected aspects of the vast and growing field; but at least it could seek to establish an interest among social anthropologists in Britain.

The outcome is this volume, which is intended as a step towards entering the wider discourse. The introductory chapter surveys the literature and identifies a series of analytical themes that broadly progress from youth to old age. It is this logical progression that has been used first to introduce and then subsequently to order the sequence of chapters in the body of the volume. A fundamental aspect of the life course has been omitted quite deliberately from this work. This is socialisation, which is a major speciality that is too extensive to consider here. The topic has, however, provided the theme of an earlier volume of this series (ASA 8, Mayer, P., 1970, *Socialisation: the approach from social anthropology*, London: Tavistock), and the present work should be regarded as a successor to this. It continues the line of discussion. By chance rather than design, there is no chapter here on age organisation, a topic often cited without discussion in the literature elsewhere. The introductory chapter therefore also takes this opportunity to explore the relevance of studies of age-sets and age systems to the various themes.

In preparing this volume for publication, my greatest debt, of course, is to the other contributors whose intellectual stimulus and patient collaboration have made its production possible. In addition, I wish to express our appreciation to all participants who enlivened the conference discussions, with special thanks to those whose papers added significantly to the conference but had to be omitted under the pressure of publication due to lack of space: Thomas Crump, Jennifer Hockey, Allison James, Dorothy Jerrome, Stella Mascarenhas-Keyes and Margaret Peil. Others whose comments have been further considered by the authors include Anne Akeroyd, Shirley Ardener, Robert Barnes, Fiona Bowie, Helen Callaway, Angela Cheater, Jean La Fontaine, Sir Raymond Firth, Joy Hendry, Roland Littlewood, Peter Lloyd, Rosalind Shaw, Marilyn Strathern, Roy Willis and the publisher's nameless reader.

Our thanks are also due to the School of Oriental and African Studies, London, as our hosts for the conference, to Anne Aggersburg as conference secretary, and to Stuart Thompson for acting as its organiser and incidentally for inspiring the title to this volume. In the course of preparing this work in its present form, I wish to express my gratitude to Sharon Lewis and Gertrude Booty for their assistance, and to Heather Gibson of Routledge for her help in steering the volume towards publication.

John Blacking's presentation was one of the conference highlights, and it was with great sadness that we have since learned of his death. This book is dedicated to his memory by all the other contributors with admiration and affection, or as he would have expressed it, to his *mudzimu*.

Paul Spencer
SOAS
February 1990

Chapter one

The riddled course: theories of age and its transformations

Paul Spencer

Theories of ageing have a very personal claim on our attention for we are all caught up in this process and affected by the upward trend of life expectancy, uncertain where it will lead. In a short space of time, ageing in this sense has become recognised as a widespread problem. But this is a narrow sense. Any anthropological study of the problem has to extend beyond the elderly to their place in a world encompassing people of all ages. The uncertainties facing youth today are not necessarily unrelated. These are the residues of societies governed by older people and of histories generated by older people, and younger people find themselves thrust into this stream of power relations and change. Ultimately, the very concept of old age is only intelligible in relation to youth and the lifelong experience of ageing. The elderly are not merely a phenomenon, but an outcome. They are those that have survived the total process of maturation and ageing, which infuses the meaning of existence.

The current concern with the aged contrasts also with research on the process of ageing in other disciplines, which has tended to focus on the formative stages of development almost to the exclusion of adult and later life. This has been noted in physical anthropology regarding the study of human growth and adaptability (Beall 1984: 85–6), in linguistics regarding the cultivation of basic language skills (Eckert 1984: 225), in ethology regarding aspects of human behaviour (Blurton Jones 1975: 69) and in developmental psychology (Neugarten 1968: 137–8). This extends to psychoanalytic theory, which assumes that in the process of character formation, the growing child has to adjust to the dilemmas of an expanding social universe, and that the earlier resolution of each stage lies embedded in adult personality. Erikson (1950: 247–74) was a clear exception in identifying eight stages of psychological development from birth to old age. Yet even he packed the first six of these into the period before sexual maturity, relegating the remaining years of adulthood to a cursory outline of the last two stages. Generally, the topic of organic growth has an appeal to growing disciplines that have arisen out of a civilisation committed to growth. Social anthropology happens to be an exception. It is weak at this younger, growing end of the age spectrum, sceptical of earlier attempts to apply psychological theories to the culture of personality development, and

1

generally silent on the topic of youth, even more than on women. It is not simply that the bias in social anthropology has been towards males, but it has been towards middle-aged males at that. And unlike the topic of gender, there is no popular reaction to this anomaly. An essential dimension of human existence too often is taken for granted.

As matters stand, the topic of ageing in social anthropology tends to be associated with age organisation as a regional speciality rather than as a relevant topic for general theory. Stratification by age was not even considered in the classification of African political systems by Fortes and Evans-Pritchard (1940: 5), and it has received only cursory mention in more recent general works. Yet an organisation of this sort was a central theme in Plato's *The Republic*, which was possibly the earliest attempt at classifying political systems. His treatise begins with Cephalus reminiscing on old age and develops into a discourse on the whole process of maturation and ageing: a contrived discourse perhaps, but clearly sensitive to the dimension of age and ageing in Greek society. It is such a discourse that has been essentially lacking in social anthropology.

This volume is not simply concerned with old people or young, but with ageing as a social process, or to use the preferred phrase, with the 'life course'. In any system of relationships, this process provides a changing and hence ambiguous element that lends itself to various levels of interpretation: this, I suspect, was the essence of the Sphinx's riddle confronting Oedipus; and it is a problem that has relevance for various theories concerning the life course. Some of these theories have been developed, notably over the past decade or so in America, but they also have drawn obliquely on earlier anthropological writings. However unfamiliar some of this recent literature for anthropologists, we are not exactly strangers to the topic. It permeates our writings, often touching on emotive aspects of social life.

This introduction, then, provides an opportunity to relate the other contributions in this volume to a variety of analytical approaches towards resolving the riddle.

Universal attributes of ageing

The physiological manifestation of ageing is too obvious and visible to ignore. It is as basic a fact of social existence as the human body itself and similarly it lends itself to symbolic elaboration, providing a basic metaphor in popular belief. In Malinowski's account of *kula* exchange, for instance, a man's success was associated with his powers of persuasion, which accrued with age. At the same time he had to make himself physically irresistible to his partners, as in love making. The cosmetics of *kula* magic, in fact, seem to have been an attempt to reverse or at least conceal the ravages of middle age. In Trobriand myth, this magic was traced back to the secret power of ancestors to rejuvenate themselves, shedding their wrinkled skins and the infirmities of age, and outshining their younger rivals with an irresistible display. The loss of this magic over time was attributed to the impatience of younger men who tried to wrest power from their senior kin before they had been taught the secrets (Malinowski 1922:308, 322–6, 336). One has here a number of ingredients that are relevant to an anthropology of ageing: the association of vital knowledge with age; the ambivalent rivalry between crafty old men and virile younger men; and a symbolic play on biological ageing and hence on time itself, projected beyond the oldest men to distant ancestors, and capable of being reversed through magic.

The Faustian appeal of this example reflects the universal problem of loss through ageing and one is led to consider briefly the biological basis of this loss, which is a very personal experience for every adult. In the absence of environmental hazards, ageing is a genetically programmed process in which organisms have a natural life span. In a perfect environment, humans have a reasonable chance of survival until their maximum expectation of about ninety years. Yet the human organism reaches its stablest and most integrated state much earlier, from about eighteen to thirty years. After this peak, ageing appears related to the cumulative inability of cells to reproduce themselves, leading to a point where the organism can no longer function. At first, reaction times increase and speed declines, while strength and endurance may still remain. Then from the age of about fifty years, metabolic rates decline, the senses convey less information, and there is a loss of adaptive capacity. In evolutionary terms, there is no evidence of any significant genetic change in these respects since long before the earliest transition towards settled agriculture. On the other hand, the genetic process of ageing has always been overshadowed by physical hazards related in part to the cultural environment. These attack the weakest parts of the body, increasing disabilities and mortality at all ages. In the course of social evolution, it is the hazards that have been dramatically reduced, increasing the chances of survival in normal times. The general shift, therefore, has not just been towards a greater proportion of humans surviving beyond their physical peak, but surviving up to two or even three times the life span up to this peak with increasing survival to old age (Beaubier 1980, Weiss 1981, Beall 1984: 90).

An alternative approach to the biological basis of ageing concerns the most rudimentary forms of social behaviour. With certain reservations, one may consider the pattern of ageing among non-human primates. There are clear differences between primate genera regarding the pattern of male and of matrifocal dominance. In relation to ageing, however, Phyllis Dolhinow (1984) has suggested a common pattern that extends to all non-human primates and may well have applied also to the earliest hominids, providing a natural base from which human society probably developed. This common pattern concerns the sequence of stages of social development specific to each sex. Between genera, the duration of each stage may vary considerably, but not the stages themselves, nor the sequence. For all primates, following the initial

3

phase of infant dependency, juveniles have considerable freedom, cultivating social and physical skills and testing the tolerance of the adult world. During this phase, the sexes diverge. Females show an early interest in caring for infants and become sexually mature, entering the adult world some time before physical maturity. As juveniles, males tend to indulge more in rough play, testing one another and older males. Then males enter a period of prolonged adolescence, too large to play with immatures and too weak to compete with adults. They become peripheral to major group activities, and remain in this limbo until they are physically strong enough to contest with mature males. Then they enter the higher ranks as full adults, or are quite likely to leave their natal group. For all genera, there is no material support from the wider group after infancy, and natural selection takes a heavy toll, with few surviving beyond their physical prime. Females normally continue to breed until overtaken by death; while ageing males tend to slip once again towards the periphery and are severely at risk. Once primates can no longer keep up with the band as it moves around to forage, whether because of ageing or accident, they become easy prey for predators. In this natural milieu and for males especially, physical and social dominance coincide.

Comparing this with an independent view of social development among humans by Nancy Chodorow (1974) suggests a clear parallel. She too portrays girls as absorbed into the role of motherhood from an early age through a continuous involvement in domestic activities and child care. Boys, on the other hand, are seen as restless, assertive and with few responsibilities as they distance themselves from the domestic domain and seek to enter the competitive ranks of their peer group. Becoming a woman is seen as natural and ascribed, whereas becoming a man is an achievement. It is a broad portrayal of human development that is firmly endorsed by other contributors to the same anthropological symposium (Rosaldo 1974: 25–6, Ortner 1974: 81–2).

Adolescence is widely regarded as a transient phase, marginal to the wider society (Lewin 1952: 142–3, Muuss 1970: 502–3). Various chapters of the present volume are concerned with aspects of this transition (Mayer, Edgar, Mars, Yates, Blacking, Jenkins). Relevant to this stage of the argument, Philip and Iona Mayer (Chapter 2) describe the adolescence among Red Xhosa boys in South Africa. Red Xhosa youth organisations are peripheral to the adult community. They are self-governing, and are tolerated only so far as they do not impinge on adult affairs; those who do intrude are beaten. At their gatherings, boys vie among themselves for status with increasing violence as they mature towards their physical prime. Significantly, their initiation is in the hands of senior elders and occurs at the critical period when this violence threatens to get out of hand. From this point, the initiates transfer to the youth organisations of young men and distance themselves from the peripheral irresponsibility of boys, cultivating values that have a central relevance for achieving status as elders. It is a transformation from 'Nature' to 'Culture', perceived by the Red Xhosa as from the 'bush' to the 'homestead', from quasi-animal to

human, as young men on the periphery become fitted to take up adult responsibilities.

Later in life, the notion of those who survive their prime drifting towards
the periphery is a feature of the more marginal areas of human existence. In a
cross-cultural survey, Pamela Amoss and Stevan Harrell (1981: 5–9, 11) noted
that security and status in old age were affected by the balance between the
relative cost of sustaining older people as against the benefit of their contribution to the group's survival. In extreme arctic conditions, where the cost was
high, older dependants were despised and might be abandoned, especially
inactive males. In less extreme conditions they were respected more, but when
food supplies were short and respect for old age was pitted against the survival
and mobility of the group, the elderly were expected to withdraw voluntarily.
Even in less marginal areas, the aged were often neglected and insecure at the
lower end of the scale of subsistence (Simmons 1945: 213, 225–8, Harlam
1964, Ortner 1978: 46–7, Sharp 1981: 106–8, qv. Halperin 1984: 176–7). This
does not at first sight tally with Marshall Sahlins's model of primitive
affluence among foraging nomads (1974: 8, 34–6), yet significantly he too
noted that this affluence was sustained by high mortality rates and selective
infanticide and senilicide, with immobilised families particularly at risk. A
prime example of effortless subsistence in his account were the !Kung San;
and yet George Silberbauer (1981: 288), working among a more remote !Kung
group that were subject to the ravages of epidemic and serious drought, suggested that few reach an age of much more than forty-five. The Northwest
Coast Indians were also cited by Sahlins as an undisputed example of wellbeing, and yet they too faced the seasonal threat of severe starvation and death
(Piddocke 1968: 285–6). Famine and disease have been twin scourges
throughout history, and during these acute episodes those that are beyond
their physical prime are doubly at risk – from the neglect of their group and
the decay of their own bodies.

The model of primate ageing is seen to have an intriguing parallel with
human society, where full adulthood is similarly bounded on its margins by
the anomalies of adolescence and old age, especially among males: those that
have difficulty in entering the arena and those that are edged out. It is close
enough to human experience to project our own concepts of maturation and
ageing in describing it (qv. Lévi-Strauss 1963: 160). It was with a model of this
kind in mind that a Samburu once drew my attention to two herds of gazelle
grazing nearby. One of them, he explained, was the herd of the 'elder' and his
'wives', while the other in which several gazelle frisked with one another, was
the herd of the young 'warriors' (*moran*) who had been excluded from the parent herd. He was, in fact, describing the rudimentary organisation of his own
society, endowing the animals with Samburu statuses. It evokes a scenario
similar to Darwin's evolutionary notion of a distant 'Brute' ancestor, who jeal-
ously horded females away from younger rivals (1871: 590). This was elaborated by Freud (1950: 141), who in his turn used a familiar metaphor – the

5

oedipal socialisation of the child – to hypothesise the transition of humanity from Nature to Culture.

This trespasses onto a mine-field of controversy: the cultural relativity of the Nature-Culture dichotomy; the inappropriateness of primate behaviour for understanding human society; and ultimately the futility of evolutionary speculation. The simplest response is to deny the relevance of biology in any social construction of ageing (qv. La Fontaine 1978: 3). But this is a difficult argument to sustain in an introduction that attempts to present a range of models, and it leaves unanswered some persistent questions that cannot easily be dismissed.

A striking shift in the process of the evolution from primate to human has been the increasing chances of survival into middle age. And this entails a shift from the physical supremacy of young adults – an ability to contest in direct encounters – to the moral supremacy of their elders. Thus Darwin's 'Brute' retained his females and held younger males at bay by brute strength; whereas his human counterpart in societies such as the Samburu is an ageing polygynist, and it is the cast-out younger males that are physically in their prime (qv. the Red Xhosa above). This regime is maintained by the constraints imposed by older men, whose ritualised display of hidden power substitutes for the more open animal display in the primate model. From a state of raw nature, the evolution of society as a moral concept has interacted with the evolution of middle age as a cultural resource in its own right. Correspondingly, the interpretation of old age has shifted from the loss of physical fitness among primates to the loss of mental agility and hence of moral authority in human society. On the one hand, one has rudimentary families and mating habits observed by primatologists, while on the other hand are the institutionalised counterparts of kinship and marriage observed by anthropologists. In evolutionary terms, this transition from Nature to Culture has been attributed to cognitive development that led to the emergence of humans as the dominant expanding species faced with the implicit choice of forming networks of alliances or succumbing to their own internecine destructiveness: marrying out or being killed out (Tylor 1889: 267, Lévi-Strauss 1949: 480–1, Washburn and Lancaster 1968: 297–9, Fox 1972: 300–1). It is a problem that forms the basis of political science, with a stark contrast between short-term physical solutions that would favour some younger men in their prime and long-term diplomatic solutions for young and old alike. Power, in the sense that Weber used the term *Macht*, holds no guarantee of a future. Those past their physical prime in particular have a vested interest in the longer term. In the very long term, paraphrasing Maine, one might argue that the movement from the most rudimentary forms of community life is a shift in emphasis from 'Nature' (or *Macht*) to 'Status', and it is only later that there is a further shift from 'Status' to 'Contract', again with relevance for the balance of power with age.

Notions of fundamental drives that motivate individuals assume the residue of 'Nature' in human behaviour. These range from Malinowski's argument of basic and derived needs, to Leach's assumption that a wish to gain power is a very general motive in human affairs, to models of gaming that underlie transactional analyses. Various approaches to the topic of ageing may broadly be described as transactional to the extent that they are concerned with the inequalities and opportunities associated with age in which calculation and self-interest are fundamental, with younger ambitious men challenging the authority of ageing leaders for control over the central arena. This is a motif that provides a narrative framework even in studies that are primarily concerned with symbolic interaction and systems of belief, as in Turner's Ndembu or Middleton's Lugbara. The rich interplay of cultural factors in such accounts overlies a common theme that has its parallel in the primate model and a basic gut appeal. It is not so much that analysis reduces to a basic contending for power as that this is one compelling construction that can be used among others, interpreting social interaction at a very fundamental level.

Such an approach may be equally apt in the interpretation of age systems. Philip Gulliver's analysis of the Arusha is a prime example (1963: 25–65). This extended beyond the life courses of individuals to the jostling for power between whole age-sets, notably in the public arena of local dispute settlement. Younger men were excluded from this arena as too inexperienced, and older men were edged out of it. Those who dominated the arena were playing both for advantage and for time. Periods of stability, when their authority was unquestioned, overlay mounting ambiguities that led sooner or later to an effective challenge. The collective aim of younger men was to enter the arena and in due course to wrest the initiative from their predecessors in early middle age, retaining it for perhaps fifteen years. Then as they dwindled in number and lost the collective will to stand up to the next age-set of younger men in some crucial debate, they in their turn would find their position of dominance discredited. The dynamics of the Arusha age system are presented in terms of a barely concealed struggle. Young men come, old men go, while the contest for power is an issue that is won by men in their political prime. The moral authority of those in power is shorn of any concern for a just settlement. True justice is subordinated to political expedience. Even collective rituals are treated as public affirmations of shifts in the balance of power between age-sets that have already taken place. It is not, in other words, a study that explores the overlayers of symbolic interaction. Nevertheless, a powerful and richly illustrated argument is built around the natural process of ageing. Following the publication of Gulliver's work, it has never again been possible to regard age systems as comfortably harmonious affairs.

The charisma of ageing and the communitas of the peer group

Weber's distinction between types of authority has a relevance for the types of knowledge and ultimately the power of older people. Where Ronald Cohen (1984: 244) suggests that the wisdom of older people is the accumulation of experience that enables them to solve problems of greater complexity, he is referring to the open system of adult roles and a very practical form of rational knowledge. On the other hand, where Gilbert Lewis (1980: 134–85) shows how ritual knowledge among the Gnau is revised and expanded with experience, he is referring to a more closed system of beliefs. Traditional knowledge especially provides the symbolic idiom in which the authority of older people is couched.

Cross-cultural surveys of homogeneous societies have repeatedly emphasised the relevance of experience and the control of information and resources for accumulating prestige and power among the elderly. Their cultural understanding, social networks and diplomatic skills are community assets that are cultivated over time. They are the repositors of the system of beliefs and symbolic superstructure, maintaining power and dignity by their ability to interpret and give meaning to social existence (Simmons 1945: 131–76, Rosow 1965: 21–3, Maxwell and Silverman 1970: 382–3, Press and McKool 1972: 304–5, Amoss and Harrell 1981: 14–19).

Here, because it is normally less explicit but nevertheless vital, I wish to draw attention to the charismatic aspect of the authority of older people which is embedded in performance. Survival to old age is not in itself sufficient: not all older people are respected, especially once their competence diminishes; and ritual is not always controlled by the oldest. It is not absolute age in itself that is displayed, but the ability to overawe from a position of superior age, using the symbolic idiom to effect, and giving it an immediacy that conveys power. Each ritual event has to be both acted and stage managed, responding to the opportunity. To the extent that it is manipulated to effect, this endows older people as repositors and the very fact of old age with a certain charisma (qv. Weber 1947: 367).

In contrast to the open competition for power among the Arusha outlined in the previous section, the manipulation of knowledge provides an alternative model, where what is concealed may be more important than the knowledge itself. This is no less concerned with political performance but offers a more positive interpretation of ritual action. The power of older people is a control over symbolic beliefs whose ambivalences are those of the very ritual institutions that elevate them. This has been vividly demonstrated for societies whose gerontocratic organisation is based on a hierarchy of secrecy. William Murphy (1980) considers the Kpelle of Liberia in this vein. All ritual knowledge was the possession of one or other of their secret societies, notably the men's Poro and the women's Sande. The content of the secrets was often insignificant compared to the privileges generated by possessing them. Belief in secrets was used by older members, masquerading as spirits to control younger men. Youths first had to submit to an extended initiation school with persistent threats of beating, poisoning or mysterious death if they betrayed the secrets. In learning to honour the code of secrecy, they learned to respect the elders. Higher status within the society entailed further initiations, and these were restricted to those that had mastered the secrets at each level and could afford the fees. The premise of knowledge placed the elders in the central arena and the premise of ignorance placed the youths on the periphery from where they had to buy their way in. However, the overall pattern was not one of elders passing on cultural traditions, but of withholding more than they taught in order to retain control over the young. In the final resort, the content of knowledge was relatively shallow and it was paradoxically the ritual display mounted around secrecy that formed the solid framework of the system.

Again, among the Baktaman of Papua New Guinea, Fredrik Barth (1975) describes a comparable system. Here, access to ritual secrets was through a hierarchy of age grades comprising seven degrees of initiation. The revelation of these secrets was shrouded in misinformation and mistrust. Even the timing and pace of each promotion was a secret and subject to false starts and delays, confusing the initiates and bringing the revealed secrets themselves into doubt. But this uncertainty did not undermine the principle of secret knowledge; and it enhanced rather than detracted from the power of those at the top who ultimately controlled the code of ritual deceit.

Analyses of this kind are relatively rare, but they serve to establish some basic features that apply to male initiation rituals more generally. Jean La Fontaine's recent survey of the topic (1985) provides a useful summary of the anthropological interpretations. A theme that is repeated in the examples she cites is this element of performance that magnifies age differences to a grotesque degree, imposing sharp discontinuities on the continuous process of ageing. Older men parade their power, overawing the initiates with dramatic revelations and threats, confusing them, exposing their childish ignorance, emphasising the termination of their childhood as a prelude to rebirth and renewal. And all this typically at the point when the initiates are entering their physical prime and those responsible for the performance are already in physical decline. A moral universe in which frail elderhood reigns is imposed on the transient physical world, and with it the prospect of an enhanced elderhood for the initiates in the longer term.

The widespread existence of group initiations introduces a further theme: the bond of fellowship among peers. This is the very antithesis of the inequality in age and authority that sets initiates apart from their seniors. While there is an element of isolated uniqueness in the mental ordeal for each initiate, they share in the prospect and retrospect as a group, lending one another moral support and emerging to share the credit. The notion of *communitas* is an especially apt expression for the shared experience of initiation. The participants are exposed to the mysteries that underlie their existence, or however the forces of gerontocratic repression are expressed. They are drawn together as mere mortals, with a prevailing emphasis on total equality, sharing everything as a group, reduced to a uniform condition that transcends all distinctions of rank, kinship and wealth.

There is, however, a shift from Victor Turner's notion of communitas

9

(1969: 119–21) which entailed the opposition between the structured inequalities that prevail in daily existence and the antistructure of rituals of transition. On the occasion of initiation – and indeed in Turner's own description for the Ndembu (1967: 151–279) – the structure of age inequality prevails and is imposed quite deliberately on the initiates. The boundary is not so much between profane authority and sacred communitas extending to humanity at large, as between elders manipulating the occasion and youths experiencing the spirit of communitas among themselves. The close fellowship of the peer group would perhaps be a less ambiguous description of this experience, but the point to stress is that, within the peer group, the sense of communitas prevails and persists even into old age, as Judith Okely and Haim Hazan indicate in their contributions to this volume.

In this volume, Iain Edgar's account of a community for highly disturbed adolescents (Chapter 3) draws some striking parallels with Turner's analysis of initiation and gives it an unexpected relevance. The process of therapy leading to rehabilitation is shown to follow the stages of a rite of transition. The residents pass through a liminal period of their lives in a setting that is itself liminal. The whole life of the community centres on creating the ethos of democratic care and shared responsibility: a communitas. It aims to stimulate a nurturing environment, counteracting earlier deprivation in their childhood and clearing the way towards adulthood (qv. Erikson 1950: 269–73). Freudian psychology underpins the therapy. In this study, however, this interpretive theory is not presented as an insight into personality development, but as an explicit premise – a cosmology – that is maintained within the community. It pervades the definition of reality, surrounding the family atmosphere with a halo of myth. In fostering this myth, the director implants his own charismatic style of leadership, shaping the sense of identity and refashioning the very meaning of becoming fully adult in the structured world outside. The ingredients of a rite of transition are evident in this example. It is the unusual setting of a bounded institution, as total as any remote society, that gives the interpretation a new and provocative edge.

Age systems and the life course of communitas

The practice of initiation may be regarded as a microcosm of other more elaborate forms of age system. In published accounts of such systems there is a similar contrast between horizontal unity and vertical subordination, and one or other theme tends to predominate according to the thrust of the analysis. But both are complementary features. Within age systems in general, the dominance of the seniors continues to cultivate the charisma of age superiority. And the equality of age mates reinvokes the close fellowship or communitas of the peer bond that cuts across rivalries in other spheres of existence.

Formal systems of stratification by age bear a certain resemblance to those of kinship and marriage. Both are symbolic elaborations rooted in a biological metaphor (Maybury-Lewis 1984: 123). But whereas formal systems of kinship are widely recognised as a structured aspect of the wider social process, there has been little recognition of this in the analyses of age systems. At best, kinship algebra can be an anthropologist's tool for modelling community relations; in practice, age-set geometry seldom is. Even the supreme classic of functional holism flatly denies any wider relevance for the Nuer age-set system (Evans-Pritchard 1940: 260). Other analyses have tended to follow this lead by default, treating age systems as esoteric and largely unrelated to the process of ageing in other spheres of social life (Spencer 1976: 171–2). Again, in the most outstanding attempt to establish the fundamentals of age systems, Frank Stewart's work (1977) should be ranked alongside Radcliffe-Brown's analysis of Australian kinship systems in its seminal rigour; and correspondingly it focuses essentially on their internal logic as self-explanatory and self-contained phenomena with little consideration for the wider context.

On one diffuse aspect of age systems, there is some agreement. The unifying ideals of age-sets are seen to cut across corporate descent groups, counteracting the divisiveness of kin-based politics (Eisenstadt 1956: 54, Baxter and Almagor 1978: 9, Maybury-Lewis 1984: 136, Bernardi 1985: 147–9). Bonds between age mates provide a form of complementary filiation, and in this respect, age systems may be compared with systems of marriage alliance or dual descent, uniting the wider society. This represents a functionalist explanation for age systems in general that does not account for their variety or their disconcerting complexities.

A widespread feature of age systems is that grouping by age tends to be partial rather than comprehensive, and rarely extends to women. It is always confined to one domain within the wider society, and normally applies primarily to early stages of development. Among the Akwe-Shavante, for instance, the age system ceases to have influence once men become established as adults and involved in the factionalism of public affairs. In the Baktaman hierarchy of ritual secrecy, the most senior grade is achieved by men generally in their thirties. The Dassanatch age system dominates their youth, but has little relevance to the network of influence built up by middle age. Even among the Nyakyusa, who are often cited as a prime example, their age villages appear to have had most significance in youth, and then either they dwindled or they prospered by becoming age heterogeneous, attracting refugees and younger men taking up their inheritances (Maybury-Lewis 1984: 134–5, Barth 1975: 96, Almagor 1978: 86–90, Charsley 1969: 88).

This transient aspect of many age systems has been noted by Philip Gulliver (1968: 159–60), although he also cites the Maasai as a classic example of an age system that carries through to old age. Yet even this has to be qualified. Maasai *moran* (young warriors) take pride in not having wives or possessions that could divide their loyalties to their age-set as a whole. Communitas is their virtue, and it is explicitly opposed to the very lifestyle that they must accept sooner or later. As they settle down to elderhood, personal responsibilities for their families and herds overshadow their loyalties to one another; and their age-sets are ultimately geared towards protecting their private interests as individuals. Taking this a step further, when Van Gennep considered Maasai initiation as a pre-eminent example of a rite of transition, preparing boys to become *moran,* he need not have stopped there. The communitas and antistructure of *moranhood* entail an extended period of marginality. *Moranhood* itself may be seen as part of an even more inclusive transition from childhood through to elderhood a decade or so later. The age system, in fact, displays very clearly a social construction of adolescence, holding men in the fullness of their twenties in a heavily ritualised suspension, which is imposed on them by much older men who are playing for time and for wives.

Elsewhere, I have suggested that the Samburu variant of the Maasai system throws further light on the life course of communitas. The dancing of their *moran,* which starts by displaying their rivalries, and progresses – or rather appears to regress – through earlier stages of social development, finally loses structure in a form of uninhibited play. It thus appears to provide a ritualised reversal of ageing, breaking down the oppositions of young adulthood and yielding to camaraderie among peers. But if this is in fact a form of regression, then it suggests that the genesis of communitas may lie in the natural play of childhood (Spencer 1985: 156).

This has an almost psychoanalytic flavour in arguing that a pattern of adult behaviour has its roots in childhood experience. Freud, however, failed to develop any theory of play among children outside the authoritarian structure of the family. In his model, there is no periphery in which children learn to interact with their peers as a counterpart to their learning to respond to parental authority. This is not to enter into any psychological argument concerning personality development or the root of symbolic behaviour, and it certainly is not to idealise every aspect of grasping childhood. But it does suggest a fundamental source of experience in human relationships: the uninhibited interaction of children as peers. The meaning of anti-authority as much as of authority for the individual appears to be nowhere more fundamental than that learned in childhood. Moreover, this is not to imply that such experience is confined to male society. Jean La Fontaine (1985: 165) notes the variety of festive occasions when women collect together, with a licence to mock the system controlled by men, deflating the dignity of male culture with an assortment of sexual innuendoes that highlight their ambiguous position. Here, they are peers by their subordinate status rather than by age; but still evoking a similar antistructure with an unstoppable counter-authority of its own. This is to suggest that perhaps the communitas and antistructure of childhood are re-enacted among adults in demonstrations against authority, typified by the element of play and licence in later life.

Amoss and Harrell (1981: 15) have suggested that the Lévi-Straussian transformation from Nature to Culture is reflected in the life course through the transition from the unruly disorder of childhood to the dignified authority of old age. In an earlier section, I modified this in the first instance to a transition from Nature to 'Status'. Age systems in their hierarchical ordering are supremely governed by Status considerations, from which uninitiated children are wholly excluded as beneath contempt. But in their horizontal bonding, a vital aspect of disorderly childhood outside the structure of authority appears to be carried over. The experience of communitas appears as a universal attribute rejuvenated in adulthood and protected within its ritualised setting. The close communitas enjoyed by age mates is revived on ceremonial occasions and at meetings and meat feasts after they have become elders, and it contrasts with the marked differences in wealth and influence in their private lives. Very generally in lifelong age systems, age-set activities may provide the nub of social order, but like those of the Kpelle secret societies, they are also separate, held away from the villages in the bush, and separated from the divisiveness of day to day existence.

Maturation, ageing and gender

In her survey of initiation, Jean La Fontaine (1985: 114–18) notes that the event of initiation marks a transformation in status from the purely domestic domain of childhood, almost invariably establishing the initiate as a sexual being, and often distinguishing males as superior to females. Female initiation is rarer and more likely to be associated with a girl's puberty as a step towards her marriage where she remains within the domain associated with women. Male initiation, on the other hand, tends to be more elaborate and a significant step towards entry into the public domain dominated by older men. A youth emerges from the obscurity of childhood with his initiation, whereas a girl is normally transformed from the obscurity of childhood to an initially obscure role as a young wife.

The subordination of young women is considered in two case studies of this volume where its persistence is tested in the context of change among ethnic minorities. In Chapter 4, Leonard Mars considers the innovation among Orthodox Jewish communities of a ceremony for girls corresponding to the established Bar Mitzvah ceremony for boys. The latter is a prestigious occasion when boys are counted as adult members of the praying congregation and accountable for themselves, shifting them ritually from the domestic domain of their mothers towards the public religious domain reserved for men. Adopting a similar ceremony for girls has been a calculated response to the increasing equality between the sexes. Yet Mars shows how this attempt has merely served to reassert the domestic inferiority of women. By comparison, the girls' ceremony plays down the occasion and any suggestion of a transition towards a fuller independence. It merely reinforces childhood training that prepares girls for marriage and the transfer of responsibility to their husbands.

In Chapter 5, Paul Yates approaches the dilemma of traditional constraints from the point of view of the girls themselves. In this instance, it is the altogether more rigid setting of Muslim immigrant families in Britain. Here, the girls are faced with the contrast between the evident freedom of their racially mixed peers at school and their own moral confinement, pressed to uphold family reputation and threatened with the prospect of an arranged marriage. Fathers, brothers of their own age, and even their mothers seek to maintain male dominance as an aspect of maintaining their ethnic identity in a hostile environment. Yates's sample of interviews reveals a range of responses among girls to this situation and provides a sensitive elaboration of the emotional cross-currents in which they are caught as they negotiate different approaches towards their uncertain future.

Sherry Ortner (1974: 83–7) has expressed the widespread subordination of women in terms of women's mediating role between culture and nature. It is not simply that women bear children, she argued, but they also nurture them and convert barely human infants into social beings. They are crucially involved in primary socialisation that is vital for the perpetuation of culture. To the extent that men have their own separate domain, this gives women a degree of autonomy and of power through the close bonds of their own informal grouping, transcending the limitations of domestic existence. The debate on this issue concerns how much power and how far this is culturally specific. But of special interest here, and anticipating Amoss and Harrell (1981: 15), Ortner has shifted the *nature–culture* dimension from a matter of gender to one of ageing. It is children who are closest to a state of *nature*.

The relevance of age to gender has been examined in several cross-cultural surveys. David Gutmann (1977: 305–12) has drawn attention to the contrast in the profiles of ageing between the sexes. Initially, the women within the domestic domain face a more restricted set of opportunities. Once these constraints are relaxed, however, there is a merging of gender differences and even a reversal of masculine and feminine roles. As they age, women become more autonomous, aggressive and competitive; whereas men tend to become more passive, expressive and dependent. This was broadly confirmed by Myerhoff and Simić (1978: 236–40) who noted that as men age and are replaced by younger men in the competitive arena of the public sphere, they lose the instrumental direction of their lives; whereas women acquire further experience within the market, household and community, when restrictions of their reproductive years are lifted, and can continue and even expand their status with age (qv. Sharp 1981: 101–2, Harrell 1981: 205–7, Brown and Kerns 1985).

A further survey on ageing in Pacific societies (Counts and Counts 1985) broadly supports this model for cultures where there are marked differences of status between genders. However, the authority developed by women within the domestic domain appears not to be because they have ceased to be parents, as Gutmann suggested, but because they continue to be parents, using their motherhood to enhance their status and expand their role. In those Pacific societies where there are no marked gender differences during the years of parenthood, there appears to be little change in old age (qv. Rosaldo 1974: 39–41).

The ability of older women to expand their role is achieved at the price of considerable emotional tension between generations. The most comprehensive and rewarding survey of this broad field is Nancy Foner's *Ages in Conflict* (1984a). She suggests that in the analysis of conflict in non-industrial societies, age inequality is often more significant than sexual inequality, and by no means confined to competition between older and younger men. As women become liberated with age, they frequently have interests that diverge widely from those of younger women, and their relationship may be one of considerable strain. They may try to compensate for their own early period of subordination by upholding practices that keep their daughters-in-law subordinate to men. In other societies, they may find it in their interests to unite with old men against attempts by younger men to seize the initiative in community affairs. And in yet others, they find themselves marginalised prematurely as the initiative passes from their hands. Even the dilemmas of older women as their sexuality wanes appear similar to those of older men, and their ambiguous position is more generally the ambiguity of old age, to be considered in a later section.

The life stages theory and the perception of time

The sociology of ageing repeatedly points back to an article by Leonard Cain (1964), who drew on anthropological writings ranging from Van Gennep (1909) to Eisenstadt (1956) to formulate the concept of the 'life course'. Cain defined this as an organising principle in any culture that gives order and predictability to individuals for the successive statuses they will occupy in the course of ageing. As a comprehensive survey, Cain's article was seminal. But at the ethnographic level, he relied uncritically on a weak selection of secondary sources. This led to a view of pre-industrial societies as typically stratified by age with rites of transition at each upgrading, and readily equated with the legislated thresholds of adulthood and old age in modern society. His interpretation – a tertiary source – was in turn accepted at face value by his successors, endowing it with the authority of a definitive statement. It was this unchecked drift from primary sources that led David Kertzer and Jenny Keith, introducing *Age and Anthropological Theory* (1984: 22), to claim that the 'identification of the social significance of age with a particular type of formal system found in East Africa has been an obstacle to thorough analysis of age in society'. It is only necessary to add that the misunderstanding extends to the very nature of these formal age systems in a way that parallels the confusion between caste stratification and class in another body of literature. Cain's survey nevertheless provided a framework for further analysis. It presented an ideal type, a formalised set of ideas that stimulated further research; and it led to further theories of ageing.

Cain's ideas on the life course as a sequence of stages were developed into a comprehensive theory by Bernice Neugarten and her associates. Sweeping to one side the whole edifice of psychoanalytic theory, Neugarten (1969) argued that we do not understand the psychological realities of adulthood by projecting forward the issues that appear to be salient in childhood. In practice, such issues have turned out to be bad predictors for adult achievements or lifestyles, for these entail a radical shift in perspective and a psychological discontinuity. Instead, she approached the life course as a changing constellation of roles and perspectives, governed by a cognitive map for ordering major life events and expectations appropriate to each age (Neugarten and Datan 1973: 59). Within any society or sub-culture, adults assess their own performance according to their internalised 'social clock', setting goals in relation to it, and moving towards the norm at the next stage if they find themselves leading or lagging behind their peers. It is, in other words, a model of conformity that seems to have stemmed from the same tradition of middle-class American achievers as William Whyte's *The Organisation Man* (1957), but it is extended in principle to all societies. Following from Cain, undifferentiated societies with tightly regulated age grades provided a model for society at large.

An illustration of this kind of society is given in this volume by Tamara Dragadze (Chapter 6), who outlines indigenous ideas concerning the development of the life course in rural Soviet Georgia. This entails a moderating set of expectations appropriate to age, and it follows parallel paths for men and for women, although they differ sharply in other respects. Within the three generation joint family, there is an indulgence towards children that continues in attenuated form even after marriage and becoming parents. Without pressure from above, there is an expectation that younger men in particular need not control their impulses or be responsible for their actions. In this way, the senior generation boost their own status, while increasing the expectation that they at least will display restraint, conforming to the ideals of behaviour appropriate to their age. Older men, and women too, are expected to exercise self-control, and to use their authority and responsibility for representing family interests wisely in order to uphold their reputation and integrity in the outside world.

Neugarten's notion of an inbuilt 'social clock' is quite apt as a metaphor for societies where consciousness of the social process of ageing is shaped by fully fledged age systems; indeed it is such societies that appear to have given Cain his initial cue. But other apt metaphors may be expressed within any culture, based on significant features of daily existence. In Chapter 7 of this volume, Stuart Thompson elaborates on the importance of metaphor in human understanding, and he considers the perception of the life course with reference to the metaphors that are familiar to irrigation rice farmers in Taiwan. Notions of the growth, fertility and recycling of plant life and of the flow of water are symbolically associated with the succession of generations. Life stems from ancestral roots that nurture their successors and live on in them. The very structure of time is vested in changes in such relationships which define the life stages. A person cannot grow old while his parents are still alive and he has a duty to ensure the continuity of the family or he is 'lost' and out of phase with the stream of time, and the harmony that should exist between people, nature and the cosmos. Expectations do not relate to age as such, but more specifically to position within the family and society.

Within the formal framework of Neugarten's theory, there has been discussion on social exchange, meaning, choice, and the changing perception of time itself. But not surprisingly, the rigidity of the assumptions has attracted criticisms that parallel those levelled against functionalism in anthropology (Fry 1976, Elder 1977: 284, Marshall 1985: 264). The notion of a general awareness of age expectations does not appear to be in question. But this is not matched by evidence of rigid time-tables of age norms and constraints. Cultures vary and there is very often a considerable flexibility which may vary over the life course, sometimes increasing with age, as among the Umeda (Gell 1975), and sometimes decreasing, as in Soviet Georgia (qv. Japan, Plath and Ikeda 1975: 117).

An alternative interpretation draws more attention to the individual's sense of development with age, shifting attention from regulation to the uniqueness of each transition for the actor (Levinson 1977, Ryff and Heincke 1983: 807). Instead of the life course as a cognitive time-table of expectations one might substitute rather the concept of a 'life text': a notional ordering of events and broad trends in the life course that acquires meaning in the way in which it is interpreted by each individual.

This alternative approach was anticipated by Anselm Strauss (1959: 89–108), who noted the element of mischance in life course transitions, emphasising at the same time the radical shifts of commitment and self-awareness that are entailed. Instead of a time-table of stages, the life course is held to be punctuated with critical dilemmas that precipitate radical adjustments, especially within the family: a life crises theory, as it were (Rapoport and Rapoport 1965, Riegel 1975: 50–5, Elder 1977: 286–7, Sarason et al. 1978, Hultsch and Plemons 1979). The thrust of this approach has been primarily by social psychologists using psychological techniques. But intriguingly, the theory follows an implicit Marxist path with a similar view of mounting contradictions between inflexible social relations and progressive forces. In the case of ageing, it is not the material forces of production that are progressing relentlessly, but life's chances and the genetic process of maturation and decay, undermining the array of power relations.

A further step towards a psychological model of life stages is to assume that successive transitions are inherently linked, the transition to each stage requiring fulfilment before further transitions can be undertaken. Doris Francis's analysis of two emigrant Jewish communities from Eastern Europe, for instance, suggested that those who had cared for their parents in old age were better able to adjust to old age themselves than those whose earlier emigration had prevented them from doing so (Francis 1984). Psychoanalysis, which Neugarten dismissed so abruptly, is another model of this kind which can be extended beyond problems associated with early socialisation to the life course as a whole (Erikson 1950, Rayner 1978). Such studies appear to open up a range of possibilities for research on adult ageing in non-western societies.

The life stages and life crises theories are not wholly incompatible. The age system of Arusha, noted earlier for instance, neatly fits both. Gulliver (1963: 27–31) presented a clear cognitive map based on their age system, where each promotion of one age-set or another is associated with a sense of maturation and a shift of expectations. However, the system provides a time-strategy – a notional text – rather than a strict time-table. Men at each stage try to work it to their advantage and this results in periods of acquiescence that build up unpredictably to a crisis and the inevitable transition.

The point holds also for societies without age systems. Paul Hiebert (1981) has outlined the elaborate life stages prescribed by Hinduism for twice-born castes. In the first stage, a man should learn to read the scriptures while still young; in the second, he should fulfil any personal ambitions as a household head; then in the final two stages, with family responsibilities behind him, he should renounce worldly goods in order to study the Vedas, reaching for spiritual perfection. But again, this programme lays down broad principles rather than firm directives, and it does not allow for family conflicts that divert men from an ideal path. Hiebert shows how elders in a south Indian village respond to these dilemmas by manipulating the prescribed pattern of stages and work them to their advantage at critical points. In this instance, the ritualised programme of stages is quite literally a life text, a script that guides progress through life, but it is open to very broad interpretation. Text and performance are complementary aspects of the life course. It is through performance that the life text is reshaped and adapted and given a specific meaning.

Altogether, Neugarten's notion of a culturally regulated internal clock within the individual raises some interesting problems. But it also reflects Cain's rigid transposition from age grades to life stages and his loose grasp of Van Gennep's work. The significance of rites of transition is not just that they upgrade the principal actors to new life stages or conform to the legal niceties of statute, but that they mark the realignments in the configuration of relations throughout the community following some life event. They bridge the ambivalent discontinuities of status in the life course and the hiatus in time from one stage to the next. Because everyone is involved, everyone is made aware of the process of ageing, and everyone ages. This is to shift the consciousness of ageing from a linear approach associated with absolute age, to a more structural approach associated with critical times of transition. The perception of time in regard to ageing goes in steps rather than a smooth flow, for it is embedded in the chequered development of social relationships.

The structural discontinuity, marked by a rite of transition, has a further relevance for the perception of ageing. Continuity and regulation are punctuated with a disorder. Time becomes symbolically dis-ordered and the notion of ageing itself is disoriented. It is characteristic of the liminal phase of a rite of transition, when the secular logic of everyday behaviour is suspended, that there is a ritualised distortion of ageing that varies with culture and context. Initiates go through a form of death and are reborn. The power of older men is grotesquely enhanced. The dead move on to another life, where they are born anew. Ancestors hover close to the living. Myths of the beginning of things are re-enacted. Indeed, one may go a step further and suggest that a major difficulty people experience in grasping the nature of time is that their awareness of its linear aspect is immobilised by formalised relationships that resist change. It is as if the ritualised parody of age and ageing at times of transition stirs this static view, introducing an element of shock and apprehension into the occasion, and reasserting social time as a dynamic process.

This metaphoric play on time is well illustrated in John Blacking's contribution to this volume (Chapter 8). Blacking is concerned with the cosmological beliefs surrounding the life course among the Venda of Southern Africa. For the Venda, the spirits of departed ancestors are the guardians of their land and people. During childhood, each person is held to be under the protection of a particular ancestral spirit while developing their own personality through social interaction. Initiation at puberty marks a major step towards adulthood as they emerge from parental protection and are given intensive instruction on adult responsibilities. This exposure to the adult world is perceived as the departure of the ancestral guardian and the emergence of a new aspect of the initiate's being, expressed as the birth of a new and responsible spiritual self. From this point, the continued maturation of the personality is seen as the development of this spirit, which will join the community of guardian ancestors after death. The notion of a new spirit within a Venda community of spirits and of recycled immortality provides a vision of spiritual continuity that overrides the biological discontinuities of social existence. Initiation rather than birth or death is the watershed between generations. Spiritual ageing is out of time with the stages of biological ageing, and this ensures spiritual continuity as a metaphor for the endurance of Venda values and traditions through community life. This example illustrates usefully how the perception of time and immortality in relation to the life course touches on the meaning of existence itself.

The age cohort theory and the interpretation of history

The age cohort theory brings together the notion of life stages considered in the previous section and the problem of social change. Karl Mannheim (1929) established the principles of the problem, following Dilthey in relation to the history of intellectual movements and Pinder in relation to world views manifested in art styles. Each *generation* in Mannheim's formulation is the repositor of prevailing ideas. Currents of intellectual expression within the generation are shaped partly by the impact of contemporary events and partly by diverse trends that crystallise into opposed world views. Successive generations fight different adversaries, both within and without, that relate to their different experiences. The impulses that determine the shifting relevance of history, he suggested, arise out of the polarisation between generations. The older generation tends to act as a conservative force, while each new generation has a radically fresh contact with prevailing conditions that leads towards novel solutions and new trends. Through the extensive work of Matilda Riley and her associates, Mannheim's problem became established during the 1970s as a central theoretical paradigm in the sociology of ageing. Here, the term *age cohort* is used for close contemporaries as less ambiguous than 'generation' or 'age stratification', by which the approach is more generally known.

The basic pattern of ageing in the age cohort theory is quite similar to Neugarten's model, with 'age strata' and 'age-related expectations'. However, the functional premise of stability is rejected, allowing for malintegration as well as solidarity. Change is immanent and both the cause and the effect of tensions. Contemporaries are seen to interact within a milieu that is different from that of their predecessors and they encounter the same historical situation differently. The theory, therefore, faces the analytical problem of disentangling the process of ageing from the trend of history. It provides a comprehensive framework that can encompass diverse social forces and even chance events. For any number of reasons, successive cohorts can vary in size and composition. Expectations and opportunities are affected by laws of supply and demand within each area of social action ranging from the market for employment to the market for marriage. The degree of mismatch between these affects the range of choice, competition and population mobility; and it has a knock-on effect for future cohorts. In the course of ageing, each cohort is uniquely marked by the imprint of history and leaves its own imprint (Riley 1972: 7–21).

This approach to ageing is well illustrated in a number of historical studies that show how even the role and perception of particular life stages, such as childhood (Ariès 1960), adolescence (Demos and Demos 1969) and old age (Fischer 1977), have themselves recently undergone change. Altogether, the way that the process of ageing is perceived is interwoven with historical change. In the present volume, Richard Jenkins (Chapter 9) considers a further concept – the changing perception of adulthood. This is revealed by a shift in attitudes in Wales as a cohort of young men and women faced prolonged unemployment in increasing numbers and followed the general trend towards unmarried partnerships. This threw into confusion the popular expectation that leaving school should lead to gainful employment and then marriage; the notion of attaining adulthood itself was now in question. However, because this problem was shared by so many young people, popular expectations were found to have modified since the 1960s. Employment had become recognised as desirable rather than a prerequisite for adulthood and alternatives to marriage were becoming accepted. In this way, the underlying notion of adulthood is shown to be robust, with a cluster of attributes, including legal entitlements, that vary in importance with circumstance. This is compared with the stigma of mental handicap, which appears to touch on a more fundamental and unchanging model of adulthood. Unlike the unemployed, those with severe learning difficulties are legally and popularly denied adult status and are virtually cast in the role of permanently dependent children, with little concession to enlightened times. For these younger people, what appears to be at issue is, in fact, the nature of their humanity.

Most strikingly in the present volume, Elisabeth Croll (Chapter 10) examines the impact of the confusion of change on successive cohorts in contemporary China. Within a few decades, sharp reversals in policies and the transition from traditional society through radical stages of revolution to the current stress on developing new professional skills has shaken the family. The role of the parent in particular is shown to have undergone radical change, first as official policies focused on schooling, marginalising the family; then, after the Cultural Revolution, when economic reforms introduced the policy of the single-child family, emphasising quality rather than quantity, but leading to a wave of spoilt and troublesome children. Particularly disoriented were the 'lost' cohort of parents whose own education had been disrupted by the Cultural Revolution, leaving them ill-prepared to prime their children. Only when this problem became manifest did the state identify the family as the principal domain of socialisation. They then took steps to end the family's independence and to reorientate parents towards their new role as agents of a leap into the future. In such a situation, a synchronic view of the life course becomes almost meaningless.

The age cohort theory touches on a problem familiar to anthropologists, whose raw field data do not conveniently separate out the process of ageing from that of social change. Without following a cohort through successive stages over a whole generation, it can never be certain how far contemporary childhood patterns generate those observed in adulthood; or how far the emergence of entrepreneurs is a totally new phenomenon or reflects a perennial opposition between young and old that is being enacted in modern dress (qv. Strathern 1972). Anthropological field studies, however deep, are relatively fleeting when matched against the time-scale of a generation, let alone the panorama of history; and this raises the problem of making historical inferences from contemporary data. The researcher is caught in a synchronic trap that centres on the immediate situation divorced from its history.

Writings associated with this theory that treat cohorts as social entities bear the unmistakable imprint of Cain's loose grasp of age systems. The problem is real, but the concept of age cohorts has no intrinsic meaning outside the contrived groupings of official statistics and opinion surveys repeated over the years. In one esoteric area of anthropological study, however, there is an apt parallel. Age systems are not only organised into real cohorts, but they sometimes pose incongruities concerning their historical development and whether their rules of succession are workable without breaking down over successive generations. It is a problem that has proved ideally suited to types of simulation that explore this diachronic dimension. Such exercises, following through successive cohorts as a set of logical transformations based on demographic data, have unravelled some of the incongruities, revealing hidden patterns. Thus, the Borana have an age system that is increasingly exclusive in successive generations. Using such a technique, Asmarom Legesse (1973: 135–62) matched the rules and oral tradition with a simulated model. This in effect ran the system backwards in time to estimate its historical point of origin, when these rules might first have been established. Another simulation has clarified the apparently unworkable age system of the Karimojong, suggesting that it is in fact viable. Evidence previously assumed to reflect a breakdown under modern conditions now revealed the inner workings of a cycle that resisted change (Spencer 1978). In areas where the historical record is sparse, age systems of this kind offer unique but rare opportunities.

A more symbolic approach to age cohort theory has been suggested by Victor Turner (1974) in his concept of social dramas, which also has a bearing on the life crises model. Turner drew attention to the role of key figures at critical moments of their careers when they faced dilemmas that were symbolic of their time, endowing them with a historical role that was only part of their making. Using Van Gennep's work as a metaphor for social change, what were life crises in the lives of these figures, casting them in the roles of martyrs or persecutors or patriots, were also key moments in history. It was not just they themselves but their whole generation and history at large that passed through a liminal phase into a new era. While Turner was not strictly concerned with ageing as such, his approach adds a touch of anthropological colour to the interpretation of history that is close to Dilthey and Pinder. Key moments in history are also key transitions in the lives of all who partake in them; and the symbolic trappings of the event itself through the myth that grows around it have the hallmarks of a rite of transition for society at large. This interpretation of history is not just concerned with a succession of cohorts, but with the symbolic elaboration of events that structure it around the careers of those that are endowed with greatness. At a less epic level, the careers of all persons are similarly structured in relation to the historical transitions of their time; and the symbols and myths that compose this structure are interwoven with those of the more personal and routine transitions of life (qv. Myerhoff 1978: 31).

The liminal status of old age

The process of adjustment to old age in the sociological literature has focused on the rival claims of activity theory as against disengagement theory. Activity theory (Cavan *et al.* 1949) may be regarded as a precursor of life crises theory applied to the onset of old age. It argued that people seek to continue their patterns of interaction as they age, and only adapt to alternative roles when old ones can no longer be maintained. More recent writers have identified strategies that the elderly can pursue to maintain an active role: they construct their own old age according to their abilities and within the cultural framework of opportunity and choice (Kerns 1980: 121–2, Myerhoff and Simić 1978: 240–3, Counts and Counts 1985: 20, Marshall 1985: 265).

In this volume, various authors are concerned with the problems of adaptation to old age. Two examples in particular consider strategies for forestalling the awkward transition between generations as parents grow older. Ray Abrahams (Chapter 11) presents a case study from rural Finland where farms are handed down as a preinheritance before the parents are too old. This is seen as an aspect of farm management, maintaining continuity and avoiding the ambiguities and tensions between generations that may arise with ageing. In this way, discontinuities within the family are underpinned by the continuity of the farm as a viable foundation for enterprise, linking successive generations as the life course unfolds.

A different strategy is revealed by Ladislav Holy (Chapter 12), who presents a novel view of Islamic marriage between close kin. Holy shows how among the Berti of Sudan, parents relinquish property with the marriage of each of their children and at first sight undermine their security against old age. However, arranging close marriages is seen as a strategy by the parents towards precisely this end, favouring different types of arrangement according to their gender and circumstance. The succeeding generation are freed from day to day control by the seniors and yet are caught up in a multiplex network of family obligation towards them. Both these chapters, in other words, introduce into activity theory the element of anticipation. Problems of adjustment in later life can be averted with foresight. By strategic giving instead of stubborn clinging, the elderly can retain the respect of those on whom they depend.

Two further chapters consider collective responses through clubs designated for the active elderly, emphasising the variety of patterns, even within one culture. In Chapter 13, Haim Hazan considers the impact of the transition from the ordered existence of adult life to the hiatus of old age, which disrupts cultural configurations that are no longer relevant. In three different types of organisation for the aged, the disengagement of individuals from their earlier lifestyle is presented as an aspect of managing the threat to their continued existence as they adopt a new collective identity: a communitas. New meanings are constructed and norms take shape through shared experience, opposed not so much to the wider social order as to the chaotic experience of old age.

In Chapter 14, the theme is elaborated in Judith Okely's study of clubs for the third age (over sixty years) in Normandy. She contrasts the ethoses of two clubs in a rural area with that of a club in the local municipal centre. In the town club, members of the bourgeois elite used their wealth and refined culture to dominate activities, marginalising the majority who did not share in this culture and introducing the class divisions of the wider society. The clubs in the rural area, on the other hand, generated ethoses that played down social and economic differences and encouraged a sense of unity and widespread participation in all their activities. This leads Okely to suggest that the communitas that is achieved in the remoter area was not just a response to the hazards of old age, as Hazan suggests (qv. Keith 1980), but was also a reaction to the wider social order. A class-free zone was generated, set apart and freed from the divisive bourgeois culture that had dominated their working lives before retirement.

Each of these examples is concerned with a positive adjustment to retirement, and illustrates activity theory for the not too old. Disengagement theory, on the other hand, appears to refer to a more terminal stage, and views old age as a natural process of withdrawal, a transition from active participation in life to passive decline and adjustment to the approach of death (Cumming and Henry 1961). Again wide variations have been observed in the extent to which people disengage, varying between and within cultures (Havighurst et al. 1964). Ultimately as health declines, the theory tends towards a truism (Maddox 1964: 80–1, Palmore 1968: 261).

In the anthropological interpretations of the symbolism of ageing, there are also two broad streams, and these may be regarded as a deification of disengagement theory on the one hand as against a perversion of activity theory on the other. Again, they tend to be culturally specific, but taken together they reflect the ambivalence that accompanies the increasingly liminal status of old age. The elderly are placed on an indefinite threshold that lies almost timelessly beyond the activities of daily life. Having arrived at old age, there is nowhere further on this earth for them to go.

Conceptually, the process of ageing points towards old age as the last surviving vestige of life. There is a resilient, cosmic quality associated with those who survive well beyond normal expectation. They have a lifelong fulfilment that lies beyond the experience of younger people, and almost outside time itself. Summarising a variety of sources, Barbara Myerhoff (1984: 315–16) noted that old people create a sense of immortality by tying the life cycle into a meaningful whole. Reliving the past and reaching back to earlier generations, they give a sense – a myth – of continuity and completeness that transcends duration and the diffuseness of life. As they rise above the rivalries of community life, they are associated with the power and awe of the already dead and with the natural forces so close to reclaiming them. As repositors of tradition they are living symbols of the continuity and endurance of culture and ultimate truths (qv. Neugarten 1969: 123). This consummating quality of old age is well illustrated in this volume in Stuart Thompson's elaboration of Chinese ideology surrounding the family and ancestors.

It is a theme that is so well trodden in the literature that Durkheim (1912) might have been better advised to follow his own earlier lead (1893: 293) and to consider the symbolic trappings of old age rather than totemism as the most basic manifestation of religious sentiments emanating from community existence. In this transposition, the elderly too are loved, feared and respected; their authority is another form of the moral ascendancy of society over its members; younger persons perceive old age as a part of themselves, elevated beyond their immediate senses, with its residence in men, but perceived as the vital principle of things (after Durkheim 1912: 220–3, with apologies). Whatever the nature of beliefs in a deity or in afterlife and whatever the emblems, the aged are closest to being the natural intermediaries with the infinite cosmos.

The principal agents of the display of the charisma of old age are not necessarily the oldest people. By nurturing a respect for age those in middle age are underpinning their own lesser claim to sharing in this authority and their own futures. Once they have arrived at old age, however, the contradiction is laid bare. It poses the anomaly of a superstructure that has outlived its base: a pinnacle of achievement with a hint of immortality and yet fragile, irrelevant and even an encumbrance. The benign view of charismatic old age is matched by a body of literature that reveals its destructive potential. Old age is not invariably benign. The alternative view of liminality typically identifies the old with the stereotype of witches, sorcerers or some other form of malevolence. Younger people may often be suspected, but the general pattern of belief is clearly associated with anomalies of ageing.

Nancy Foner (1984a: 157–91) presents a detailed analysis of this insidious aspect in the anthropological literature, yielding three types of interpretation. The first identifies the frustrations of younger people who resent the overbearing power and ingratitude of the elderly. Generally, as the old shake free from conventional restrictions, there is less tolerance for their desocialised irresponsibility than for the unsocialised innocence of children (qv. Myerhoff 1984: 308). A second interpretation identifies the stereotype of elderly malcontents with increasing psychological stress as they fail to adapt to the physical process of ageing within their own bodies and resent their loss of control over others. This switches the focus from the grounds for resentment among the young to the characteristics of resentment among the old; and it inverts activity theory in suggesting a refusal to adjust to the realities of ageing. They may threaten others too readily, displaying greed, envy, uncontrolled anger, and even intolerance for young children. The desocialised in a sense are competing with the unsocialised as dependants. A third interpretation is the natural isolation of those that have survived to old age, outliving their peers. Like witches and tyrants, they are cut off from the communitas of the peer group. The sense of communitas is a wasting asset as their power and isolation increase, and they are led towards a corruption of this power. The charisma of old age becomes inverted, exposing them to resentment from all sides.

While the pattern of belief and accommodation surrounding old age varies widely, the onset of physical and mental incapacity normally leads to a loss of deference and self-regard (Simmons 1945: 62, Neugarten 1974: 198, Amoss and Harrell 1981: 4). Besides the loss of ability and competence in old age, various writers have pointed to bereavements and emotional loss, loss of role and normlessness. The common experience of old age is one of loss (Counts and Counts 1985: 5, Neugarten and Hagestad 1976: 40).

One has therefore two aspects of liminality associated respectively with the ideals of youth as against the isolation of those that have survived to old age: communitas as against cosmic forces, unstructured human sociability as against loss and isolation. They are the two periods commonly associated with a crisis in identity and sometimes with a certain bond of sympathy. Between these two lies the prime of adulthood, framed as it were by those whose time has not yet come and those for whom time has stopped.

Modernisation theory and the evolution of age relations

Most of the chapters in this volume bear directly or indirectly on the processes of modernisation that inevitably affect any anthropological study: the changing roles of the sexes and breakdown of traditional notions of marriage (Mars, Yates, Jenkins); changing metaphors (Thompson); urban drift and the erosion of rural society (Abrahams, Okely); and the effect of state paternalism on wider family ties through local bureaucracy (Dragazde), institutions for the elderly (Hazan) and those for adolescent delinquents (Edgar). Most striking among these, however, is once again Elisabeth Croll's example of increasing state control over the family in China. There is here an intriguing parallel with the Cleisthenean reforms in Athens around 500 BC and with the successive changes in Roman law that occurred later. These reforms also aimed at consolidating the unity of the state by limiting the power of the family. It is the attenuation of the family with increasing urbanisation that has raised questions concerning the status of the elderly.

The concern over the loss of status among the elderly in disengagement theory has combined with the concern for history in the age cohort model to produce *modernisation theory*. This term was coined by Cowgill and Holmes (1972) in a cross-cultural study that suggested that the loss of status is a product of industrial society. New ideas and technologies and greater mobility and longevity, they argued, have undermined traditional attitudes, shifting the initiative towards younger people. The concentration of interest in this theory reflects an increasing awareness of the dilemma of old age with the increasing privacy of the nuclear family and the attenuation of responsibility towards more distant kin (Hareven 1978: 209–13).

Questioning this theory, Nancy Foner (1984b: 197–204) has pointed to the diversity of responses to modernisation that makes generalisation virtually impossible. Historically, the status of the elderly was not invariably high in earlier centuries (Laslett 1976: 205), and their authority in America was undermined before industrialisation rather than as a result of it (Fischer 1977: 99–101). More recently, the development of welfare systems for some has led to a reversal of their depressed segregation (Palmore and Manton 1974: 209–10). It is a reversal, reminiscent of Foucault's analysis of the segregation of the insane during the Enlightenment when they posed an anomaly for the prevailing ideology, followed by their partial rehabilitation subsequently (Foucault 1977, qv. Hareven 1978: 212). This somewhat patchy historical trend in the West is matched in Foner's survey of anthropological findings elsewhere with as many exceptions as confirmations (1984a: 211–22). The status of the elderly in traditional societies also was not invariably high. In recent times, younger people have not always benefited from new opportunities: work available to them is normally unskilled and poorly paid. The old, on the other hand, may sometimes have benefited, consolidating their control over land as it has become increasingly valuable, and capitalising on the security of imposed colonial rule. They might even recover from an initial lapse in status, taking the initiative during a revival of ethnic traditions in the face of change.

A further criticism of modernisation theory is that the recent loss of status primarily involves the public sphere and property dominated by males, and it has affected women only to a lesser extent (Van Arsdale 1981: 121, Sinclair 1985: 27–9). Unlike male skills, those that are passed on within the family are not outmoded by the pace of change, and this is reflected in a 'matrifocal tilt' in modern families, except in so far as increasing mobility has separated women from their offspring (Hagestad 1985: 150, Abendstern 1986: 12–13). Thus a criticism of disengagement theory, that it is men in the first instance whose status is affected by ageing, applies also to modernisation theory.

This lack of a clear trend in the transition to modern society is also discernible in relation to other stages of the life course. It has been suggested, for instance, that adolescence as a distinctive stage emerged for the first time in urban America after 1880 (Demos and Demos 1969: 632). Yet clear parallels in lifestyles and ideologies have been noted between gangs of adolescents in Chicago in the 1950s and cohorts of *moran* in the age-set societies of East Africa (Baxter and Almagor 1978: 3–4, Keiser 1969). One also has the impression from de Tocqueville (1961: 229) of the suspension of adolescence for only a brief while in young America: a hiccup in the history of ageing, rather than an innovation. Or again, Philippe Ariès is widely regarded for his work indicating that childhood was first recognised as a distinct phase in the life course in middle-class urban families in the early nineteenth century. Yet, his study was explicitly concerned with the transition from medieval to modern society and avoided any assumption that childhood as a distinct life stage had never existed previously (Ariès 1960: 34). The thrust of the earlier section on initiation concerned a precise distinction of this sort between childhood and adulthood in many pre-industrial societies.

The problem, I suggest, is that the modernisation model, concerning the redistribution of power as it affects older people, rests on an argument that has too narrow a base historically. As with the age cohort approach, one is led towards the particularism of individual instances, many of which seem to confirm the theory, while others clearly do not.

This suggests broadening the theory. The emphasis has to extend beyond the aged to the total array of power with age and for each sex. And it has to be cast against the backdrop of grand theories concerning the more general transition from rural to urban society: in other words, social evolution as macro-history rising above the unique variations of micro-history. Modernisation theory was foreshadowed by the general interest in the transition to modern society in the nineteenth century. Indeed, it was in this climate that the social sciences, notably anthropology, may be said to have been born. The climate has changed, and the thrust of philosophical speculation in anthropology has shifted towards ahistorical issues. Yet the problem and the opportunity remains, and it is pertinent to recall three earlier commentators who touched on a grand theory of social evolution, placing modernisation theory within a broader setting.

Alexis de Tocqueville was one of the earliest and most fluent writers to outline the process of modernisation from personal experience. He was struck by the contrast between the lifestyles of European societies that were still largely in the grip of feudalism and the new American democracy that had liberated the individual from close family ties. He described a clear-cut transition from ascription to achievement, breaking down the formalities between father and son, but also one that broke the thread of continuity between generations, condemning each new generation to itself alone – and indeed each person, not just the elderly, but everyone to a greater or lesser extent (Tocqueville 1961 vol. 2: 118–20, 229–36, Oster 1984: 291).

Henry Maine (1861: 126–70) interpreted this transition as it was reflected in long-term trends in Law; and his analysis anticipated the problems of generalisation in modernisation theory. The transition from Status to Contract – from the Family to the Individual – was a chequered trend from early Roman times to Maine's own time and was still proceeding. It was actually reversed in relation to the position of women, when the early Christian emperors consolidated the power of the husband that still survived even in Maine's time. Similarly, the extension of Roman citizenship to colonised peoples had also extended the principle of Patria Potestas. This appears, in fact, to have been very similar to the consolidation of the power of elders under recent colonial rule, noted by contemporary writers. Apart from the particular exceptions, however, the broader historical trend is clear. Adults increasingly became free of parental control, and filial dependency within the family remained only for the immature young. In this way, the progress from Status to Contract applies also to the life course, and the broad experience of history is also the experience of the individual on reaching adulthood. It is a model that focuses on the liberation from ascribed junior status as it affects the young; whereas the anomaly of old age, freed of ascribed seniority at the other end of adulthood, is that it has no place.

Maine has been generally criticised for his failure to conceive of alternative systems of kinship other than that of patriarchal Rome. However, if one substitutes the broader term *ascription* for *Potestas*, he could almost have been making an important evolutionary point in suggesting that: 'Where the Potestas begins, Kinship begins.... Where the Potestas ends, Kinship ends' (Maine 1861: 149). For this is to conceive of the rise as well as the fall of the ascriptions of extended kinship: an evolutionary trend from Nature to Status to Contract.

It is at this far-reaching level of social evolution that Lewis Henry Morgan (1877: 498–508) pitched his work. His notion of the development of the human family from its inception to the rise of civilisation was in effect an attempt to extrapolate the thrust of Maine's argument backwards in time. But more interestingly, implicit in Morgan's analysis of kinship systems as institutions of ascribed relationships, one has again the notion of the rise and fall of kinship itself with the evolution of the concept of property. Thus, while David Maybury-Lewis (1984: 135–6) has suggested that kinship, grounded in property ownership, tends to be more enduring than age systems, even kinship has become outmoded with the demise of peasant economies. But these changes affect the status of the aged. The evolutionary boom of kinship based on property has entailed the rise and fall of the power of the old to constrain the young. Morgan's scheme bears on the evolution of age relations.

With regard to the future of the anthropological study of ageing, there appear to be three strands. The first relates directly to the esoteric study of age systems which will surely continue for some while and should find its place within any theories of ageing. The second relates to the symbolic analysis of relations of ageing, both at liminal times of transition and in the more general interpretation of the life course. For this is a topic that is only beginning to find its way into the sociology of ageing. And finally if anthropologists wish to contribute to the current debate on modernisation, then I suggest the third is to return to the major focus of interest that concerned nineteenth-century evolutionists. This is to suggest that the social and historical context of ageing in any society may usefully be seen in the context of broader evolutionary forces. It is to look at the changing relations of power with age and by sex in terms of the rise and fall of systems of extended kinship. This is not to speculate on remote origins, but to recognise the logic of a broad evolutionary process within which each society is placed. And indeed, it is a process within which traditions are often seen, with myths of the coming of culture and responses to its recent loss. It is the systems of kinship and not just the very old that have been involved in disengagement, and geographic mobility and the process of urbanisation must surely have played a significant role in this. Where the old retain status in the modern situation of change, this should be examined in the context of the retention of their control over the kinship nexus for the time being. Where their status was low before, this raises the question of whether perhaps the kinship system had already dwindled, or perhaps it had never developed beyond a rudimentary level. In other words, it is not just age systems that should be re-examined in terms of their links with the system of kinship, but also the changing profile of relations of ageing in other types of society. If we are to study change in modern times, do we dare to disinter grand theories of the past?

©1990 Paul Spencer

References

Abendstern, M., 1986, 'Life Histories and Ageing' (ms), ESRC Research on Ageing Workshop.

Almagor, U., 1978, 'Equality among Dassanetch age-peers', in Baxter and Almagor.

Amoss P.T. and S. Harrell (eds), 1981, *Other Ways of Growing Old*, California: Stanford University Press.

Ariès, P., 1962 (1960), *Centuries of Childhood*, New York: Vintage Books.

Barth, F., 1975, *Ritual Knowledge among the Baktaman of New Guinea*, New Haven: Yale University Press.

Baxter, P.T.W. and U. Almagor (eds), 1978, *Age, Generation and Time*, London: Hurst.

Beall, C.M., 1984, 'Theoretical dimensions of a focus on age in physical anthropology', in Kertzer and Keith.

Beaubier, J., 1980, 'Biological factors in aging', in Fry.

Bernardi, B., 1985, *Age Class Systems*, Cambridge: Cambridge University Press.

Binstock, R.H. and E. Shanas (eds), 1976, *Handbook of Aging and the Social Sciences*, New York: Van Nostrand Reinhold.

Blurton Jones, N., 1975, 'Ethology, anthropology, and childhood', in Fox, R. (ed), *Biosocial Anthropology*, London: Malaby.

Brown, J.K. and V. Kerns (eds), 1985, *A New View of Middle-Aged Women*, South Hadley: Bergin and Garvey.

Cain, L.D., 1964, 'Life course and social structure', in Faris, R.E.L. (ed), *Handbook of Modern Sociology*, Chicago: Rand McNally.

Cavan, R.S., E.W. Burgess, R.J. Havighurst, and H. Goldhamer, 1949, *Personal Adjustment in Old Age*, Chicago: Science Research Associates Inc.

Charsley, S.R., 1969, *The Princes of Nyakyusa*, Nairobi: East African Publishing House.

Chodorow, N., 1974, 'Family structure and feminine personality', in Rosaldo and Lamphere.

Cohen, R., 1984, 'Age and culture as theory', in Kertzer and Keith.

Counts, A.C. and D.R. Counts (eds), 1985, *Aging and its Transformations*, Honolulu: University Press of Hawaii.

Cowgill, D.O. and L.D. Holmes (eds), 1972, *Aging and Modernization*, New York: Appleton-Century-Crofts.

Cumming, E. and W.E. Henry, 1961, *Growing Old: the process of disengagement*, New York: Basic Books.

Darwin, C.R., 1871, *The Descent of Man, and Selection in Relation to Sex*, London: Murray.

Demos, J. and V. Demos, 1969, 'Adolescence in historical perspective', *Journal of Marriage and the Family*, 31: 623–39.

Dolhinow, P., 1984, 'The primates: age, behaviour, and evolution', in Kertzer and Keith.

Durkheim, E., 1933 (1893), *The Division of Labour in Society*, New York: Free Press.

Durkheim, E., 1915 (1912), *Elementary Forms of the Religious Life*, London: Allen & Unwin.

Eckert, P., 1984, 'Age and linguistic change', in Kertzer and Keith.

Eisenstadt, S.N., 1956, *From Generation to Generation: age groups and social structure*, New York: Free Press.

Elder, G.H., 1977, 'Family history and the life course', *Journal of Family History*, 2: 279–304.

Erikson, E., 1950, *Childhood and Society*, New York: Norton.

Evans-Pritchard, E.E., 1940, *The Nuer*, Oxford: Clarendon.

Fischer, D.H., 1977, *Growing Old in America*, New York: Oxford University Press.

Foner, N., 1984a, *Ages in Conflict: a cross-cultural perspective on inequality between old and young*, New York: Columbia University Press.

—— 1984b, 'Age and social change', in Kertzer and Keith.

Fortes, M. and E.E. Evans-Pritchard, 1940, *African Political Systems*, London: Oxford University Press.

Foucault, M., 1977, *Madness and Civilization*, London: Tavistock.

Fox, R., 1972, 'Alliance and constraint: sexual selection in the evolution of human kinship systems', in Campbell, B. (ed), *Sexual Selection and the Descent of Man 1871–1971*, Chicago: Aldine.

Francis, D., 1984, *Will You Still Need Me, Will You Still Feed Me, When I'm 84?*, Indiana: Indiana University Press.

Freud, S., 1950 (1913), *Totem and Taboo* (trs. Strachey), London: Routledge & Kegan Paul.

Fry, C.L., 1976, 'The ages of adulthood: a question of numbers', *Journal of Gerontology*, 31: 170–7.

—— (ed), 1980, *Aging in Culture and Society: comparative viewpoints and strategies*, New York: Bergin.

Gell, A., 1975, *Metamorphosis of the Cassowaries*, London: Athlone.

Gulliver, P.H., 1963, *Social Control in an African Society*, London: Routledge & Kegan Paul.

—— 1968, 'Age differentiation', in *International Encyclopedia of the Social Sciences*, 1: 157–62.

Gutmann, D., 1977, 'The cross-cultural perspective: notes towards a comparative psychology of aging', in Birren, J. and K.W. Shaie (eds), *Handbook of the Psychology of Aging*, New York: Van Nostrand Reinhold.

Hagestad, G., 1985, 'Older women in intergenerational relationships', in Haug, M., *The Physical and Mental Health of the Aged Women*, New York: Springer.

Halperin, R., 1984, 'Age in cultural economics: an evolutionary approach', in Kertzer and Keith.

Hareven, T., 1978, 'The last stage: historical adulthood and old age', in Erikson, E.H. (ed), *Adulthood*, New York: Norton.

Harlam, W.H., 1964, 'Social status of the aged in three Indian villages', *Vita Humana*, 7: 239–52.

Harrell, S., 1981, 'Growing old in rural Taiwan', in Amoss and Harrell.

Havighurst, R.J., B.L. Neugarten and S.S. Tobin, 1964, 'Disengagement, personality and life satisfaction in later years', in Hansen, P.F. (ed), *Age with a Future*, Philadelphia: Davis.

Hiebert, P.G., 1981, 'Old age in a South Indian village', in Amoss and Harrell.

Hultsch, D.F. and J.K. Plemons, 1979, 'Life events and life-span development', in Baltes, P.B. and O.G.Brim (eds), *Life-Span Development and Human Behaviour: volume 2*, New York: Academic Press.

Keiser, R.L., 1969, *The Vice Lords: warriors of the streets*, New York: Holt, Rinehart & Winston.

Keith, J. (1980), ' The best is yet to be, toward an anthropology of age', *Annual Review of Anthropology*, 9: 339–64.

Kerns, V., 1980, 'Aging and mutual support relations among the Black Caribs', in Fry.

Kertzer, D.I. and J. Keith (eds), 1984, *Age and Anthropological Theory*, London: Cornell University Press.

La Fontaine, J.S. (ed), 1978, *Sex and Age as Principles of Social Differentiation*, London: Academic Press.

—— 1985, *Initiation*, Harmondsworth: Penguin.

Laslett, P., 1976, 'Societal development and aging', in Binstock and Shanas.

Legesse, A., 1973, *Gada: three approaches to the study of African society*, New York: Free Press.

Levinson, D.J., 1977, 'The mid-life transition', *Psychiatry*, 40: 49–112.

Lévi-Strauss, C., 1969 (1949), *The Elementary Structures of Kinship*, London: Eyre & Spottiswoode.

—— 1963 (1962), *Totemism*, Boston: Beacon Press.

Lewin, K., 1952, *Field Theory in Social Science*, London: Tavistock.

Lewis, G., 1980, *The Day of Shining Red*, Cambridge: Cambridge University Press.

Maddox, G.L., 1964, 'Disengagement theory: a critical evaluation', *Gerontologist*, 4: 80–2.

Maine, H.S., 1861, *Ancient Law*, London: Murray.

Malinowski, B., 1922, *Argonauts of the Western Pacific*, New York: Dutton.

Mannheim, K., 1952 (1929), 'The problem of generations', in *Essays on the Sociology of Knowledge*, London: Routledge & Kegan Paul.

Marshall, V.W., 1985, 'Conclusions: aging and dying in Pacific societies: implications for theory in social gerontology', in Counts and Counts.

Maxwell, R.J. and P. Silverman, 1970, 'Information and esteem, cultural considerations in the treatment of the elderly', *Aging and Human Development*, 1: 361–92.

Maybury-Lewis, D., 1984, 'Age and kinship: a structural view', in Kertzer and Keith.

Mayer, P. (ed), 1970, *Socialization, the approach from social anthropology*, A.S.A. Monographs 8, London: Tavistock.

Morgan, L.H., 1877, *Ancient Society*, New York: World Publishing.

Murphy, W.P., 1980, 'Secret knowledge as property and power in Kpelle society: elders versus youth', *Africa* 50: 193–207.

Muuss, R.E., 1970, 'Puberty rites in primitive and modern society', in Muuss, R.E. (ed), *Adolescent Behavior and Society*, New York: Random House.

Myerhoff, B.G., 1978, *Number our Days*, New York: Dutton.

—— 1984, 'Rites and signs of ripening: the intertwining of ritual, time and growing older', in Kertzer and Keith.

Myerhoff, B.G. and A. Simić (eds), 1978, *Life's Career-aging: cultural variations in growing old*, California: Sage.

Neugarten, B.L., 1968, 'Adult personality: towards a psychology of the life cycle', in Neugarten, B.L. (ed), *Middle Age and Aging*, Chicago: University of Chicago Press.

—— 1969, 'Continuities and discontinuities of psychological issues into adult life', *Human Development*, 12: 121–30.

—— 1974, 'Age groups in American society and the rise of the young–old', *Annals of the American Academy of Political and Social Science*, 415: 187–99.

Neugarten, B.L. and N. Datan, 1973, 'Sociological perspectives on the life cycle', in Baltes, P.B., and K.W. Schaie (eds), *Life Span Development Psychology*, New York: Academic Press.

Neugarten, B.L. and G.O. Hagestad, 1976, 'Age and the life course', in Binstock and Shanas.

Ortner, S.B., 1974, 'Is female to male as nature is to culture?' in Rosaldo and Lamphere.

—— 1978, *Sherpas through their Rituals*, New York: Cambridge University Press.

Oster, A., 1984, 'Chronology, category, and ritual', in Kertzer and Keith.

Palmore, E.B.,1968, 'The effects of ageing on activities and attitudes', *The Gerontologist*, 8: 259–63.

Palmore, E. and K. Manton, 1974, 'Modernization and status of the aged', *Journal of Gerontology*, 29: 2, 205–10.

Piddocke, S., 1968, 'The potlatch system of the southern Kwakiutl: a new perspective', in LeClair, E.E. and H.K. Schneider (eds), *Economic Anthropology*, New York: Holt, Rinehart & Winston.

Plath, D. and K. Ikeda, 1975, 'After coming of age: adult awareness of age norms', in Williams, T.R., *Socialization and Communication in Primary Groups*, The Hague: Mouton.

Press, I. and M. McKool, 1972, 'Social structure and status of the aged: toward some valid cross-cultural generalizations', *Aging and Human Development*, 3: 297–306.

Rapoport, R.N. and R.V. Rapoport, 1965, 'Work and family in contemporary society', *American Sociological Review*, 30: 381–94.

Rayner, E., 1978, *Human Development: an introduction to the psychodynamics of growth, maturity and ageing*, London: Allen & Unwin.

Riegel, K.F., 1975, 'Towards a dialectical theory of development', *Human Development*, 18: 50–64.

Riley, M.W., 1972, 'Elements in a model of age stratification', in Riley, M.W., M. Johnston and A. Foner (eds), *Aging and Society, vol. 3: A sociology of age stratification*, New York: Russell Sage Foundation.

Rosaldo, M.Z., 1974, 'Woman, culture and society: a theoretical overview', in Rosaldo and Lamphere.

Rosaldo, M.Z. and L. Lamphere (eds), 1974, *Woman, Culture, and Society*, California: Stanford University Press.

Rosow, I., 1965, 'And then we were old', *Trans-action*, 2 (2): 20–6.

Ryff, C.D. and S.G.Heincke, 1983, 'Subjective organization of personality in adulthood and aging', *Journal of Personality and Social Psychology*, 44: 807–16.

Sahlins, M., 1974, *Stone Age Economics*, London: Tavistock.

Sarason, I.G., J.H. Johnson and J.M. Siegel, 1978, 'Assessing the impact of life changes: development of the life experience survey', *Journal of Consulting and Clinical Psychology*, 46: 932–46.

Sharp, H.S., 1981, 'Old age among the Chipewyan', in Amoss and Harrell.

Silberbauer, G.B., 1981, *Hunter and Habitat in the Central Kalahari Desert*, Cambridge: Cambridge University Press.

Simmons, L.W., 1945, *The Role of the Aged in Primitive Society*, New Haven: Yale University Press.

Sinclair, K.P., 1985, 'Koro and Kuia: aging and gender among the Maori of New Zealand', in Counts and Counts.

Spencer, P., 1976, 'Opposing streams and the gerontocratic ladder', *Man*, 11: 153–75.

—— 1978, 'The Jie generation paradox', in Baxter and Almagor.

—— (ed), 1985, *Society and the Dance*, Cambridge: Cambridge University Press.

Stewart, F.H., 1977, *Fundamentals of Age-Group Systems*, New York: Academic Press.

Strathern, A., 1972, 'The entrepreneurial model of social change, from Norway to New Guinea', *Ethnology*, 11: 368.

Strauss, A.L., 1959, *Mirrors and Masks: the search for identity*, Glencoe, Ill.: Free Press.

Tocqueville, A. de, 1961 (1835–40), *Democracy in America*, New York: Schocken.

Turner, V.W., 1967, *The Forest of Symbols*, Ithaca: Cornell University Press.

—— 1969, *The Ritual Process*, London: Routledge & Kegan Paul.

—— 1974, *Dramas, Fields and Metaphors*, Ithaca: Cornell University Press.

Tylor, E.B., 1889, 'On a method of investigating the development of institutions:

applied to laws of marriage and descent', *Journal of the Royal Anthropological Institute*, 18: 245–69.

Van Arsdale, P.W., 1981, 'The elderly Asmat of New Guinea', in Amoss and Harrell.

Van Gennep, A., 1960 (1909), *The Rites of Passage*, London: Routledge & Kegan Paul.

Washburn, S.L. and C.S. Lancaster, 1968, 'The evolution of hunting', in Lee, R.B. and I. Devore, *Man the Hunter*, Chicago: Aldine.

Weber, M., 1947 (1925), *The Theory of Social and Economic Organization*, New York: Free Press.

Weiss, K.M., 1981, 'Evolutionary perspectives on human aging', in Amoss and Harrell.

Whyte, W.H., 1957, *The Organisation Man*, Harmondsworth: Penguin.

Chapter two

A dangerous age: from boy to young man in Red Xhosa youth organisations

Philip Mayer and Iona Mayer

South Africa, in line with its colonial origins, provides a violent social climate to grow up in, including violence by the state among the population, and violence among the population occasioned by deprived and alienating conditions of life. In the 1960s, to which this chapter refers, black people had become widely concerned about 'senseless violence' and gangsterism among their youth, apparently spreading from towns and mines to rural areas by way of migrant labour.[1] In the 1970s, black school-children were to experience the full weight of state violence in a context of quasi-revolution.

Rural Xhosa communities have had their own ways of socialising youth in regard to violence. One was through the youth organisations. As Philip Mayer's extensive fieldwork in 1960–5 showed, these self-organising groups of local youth, typically from early teens to late 20s or after, have been a key institution throughout the Transkei and Ciskei (Xhosa reserves, so-called 'homelands' or Bantustans). Meeting at leisure to entertain themselves, they were also transmitting significant ideologies and social skills.

This chapter focuses on 'Red' communities, implying conservative, unschooled and pagan as against 'School' or missionised ones (cf. Mayer and Mayer 1974: Ch. 2; Mayer 1979: Ch. 1), and illustrated by Shixini in Transkei and Khalana in Ciskei, 20 miles from East London. Both places had the classic Red organisations, namely the Mtshotsho for boys and the Intlombe for young men, each also associated with girls of corresponding status. As everywhere in Xhosa society, the dividing line between boys and young men was manhood initiation, undergone most commonly at an age between 18 and 23.

Regional archives recorded conflicting opinions about these organisations from early colonial times. In many places local adults had tried at some time to suppress at least some of their activities with the help of white magistrates or black chiefs. Some administrators and missionaries had seen them as harmless entertainments. Others deplored the unsupervised mingling of the sexes. Some School Xhosa people too had come to mistrust them as pagan indulgences. But also, much had been made of the physical dangers posed by Mtshotsho boys fighting with dangerous weapons.

In an earlier paper on the Red Xhosa youth organisations (Mayer and

Mayer 1970), we were firmly in their favour and described their organisations as 'notably successful in a number of senses'. They had maintained themselves right down to the present, in face of all criticism – and in some cases competition – from, for example, Christian and urban sources. The youth seemed to enjoy them greatly, so much so that young migrant workers would maintain that they 'must' come home frequently so as not to miss too many meetings.

The most notable success seemed to be in regard to socialisation. In the Mtshotsho and Intlombe, as we saw it, youth socialised each other into adult-approved values and behaviour, particularly in the two important areas of sexuality and violence, even though the organisations were strictly peer-group ones without any adult participation or control.

Thanks to these organisations, we suggested, Red Xhosa parents and communities in the 1960s seemed relatively untroubled by the 'youth problems' that were causing great anxiety elsewhere, notably premarital pregnancies and 'senseless violence'. On the whole, their youth showed more lasting attachment to home and respect for parents than either School or urban youth. Red adults proudly referred to the organisations as 'the schools of Red people', and all sections seemed to agree that 'Red children are the best controlled'.

Looking back and reinterpreting, we now see a need to qualify that optimistic picture at one point: the socialisation by peers seems more ambiguous and the Red youth problem more noticeable than we allowed for. It relates to violent fighting, specifically by what were called the 'senior boys'. The Mtshotsho did not match the Intlombe for consistency in socialising out senseless violence because its leaders – the senior boys – were the very people most apt to become 'senselessly violent'. This topic also raises some wider questions about the ambiguous values of fighting itself in a long-standing colonial situation.

Boy and man

In Red Xhosa eyes the most crucial aspect of training boys into manhood was to get them to give up force and commit themselves instead to the rule of law (*umthetho*) and respect (*imbeko*). Precisely for that reason, manhood initiation was seen as a critically important institution and event, not only for the individual but for family, community and society.

According to Red Xhosa folk wisdom, boys are irresponsible and often pugnacious as part of human nature itself. They therefore needed to be kept under control and within bounds by plenty of parental discipline, including thrashing. Conversely the hallmark of an adult (i.e. initiated) man was that he can and does control himself in the interests of social order. Nobody has a right to lay hands on him, but by the same token he refrains from blows, and fights his own battles 'with words only'.

The distinction or opposition between boy and man had become axiomatic in the Red Xhosa way of thinking in a variety of contexts. It was culturally associated with other oppositions, for instance between 'bush' and homestead; between animal – 'a boy is a dog' – and human; between unrestrained sexuality ('bull') and socialised sexuality ('ox'). As to behaviour, 'boy' implied inconsiderateness and a lack of restraint, dignity and sense, which easily combined into an enjoyment of fighting for its own sake. In principle any adult man had the right or duty to chastise any boy whom he found misbehaving, much as with an actual dog, and the boy had to take it submissively. In short, a boy was seen as incompletely socialised and therefore still partly in the realm of nature, while a man was fully in the realm of society.

The boy–man opposition has traditionally been dramatised and acted out in the long-drawn-out procedures of Xhosa manhood initiation, but also in numbers of customary etiquettes – almost amounting to avoidances or taboos – designed to separate and distinguish between boys and men in everyday contexts. Red people valued these as the essential manifestations of respect. They could sometimes assume exaggerated importance in interactions involving fairly recent young men with senior boys, since that was when young men were keenest to emphasise their distinction from boys and boys were most touchy and resentful about it.

The senior boys, so-called, were the set who had worked through to the top seniority echelon or 'first grade' of their local Mtshotsho. They would be the next candidates for manhood initiation and promotion to the Intlombe: meanwhile, at the age of 17 to 20-plus, they had adult or near-adult physique and physical powers. Some were already migrant workers, earning for the family homestead and/or their personal wants or coming initiation expenses.

The senior boy, then, with his grown-up bodily strength, was perceived by adults as having lost a younger boy's controllability but not acquired a man's self-control or sense. 'He is big in body but not in mind' was a stereotyped formula by which they characterised this age. But the danger must surely be multiplied in the collective context of the Mtshotsho. There the senior boys joined forces and took command of their juniors, without any adult presence to restrain them. They were by definition the strongest and most experienced fighters, and in some cases also had money for weapons, over and above the pair of cudgels that every boy traditionally made for himself.

We shall be illustrating the perceived dangerousness of this age, and the adult fear of it, from the events known as 'battles' (*amadabi*, sing. *idabi*). Battles contrasted markedly with the adult-approved stick-fighting games or matches which were part of Mtshotsho routine. They were much more violent and lawless, but also they could not be kept segregated from the adult community and its interests.

It can be seen that Red Xhosa boys were to be initiated into manhood at the very time of life when they had become most prone to 'unmanly' behaviour, in the sense of uncontrolled and anti-social. Many of the initiation procedures can be looked at in this light. Older men had a prominent role to play in them: for example, at open-air gatherings where they stepped forward and publicly harangued the silent novices on the necessity of putting off boyish irresponsibility and taking on manly attitudes. It was as if the task of taming the dangerous age was more than could be left to the family and peer group who handled it for younger ages. After initiation the novice young men would be returned to peers and near-seniors in the Intlombe, where several years of attendance were thought necessary to consolidate their education in manliness.

The boy–man contrast in the youth organisations

The wider meaning of 'Intlombe' is a ceremonial round dance, while 'Mtshotsho' or 'Tshotsha' is the name of a juvenile dance style. Local Intlombe and Mtshotsho groups both held dances at weekends, using empty living-huts borrowed from absent owners. All local Red youth were expected to be there right through from Saturday evening to Sunday morning. They dressed up festively for the occasion in 'traditional' style, the girls in red-ochred skirts, the males with heavy multicoloured beadwork decorations round the neck, chest and arms. Red girls, on top of their home chores, spent long hours threading quantities of tiny beads into impressive designs for their sweethearts.

Both parties were occasions for male display. The males formed a dancing ring in the centre while the girls provided the music by clapping and singing (*ombela*) to order. During rest breaks a boy or young man could take a chosen girl out into the night and, as they said, 'propose love' to her. However, there were differences of style and atmosphere: the Mtshotsho – one could say – giving relatively more display to physical prowess and the Intlombe to social skills.

Mtshotsho dancing was fast and vigorous, sometimes noisy. The young men's dance movements were statelier, and their decorations richer, revealing less bare torso, for they had more money and more girlfriends to do beadwork for them. Boys commonly danced naked below as well as above the waist except for a penis sheath; young men wound a blanket around the loins. Girls also dressed more maturely for the Intlombe, with longer skirts and bare breasts, indicating marriageable status. Where boys were often hesitant or clumsy in 'proposing love' young men would be expected to show more sophistication.

A major Mtshotsho activity was 'playing sticks' – cudgel duels which were seen as both sport and fighting practice. The boys played regularly on Sunday mornings on the veld after the dance had ended. Girls were not allowed to come near these games. The Intlombe on the other hand had nothing to do with stickplay. Their typical pursuit was to 'discuss things' or 'hear cases' (disputes between members) with adult-style oratory and formality. This was often done during dance nights, with the girls sitting by quietly or speaking when called on. Sometimes the young men drank beer (not allowed in the Mtshotsho) with appropriate ceremony.

In Xhosa idiom almost any organisation or identifiable group claims to have its own 'law', meaning internal rules, conventions and codes of conduct. In principle a local youth group could interact with its peers anywhere else on the basis of common Intlombe or Mtshotsho 'law'. Xhosa seniority etiquettes were 'law' in both organisations, e.g. that the seniors present are entitled to the first pick of anything desirable, from food to beer to girls; that they must be allowed to speak their opinion and be listened to, and that juniors must not answer back or contradict them. In addition the Mtshotsho had a whole body of law regarding stick fighting, designed to keep it chivalrously regulated while also highly competitive: e.g. not to match unequal opponents, not to go on hitting after the opponent calls 'stop', or if he is on the ground. Senior boys were responsible for impressing the chivalrous code on juniors as much as showing them the technicalities of play.

The Mtshotsho was stratified into three grades or echelons, reflecting age, strength and experience. (Sometimes there would be additional fourth and fifth grades, jointly called the Intutu or children's Mtshotsho.) Only members of the same grade played each other at sticks. Generally the grade members were to interact as equals while requiring deference from those below and offering it to those above. There were no individual leaders: the Mtshotsho was controlled by its top echelon as a whole, though the most successful fighters enjoyed extra prestige.

Promotion came about automatically *en bloc*. Whenever the local first grade (called 'the senior boys') chose to go for initiation, thus leaving the Mtshotsho, they would be succeeded by the erstwhile second grade ('dyongos' – from Afrikaans, *jong*, 'boy') and the third grade would become second, with a new intake below them. Alternatively, however, a specially capable dyongo might fight his way to individual promotion. If he could personally challenge and defeat every member of the first grade they would have to accept him as their equal. First graders were often unwilling to grant this personal promotion and would refuse the dyongo's challenge accordingly. An underlying ambivalence could be perceived between adjacent grades, as between adjacent generations: the seniors wanting to defend their distinctiveness and prerogative precisely when and because the juniors began aspiring to them.

In the Intlombe only two grades were recognised, the *abafana* or full young men and the *amakrwala* or 'unripe fruit'. In wider social contexts 'unripe fruit' was a formal status lasting a few months after initiation was completed, but in the Intlombe context it was extended to several years. In contrast to the Mtshotsho the Intlombe had several specially designated functionaries. The most important was the so-called 'Magistrate' (*iMantyi*), with special responsibilities in hearing cases. To become 'Magistrate' one needed to be 'good at speaking' and 'persuading people' – typically adult male values.

Besides age and life stage, seniority could turn on the years spent by a member in the given stage relative to those spent by another member. In certain contexts a young man with two or three 'years of manhood' ranked above another with only one year, and in others, the emphasis would be on parity within the category. Intlombe 'cases' pursued the protocol endlessly, while the bored girls yawned in the background.

Both Mtshotsho and Intlombe groups would visit their opposite numbers in other locations. Although an overt aim of both was to 'dance together and establish harmony', relations between Mtshotsho groups tended to be shifting and quasi-political. Tension could often be sensed in the air as a visiting group arrived, and though they had to lay their sticks down before entering the dance hut, as a token of friendly intentions, a fight could easily be sparked by something or other. Cudgel play too was formalised in a more confrontational and warlike style than the fairly relaxed practising at home. A rupture of relations – 'We do not dance with them any more' – was often attributed to a fight at a past inter-group occasion.

By contrast, Intlombe inter-visiting was essentially peaceful and polite. The circuits were wider than Mtshotsho ones, sometimes covering scores of miles. Also, young men were entitled to visit other Intlombes singly and on their own initiative, not only on prearranged group expeditions. It was Intlombe 'law' that a visiting young man must be welcomed at any Intlombe regardless of whether he or his group had had any relations there before.

The ideal of wide-range peaceful visiting had explicit associations with manhood as against boyhood. During the seclusion period of initiation, novices were supposed to roam around visiting other lodges near and far. The contacts had to be friendly since fighting of all sorts was strictly forbidden to novices. The Intlombe itself, as a young man put it, 'teaches us to love each other. Late in life many are still great friends with those they met at Intlombe.'

From a mature adult standpoint – as our earlier paper noted (Mayer and Mayer 1970) – the youth in both organisations formed a somewhat marginal category. The autonomy they were allowed from the adult world was in a sense a *quid pro quo* for their non-interference in it, and for not troubling adults with their sexuality, fights or problems. Their meetings were extra-domestic, and in some senses extra-community, in disused or borrowed huts or out in the veld. In adult terms, the so-called 'Magistrate' of the Intlombe had no real power – domestic, political, legal or ritual.

But unlike Mtshotsho cudgel games, the beer-drinks and case-hearings of the Intlombe were kinds of play that foreshadowed 'real' equivalents in the adult world. An Intlombe 'Magistrate' would often be carefully watched in the adult community, because, as I was told, 'We may expect such young men to become future headmen or councillors one day.' An investigation into the backgrounds of a number of serving headmen confirmed that a high proportion actually had been Intlombe officials in their youth.

Law and force

The concept of the relation between law, respect and force differed significantly between Intlombe and Mtshotsho. In the Intlombe the young man had to carry the image of the socialised adult whose respect for the law and for his fellows was evinced above all by never using blows to gain his ends. In the Mtshotsho, law itself was something that had ultimately to be enforced by blows. The idea of using physical force to 'make others respect us', which would be sheer contradiction in Intlombe terms, was a recurrent theme and temptation here.

'How can I lead', said a Shixini senior boy answering my questions, 'if when contradicted I am unable to use force effectively?' It was no surprise to find that becoming a cudgel champion was a great ambition among boys: more interesting was the way they tended to equate it with being able to lay down the law. 'His words will be final when a final word is needed.' 'It is the same as having much money is to a European. He is respected and has a good position in the community.' 'It is human nature to wish to be ruler over others whenever possible.' Perhaps getting beaten 'like a dog' by fathers and other men (p. 37, above) reinforced the desire to be top dog among the peers.

Shixini boys were indignant because the local Intlombe had, as they saw it, been over-exercising their prerogative to claim the pick of the girls of all ages to attend at their dances. (Seniority 'law' required that a boy must yield if a young man beckons to his girl.) Senior boys explained the situation for my benefit with a heady mixture of the rhetorics of respect and of violence. 'We boys have much respect for the young men,' said one. 'But the young men have no respect for us at all. They sometimes came to take our girls to their Intlombe against our will. They would take away the best girls and we would be left with the useless ones. That was not right.' He went on: 'Now that we have got our axes we have refused them making such free use of our girls.' Another put it: 'If they do not show respect for us we will demand it with our axes.'

The Khalana Mtshotsho used to embrace boys from two local geographical sections. Then the senior boys from section A angered the dyongo grade from section B by high-handed treatment. It led to rupture: 'These seniors still called us "children". So we decided to thrash them, to force them to give us respect.' That proved to be the end of the single Mtshotsho group: 'They could no longer come to a common meeting place for fear we hit them again.'

Battles (*amadabi*) were mass confrontations between Mtshotsho groups of different locations or sub-locations (local administrative and neighbourhood units). Being fought in earnest, they were much less ruled by chivalrous conventions than ordinary cudgel games or matches, and much grimmer in their consequences. Battles were not frequent, but those that did occur were recalled by the participants long afterwards in considerable detail. While they differed in their underlying origins, in nearly all cases the rationale was that one side claimed to have been insulted or treated without respect by the other.

A battle was supposed to be preceded by a formal challenge when time and place would be arranged. Surprise attacks did occur but were regarded as cowardly. At the appointed time the two groups advanced on each other with horns blowing (the traditional challenge signal). The added noise of whistles and loudly chanted praises and war songs intensified the bellicose atmosphere.

Mtshotsho boys did not use knives as did fighting gangs in town, but they allowed themselves a generous interpretation of the 'stick' or cudgel which was the only weapon allowed to boys in Red Xhosa tradition. They would add knobkerries, heavy bent sticks (which overshoot the opponent's defence cudgel) or sharp pointed sticks, and in parts of southern Transkei battle axes too. No wonder there were occasional deaths or permanent disability.

This was the boys' most open challenge to adult authority. Chiefs and headmen constantly issued prohibitions against carrying dangerous weapons. Boys simply ignored them whenever they chose. Thus at Shixini Mtshotsho's victorious battle against Groxo four years earlier – supposedly avenging an 'insulting' attack at a party but really reflecting chronic rivalry over girlfriends – some defiantly carried small picks brought from the mines and 'sharpened to a point that easily goes through bones'. One pressed a sharpened axe against his fallen opponent's spine and, ignoring his pleas for mercy, 'kept chopping so as to ruin him completely'. Even his own side rated this 'a very cruel deed'. That Groxo boy still cannot walk. Criminal charges were brought before the (white) district magistrate, who imposed fines. The two groups had been feuding ever since. Boys appeared to deprecate such incidents but not the fighting of battles as such.

Pacification

If the obligation of the initiated young man to renounce fighting was a cornerstone of Xhosa tradition, so until not long ago was his obligation to be a fighter: that is, until colonial appropriation of the complementary opposites of 'law within and war without'.

Warfare has been prominent in Xhosa history for as far back as there are records. Chiefs were war leaders among other things. In particular the Xhosa have a longer history of wars against colonial aggression and associated internal wars than any other people in Africa. It takes up much of the hundred years from the late eighteenth century onwards when the British Cape Colony kept advancing its frontiers eastwards at Xhosa expense. The last war was fought in Transkei only eighty years before the fieldwork.

After conquest, the coming generation were no longer allowed to be trained for war. The pacification of young men by initiation needs to be considered *inter alia* in relation to colonial pacification. As long as there was war, young men were the warriors *par excellence*, and initiation was a step up in military as much as civil status. It promoted them to own and use the adult weapon – the lethal spear. At the time of fieldwork, the authorities had long prohibited the possession of spears except for ritual purposes, but initiation procedure still made symbolic connections between young man and spear. Not only was a spear blade used to circumcise the novices, but each was presented with a spear during seclusion, along with a stick which seemed to symbolise his changing civil status. The stick was white when presented; it had to be gradually blackened in the seclusion fire; in later life the man would carry his black stick whenever he went on important business. In everyday situations, if a young man lost his temper and seemed on the point of fighting, elders would sometimes say: 'It seems as if the spear has not changed his mind.'

The Xhosa did not take kindly to enforced pacification or disarmament, particularly the Red Xhosa, who were not exposed to Christian mission ideologies. At the time of fieldwork Red men still spoke of it grudgingly as one of the deprivations the conqueror had imposed. The public insistence on the unmanliness of fighting or interest in fighting might therefore be suspected of covering more ambivalent attitudes. Dignity forbade grown men to attend boys' fighting games, but they would sometimes stand and watch keenly from perhaps a hundred yards off. Even battles might be tacitly condoned. On at least one occasion boys describing a battle said that men who met them setting out with their weapons had made no attempt to remonstrate: 'They rather seemed to be egging us on.'

Old men said that boys' battles were very similar in style to inter-communal fighting or petty warfare of many years ago. That had been suppressed by the authorities, they said, but the boys went on having these battles despite almost certain police intervention, and there seemed no way of preventing them. In saying so, the elders were representing the boys as the one remaining pocket to have defied pacification; perhaps even a kind of shadow fighting arm in succession to the vanished spearmen of former times. Defining boys as 'irresponsible' and 'hard to control' was necessary if elders were to draw vicarious satisfaction from their continued fighting spirit without appearing to be compromised themselves.

Pacification of the individual, obviously, also had limits in real life. Red Xhosa communities were by no means havens of peaceful behaviour disturbed only by boys. Some young men, and older ones too, would continue to get into quarrels and use some force, particularly when drunk. Some elders would so overdo disciplinary thrashings as to move the victim's family to protest. But the response to an assault involving an initiated man would be a 'case', whether in the Intlombe, adult moot, chief's or magistrate's court. He could never mobilise his peers for a collective fight as boys did. In this essential respect the model held.

© Philip Mayer and Iona Mayer

Notes

1. Fieldwork was supported by the Institute of Social and Economic Research at Rhodes University and the Human Sciences Research Council of South Africa.

Acknowledgement is made to these and to the late Percy Oayiso and Enos Xotyeni, principal field assistants.

References

Mayer, P. (ed), 1979, *Black Villagers in an Industrial Society*, Cape Town: Oxford University Press.

Mayer, P. and Mayer, I., 1970, 'Socialisation by peers', in Mayer, P. (ed), *Socialisation: the approach from social anthropology*, ASA 8, London: Tavistock.

Mayer, P. and Mayer, I., 1974, *Townsmen and Tribesmen*, Cape Town: Oxford University Press.

Chapter three

The social process of adolescence in a therapeutic community

Iain Edgar

This chapter will focus on the relationship between adolescent ageing, thera-peutic intention and charismatic authority in a therapeutic community for adolescents. After describing the community and my role, I present the anticip-ated therapeutic progress of residents as both a chronological and a develop-mental sequence in which age and status are mediated through the concepts of peer-group therapy and democratisation, two principles of the therapeutic community approach. The chapter explores the partial state of communitas existing in the community. Adolescence in this community is analysed as exemplifying the features of a socially constructed liminal period, designed with both a therapeutic and a social intent.

The community

The community in question describes itself as a therapeutic community for adolescents. It is situated in Britain. It is physically located in a large Georgian house which is set in several acres of rolling parkland. The community can cater for approximately fifty residents at any one time. When I was living and studying the community in 1981 there were forty male and ten female resi-dents. This was the first year that female residents were admitted to the com-munity. There were twenty staff combining therapeutic and educational roles. The planned length of stay for residents is between four and five years with forty-four weeks a year spent in the community. The age of entry is between thirteen and seventeen . All the residents are placed in the community by local authority social service departments and are on Care Orders which vest al-most all parental rights with the local authority. Most residents came to the community from a residential establishment, usually a local authority assess-ment centre. Many had been in several residential establishments prior to coming to the community. According to an internal study, half of the children were of above average intelligence and one-third of them had high academic potential though they were often underachieving in school prior to admission. Most residents had suffered the trauma of family breakdown, often at an early age. A high percentage of residents had previous behaviour problems ranging from truancy, and offending, to alcohol/drug offences. Residents had not usually committed very serious offences such as murder or rape before admission, though one resident had been charged with attempted murder of his father, and another had been charged with attempted assault on a three-year-old girl. Little information was available on residents' psychological health prior to admission, though it was the community's policy not to admit psychotic adolescents.

The community was run according to the therapeutic community principles as defined by Rapoport (1960), Jones (1968), Clark (1965), Bettelheim (1974), Kennard (1983) and Sugarman (1984). Emphasis was placed on the social processes of communalism, permissiveness, democratisation and confrontation (Rapoport: 1960) and the principal arena for therapy was the daily one-hour community meeting at which attendance was obligatory for all educational/caring staff and residents. There were also occasional emergency community meetings. The treatment philosophy was based on psychodynamic theory, and staff particularly employed Freudian theory to convey insight to residents. The use of the peer-group to provide residents with support, insight and confrontation is termed peer-group therapy and was a crucial therapeutic ingredient. No attempt was made to restore previously successful social functioning and role performance. The therapeutic aim was treatment rather than rehabilitation. The aim of the therapeutic community was to change or modify the 'individual personality towards better intra-psychic integration' (Rapoport: 1960: 28).

I lived in the community for the eleven-week Summer term of 1981. I went to the community as a social work teacher who needed to gain experience of residential social work. I participated in the community as a temporary staff member who also had a general brief to 'study' the community. I became deeply interested in understanding the particular therapeutic milieu of this community and subsequently made a retrospective anthropological study of the use of myth, ritual and symbol in the construction of the treatment milieu. I primarily used a participant/observation methodology combined with unstructured interviewing of staff members and a detailed study of secondary written sources about the community.

Stages of residents' development

Residents are expected to progress through three main developmental stages during their typical four–five-year stay in the community. The first stage lasts approximately a year to eighteen months. During this time residents are expected to absorb the culture, norms and values of the community. They are not expected initially to give anything to the community by, for example, speaking in community meetings. It is understood by the community that all they can probably achieve is to learn to receive from other residents and staff, to relax and to learn to trust adults as consistent carers, possibly for the first time. During this period residents are expected to begin to 'open-up' and slowly reveal in community meetings and in other pertinent therapeutic situations their inner life and especially their difficulties and their feelings about their past and present life. New residents learn how to 'open-up' by modelling their behaviour on that of more experienced residents. Such an excavation of the 'catastrophic relationship' (Ezriel 1956) leads to severe behavioural responses by some new residents. New residents frequently abscond, are verbally and physically abusive to staff and their peer-group, and damage the building. To foster abreaction residents are free to 'doss' about all day and are not allowed to be involved in formal educational programmes, as the community intends the residents first to be integrated into the culture of the community and to 'work' on their own problems. This description of the first stage of the therapeutic process illustrates Rapoport's theme of 'permissiveness' as being a key principle of therapy. Permissiveness refers to the therapeutic community's decision to allow members a 'wide degree of behaviour that might seem distressing or seem deviant according to "ordinary" norms' (Rapoport 1960: 58). Such a first therapeutic stage is analogous to Almond's cross-cultural analysis of healing communities in which the first stage of resident development is termed 'imitation'(Almond 1974: 301–6).

The second stage of the therapeutic process typically begins after eighteen months of residence and extends up to about the third year of residence. This period should be the period when the resident has joined and accepted the community and is consequently able to take advantage of its ego-nurturing opportunities, be they therapeutic, recreational or educational. She or he will be beginning to internalise the norms of the community and will see it as their 'home'. They will typically have joined the formal educational programme. I observed that two notions, defined as therapeutic by the community and constituting a type of 'folk-psychology' (Weiss 1977: 10), would be stressed particularly during this stage, although staff would encourage their adoption at any point in a resident's stay. The first notion was that of 'containment'. 'Containment' refers to the idea, often expressed in the daily community meetings, that the residents had to learn to 'contain' or hold onto their feelings by becoming able to express and to share their feelings appropiately with others. The peer-group and staff would help this containment process by providing support, guidance and confrontation where necessary. In this way the residents learnt how to handle their difficult feelings without resort to destructive action. Following the community meeting, I would regularly notice residents giving physical and emotional support to their peers who had been distressed in that meeting. 'Control' was the second notion referred to particularly by staff in this stage of the resident's progression. Learning 'control' followed on from the gaining of skill in containing emotion as it referred to the development of ability in making what the community considered to be constructive choices of behaviour. For instance, one senior staff member would frequently state that there was a world of difference between wanting to steal something and actually doing it, and there was a much greater chance of understanding the deeper dynamic reasons for 'negative' thought patterns and impulses if the destructive behaviour could be contained and then controlled by the resident with support from the community.

The anticipated third stage of residents' development covers the last year or so of their stay in the community. During this time the resident is expected to participate in co-leading both within community meetings and potentially within all the community's activities. Co-leading refers primarily to situations designated as 'therapeutic', such as the physical restraint of a violent resident or the giving of an interpretation of behaviour in a meeting, and not to the administrative functioning of the community. Often residents in this final stage of their therapeutic career are studying for academic achievements such as 'O' and 'A' levels. Residents at this stage can still use the therapeutic resources of the community for their own development but will have fully identified with the norms of the community and be finally preparing to leave the community.

Two more therapeutic notions structure the community's understanding of residents' development during this last stage. These notions are 'understanding' and 'care'. 'Understanding', especially in community meetings, means the application of Freudian psychodynamic theory. Thus when an individual was seen to discover the mainsprings of their neurotic, destructive and compulsive behaviour and undergo a corrective emotional experience this would be recognised as 'understanding'. This usually meant the staff and/or peer-group relating a particular resident's behaviour to early life experience in her or his distorted family life and relationships. 'Understanding' operated on a community level too. There was an assumption that each person's experience was significant for everyone else in that people share similiar emotions and mentalities. Residents' ability to empathise with each other was developed in this way and links were sought between seemingly disparate events such as the theft of clothes and residents' fear of the loss of senior residents at the end of the year.

The final therapeutic notion utilised primarily in the last chronological stage of the resident's career is that of 'care'. In this community the goal of therapy was described as the development of the ability to care positively about oneself and others. Bettelheim, founder of the famous therapeutic community, the Orthogenic school of the University of Chicago, has described the importance of self-care thus: 'The most important task of therapy is not to have the patient gain insight into his unconscious, but to restore him to a high degree of justified self-esteem' (Bettelheim 1974: 19). It was a constant refrain in this community that the need fully to care about oneself was linked with the understanding that this could only be done by caring equally about each other. The whole life of this community revolved around the creation of this ethos of care, especially in the many uses of peer-group therapy. The community's view of 'caring' as being self evidently good allows us to see 'care' as an axiomatic symbol, after Myerhoff (1977: 210).

Status for residents in this community is determined by their age in relation to their identification with the norms of the community and in particular their development in relation to the chronological and developmental sequence outlined already. The theory and practice of peer-group therapy, for instance, clearly potentially contributes to an equalising effect on the relationship between staff and residents. So also should the application of Rapoport's notion of 'democratisation', which refers to the deliberate sharing of both therapeutic and administrative power in the community in the interests of residents' participation and development. In particular Rapoport saw democratisation as being a prerequisite for creating an open, trusting group climate in which the purposeful expression of feelings can be encouraged and where the often habitual anti-authoritarian transferences of residents can be diminished. Both of these concepts, peer-group therapy and democratisation, refer to an ideal situation rarely, if ever, achieved (Morrice 1979: 50–2). In this community the principle of democratisation, which Rapoport had developed in relation to communities of adults and not adolescents, was compromised by the Director's blending of charismatic and legal–rational authority. The Director had redeveloped the previous residential facility for adolescents into the present well-known therapeutic community. He had been Director at that time for over ten years. He combined a charismatic authority that would express itself in, for example, imaginative conceptualisations of individual and community need with a strong use of rational–legal authority. This combination of personal and institutional power gave him the ability to largely define the therapeutic way of life in the community as well as to control residents' perceptions of themselves and each other. An example of the latter would be his defining in community meetings who was progressing in the community and who was not. Democratisation as an ideal was also compromised by the fact that staff used staff meetings to share emotionally vulnerable aspects of their character and performance in the community rather than share these personal characteristics in the community meetings when residents were present. For staff there remained a sense in which community meetings were frontstage and staff meetings backstage, to use Goffman's theatrical distinction (Goffman 1959: 109–15).

The five therapeutic notions, 'opening-up', 'containment', 'control', 'understanding' and 'care', used to structure the resident's progress in the community, constituted the ideological core of this community's 'folk psychology' and, as indicated, was the particular belief system outlined to residents in community meetings and advocated by staff and the Director as leading to a successful therapeutic outcome for residents. I have formulated the use of these notions into a structured sequence from my observation of the discussions in the daily community meeting. The relative simplicity of such a therapeutic understanding has been noted before with respect to other therapeutic communities. Kennard refers to the Syanon therapeutic communities for drug addicts where the community has certain 'concepts' to explain both the causes of drug addiction and its cure: 'The availability of simple, direct concepts, rather than the more tentative or complex theories which professionals tend to use (such as psychoanalysis) helps residents to experience a sense of mastery over their previously helpless situation' (Kennard 1983: 69). At the centre then of this therapeutic community's explicit therapeutic process we find the idea of the importance of 'care'. It may appear surprising that such a radical community as this one was known to be should rely implicitly or explicitly on traditional sources of wisdom and insight as the idea of caring for others connotes in our society. 'Caring' is after all the second most important Christian commandment! Moreover the other 'therapeutic notions', stripped of their appeal in the community meeting, appear very homespun and well known. One could easily expect to hear such ideas, even if they are not formulated into a therapeutic process, prevalent in many residential settings such as community schools, mental hospitals and even prisons. People everywhere are after all exhorted to care about others, to contain or 'bottle' up difficult emotions, to 'open-up' or to 'get things off their chest'. Why then is the banal perceived as 'wisdom' and the commonplace treated as if akin to sacred instruction? The answers to these questions lie in first analysing the community as a liminal zone, as Turner used the concept of liminality (Turner 1969: 83–95), and then in the related analysis of the Director's charismatic leadership style, as evidenced by his mythogenesis.

The community as a liminal zone

Turner based his theory of liminality on Van Gennep's well-known study of rites of passage (1960). Van Gennep asserted that there was a common structure to rites of passage throughout the world. This common structure consists of three stages, that of separation from the previous social state, the liminal or marginal state and the final stage of reaggregation of the individual or group back into a new position or positions in the social structure. The separation from the social structure is accomplished through the process of the admission interview and the resident joining the new persons' group in both of which the particular norms of this community are articulated and transmitted. The return of the resident to mainstream society is particularly symbolised by an extravagant feast which the whole community spends weeks preparing for and is clearly the transitional vehicle for the leaving resident. I will concentrate now on demonstrating the features of liminality found in this community as Turner (1977: 37–9) describes them, for example: (1) new rules and social processes, (2) permissible regression and reconstruction of the personality, (3) mythogenesis by the Director, (4) a paradoxical state for residents, both elevated and special, yet also outcast and abnormal, very young and adolescent, (5) symbolic inversion, (6) dramatic performances, (7) the dramatisation of community problems through crisis community meetings,

(8) the blurring of work–play categories, and finally (9) the creation and combination of symbols. Turner asked: 'whatever happened to liminality in post-tribal society?' (1977: 39). In this community we can see elements of liminality used for therapeutic purpose.

(1) New rules and social processes

The construction of a therapeutic community environment necessarily involves the use of atypical social norms such as permissiveness and democratisation. New residents are shocked by the empowerment and the responsibility given by the community to longer established residents through, for example, the latter's involvement in the selection process and the therapeutic process already outlined as evident in community meetings. Formally there are few 'rules' in this community – alcohol and other drugs are forbidden and residents must attend every community meeting – otherwise there is a system of 'agreements' covering the ordering of the day and the allocation of responsibilities which was rarely challenged during my stay. Such a lack of rules is in stark contrast to the disciplinary regime of a typical children's assessment centre. The reason for so few rules in this community was linked to the absence of punishment. There are no individual punishments or sanctions available to staff except that of final dismissal from the community. Instead, residents who display what the community regarded as 'negative' behaviour, such as bullying or stealing, are 'confronted' (Rapoport 1960: 63) in the community meetings by both staff and other residents' interpretations of their behaviour. Moreover the problematic behaviour being challenged by the community was interpreted both as being related to earlier life-events experienced by the individual and as being relevant to the current preoccupations of the community. Burridge has written about the lack of rules in transitional states:

> the transient is separated off, placed apart until he can be inducted into a new set of rules. And this suspension of the human condition, a situation of 'no rules', appears as a necessary stage in the progression from old rules to 'new rules'.

> (Burridge 1969: 166)

(2) Permissible regression

Residents were not allowed to participate in formal education during their first year to eighteen months in the community. This was because their therapeutic development was seen as a priority, and new residents were expected to get in touch with their life experience to date and especially their 'catastrophic relationship'. Residents were also intended to absorb the culture of the community during this time. However, education in its broader sense was available from day one for the resident. Various art and humanities activities were scheduled throughout the day and any resident could join in. In particular there was a basic workshop where residents could undertake any play or artistic activity. This workshop was viewed by staff as akin to a nursery educational facility which allowed residents to start again their experience of play, exploration and learning.

(3)   Mythogenesis

I suggest that it is valuable to perceive the therapeutic definition of reality evident in this community as a process of mythical creation, involving the ritual ordering of time and space in the annual cycle of the community. Therapeutic community theory, as we have seen, emphasises the therapeutic potential of all social interaction occurring in the community throughout the twenty-four hours. There is then, in any functioning therapeutic community, an awareness that all social encounters carry an additional potential meaning, that of 'therapy'. I suggest that it is helpful to analyse this 'extra' meaning as being an example of mythogenesis. I am using the term 'myth' not to denigrate the idea of constructing a therapeutic environment but rather to stress the importance of resident and staff's belief in it. I am basing my use of the term 'myth' on Leach's definition of myth as being 'a sacred tale ... divinely true for those who believe and a fairy tale for those who do not' (Leach 1970: 54).

Lewis (1976: 120) similarly describes myths as 'sacred tales'. If, instead of 'divinely' in Leach's definition, we substitute 'therapeutically' we have a notion of myth as being 'therapeutically' true if it is believed. I suggest an analogy between societies such as the Tikopian Islanders (Firth 1936) wherein all aspects of life are impregnated with a sacred meaning through their relationship with unseen powers, and the community under discussion where all aspects of life within the community, from the material surroundings to the social processes, are imbued with an unseen 'therapeutic' meaning. Moreover this 'therapeutic' meaning is dependent on continual assertion by the Director. I further suggest that this mythogenesis by the Director is part of the explanation of both the special intensity of life in this therapeutic community, and the positive sense of specialness felt by residents themselves due to their presence in the community. Almond has described the importance of this sense of specialness in his cross-cultural study of healing communities (1974: xxv), and Lévi-Strauss has written of how cultural identity needs the community to feel special and original: 'In order for a culture to be really itself and to produce something, the culture and its members must be conscious of their originality, even to some extent of their superiority over others' (Lévi-Strauss 1978: 20).

I have identified three parts to this mythogenesis. First was the renaming of the community by its original Anglo-Saxon placename to symbolise a change of identity and to indicate a community with ancient and historical roots which would give a sense of security to residents in their personal confrontations with the past. The second aspect of mythogenesis, that I call the 'myth of symbolic compensation', was the continual assertion by the Director that the whole physical environment of the community was imbued with therapeutic meaning for the resident. For example, the kitchen/dining area was described by the Director as replicating at a symbolic level the good feeding experience that the fortunate infant experiences with its mother. Such replication was achieved through the attention given to the possible meaning for the disturbed adolescent of each and every object and decoration in that environment. The third aspect of mythogenesis observed in this community was the calendrical structuring of time. The community had developed its own forms of celebration for Christmas and other seasonal festivals as well as developing its own 'special' celebrations such as the feasts at the end of Summer term. These feasts involved the production, by the community, of artistic and symbolic forms such as, at the 1981 Summer feast, larger than life effigies of Superman and Superwoman and the decoration of the largest room as an intergalactic space.

(4) Paradoxical state for residents

Residents in this community are among the most marginal and outcast children in our society. Yet, paradoxically, I found a strong sense of identity with the community among most of the residents. This was illustrated positively in residents' frequent modelling of and verbal commitment to the developmental process already outlined. Many residents clearly felt considerable pride in belonging to the community and showed this to visitors by their descriptions and evaluations of the community. Residents were aware that they were somewhere 'special' and were often told this! Many of the residents, on leaving the community after four or five years, went on to college or university and such an outcome allows us to see the process of change aimed for in this community as the elevation of the structurally inferior. Moreover residents were perceived as chronologically aged adolescents yet emotionally aged infants as shown in the nursery style educational provision and in the dining-area symbolism.

(5) Symbolic inversion and (6) Dramatic performances

Feasts were demarcated as special events in the life of the community by staff, instead of the residents, cooking all the food. Indeed the most recent and disruptive residents welcomed the guests to the feast. Feasts, which happened approximately three times a year, were the most obviously dramatic performances with, as mentioned, lengthy preparation of both food and room decoration. Feasts typically involved music and speeches as well as the giving of gifts to those leaving.

(7) Dramatisation of community problems

The use of regular community meetings has already been described. There were also, however, emergency community meetings held at any hour of the day or night which would be called by staff or a group of residents as a way of dealing with a critical problem facing the community. At these times all other engagements were forgone and the whole community engaged in the task of confronting, managing and using the evident problem. The therapeutic processes apparent in these meetings represented an intensification of the previously described folk psychology and the advocacy of the developmental process.

(8) Blurring of work–play categories

I have shown how residents were seduced back into education by reframing work as play.

(9) Combination and construction of symbolism

The symbolic creation and description of this community was based on the idea of the importance and potential of each and every aspect of the environment from the choice of a water jug to the planning of an expedition. Bettelheim, that famous pioneer of therapeutic communities for adolescents, describes the profound importance of the local environment to a child:

> When planning a mental institution one must realise that mental patients can see one thing as safe, and another as personifying persecution or despair. Irrespective of how the rest of us view the object, everything becomes a symbol. Most of the patient's mental energy goes into ruminating on the hidden meaning of each colour, each object, and its placement; what it tells him about the institution's intentions and his future. Everything has its private meanings and secret messages which he tries to decipher ... this is even more true for emotionally disturbed children.
>
> (Bettelheim 1974: 99)

I would contend that both the living space and the social processes in this community are symbolised by the Director and staff in the context of a particular treatment world which has the following aims: to attract residents whose habitual response to institutionalised care is one of rejection; to provide a highly stimulating, rewarding and nurturing environment which will counteract early deprivation; and to foster social integration and identification with the community by the residents.

Conclusion

We can see, then, many of the characteristics of liminality present in the community and particularly in the daily community meetings. The therapeutic intention in these meetings is the refashioning of the person. Turner describes the 'wisdom.... .imparted in sacred liminality' as not merely 'an aggregate of words and sentences: it refashions the very being of the neophyte' (1969: 89). Residents come to the community with the explicit intention of changing themselves and the centre of this change is located in the community meeting. In these community meetings we see an intensification of the elements of therapeutic communities so far described, such as democratisation, permissiveness, confrontation and communalism. Whilst such elements are meant to be present throughout the community they are particuarly focused in the processes of the meeting itself. Democratisation is intended but only partly achieved. Permissiveness is the principle underlying the first aspect of the therapeutic process. 'Opening-up' and confrontation describe powerful ways of reaching the inner person. Rapoport's notion of communalism, which emphasises the therapeutic importance of close and egalitarian group feeling and attachment, is identical to Turner's notion of 'communitas', as Almond agrees (Almond 1974: xxv). Turner describes communitas thus: 'we see communitas rather as a relationship between persons, an I–thou relationship in Buber's terms or a We, the essence of which is its immediacy and spontaneity' (1974: 251). Both communalism and communitas aim for the creation of intimate, affective relationships. Moreover in liminal settings we find appeals to a generic identity of all individuals in the group as was affirmed in this community through the use of the notion of 'understanding' and 'care', already outlined, as features of the third stage of residents' development.

The resident is, as in liminality (Turner 1969: 89–90), made a *tabula rasa* on which 'is inscribed the knowledge and wisdom of the group, in those respects that pertain to the new status'. The transmitted wisdom in this community is the wisdom of growing up to live well in British society by following and incorporating the chronological and developmental sequence described early in this chapter. The ingestion of this wisdom leads to new status both in the therapeutic community and, hopefully, upon return to wider society, as no longer a marginalised member of society but as structurally elevated through successful participation in this lengthy therapeutic process. In the community meetings the notion of 'opening-up' is effectively an emotional stripping out of the past, preparing the resident for the new 'knowledge' – that is the 'folk-psychology' of the community.

If then the community meetings are perceived as periods of intense liminality this answers our question as to how the banal becomes wise, for as Turner writes: 'The powers that shape the neophytes in liminality for the incumbency of new status are felt, in rites all over the world, to be more than human powers, though they are invoked and channelled by the representatives of the community' (1969: 92).

If we adopt Moore and Myerhoff's (1977: 3) definition of the sacred as encompassing the portrayal of 'unquestionable ... social and moral imperatives' we can see a making sacred of the therapeutic process in this community, and especially in the community meetings, through the institutionalisation of liminality.

In this chapter I have described a unique combination of social structure and partial communitas, of authority/status and therapeutic egalitarianism. The community has created and sustained a setting in which can be observed many features of liminality used not only for the purposes of social initiation and education but also for personal reconstruction and the animation of the community.

More generally this example of a therapeutic community offers a contemporary model of a society for adolescents that compensates, through its cultural production, for the widely reported loss of religious, philosophical and social forms during the adolescent's transition (Laycock 1970). Such a society also compensates, through its community organisation, for the loss of a familial world for these adolescents. The feelings of belonging and of specialness were, as Turnbull (1985: 116) has described for adolescence in general, the foundations from which a sense of self, both as an individual and as a social being, could grow.

© 1990 Iain Edgar

References

Almond, R. (1974) *The Healing Community*, Jason Aronson Inc., New York.

Bettelheim, B. (1974) *A Home with a Heart*. Thames and Hudson, London.

Burridge, K. (1969) *New Heaven, New Earth*. Blackwell, Oxford.

Clark, D.H. (1965) 'The Therapeutic Community Concept, Practice and Future'. *British Journal of Psychiatry*. Vol. III, pp. 947–54.

Ezriel, H. (1956) Freud Centenary number of the *British Journal for the Philosophy of Science*. Vol. VIII, No. 25.

Firth, R. (1936) *We, the Tikopia*. Allen & Unwin, London.

Goffman, E. (1959) *The Presentation of Self in Everyday Life*. Doubleday, New York.

Kennard, D.K. (1983) *An Introduction to Therapeutic Communities*. Routledge & Kegan Paul, London.

Jones, M. (1968) *Social Psychiatry in Practice*. Penguin, Harmondsworth.

Laycock, A.L. (1970) *Adolescence and Social Work*. Routledge & Kegan Paul, London.

Leach, E.R. (1970) *Lévi-Strauss*. Fontana, London.

Lévi-Strauss, C. (1978) *Myth and Meaning*. Routledge & Kegan Paul, London.

Lewis, I.M. (1976) *Social Anthropology in Perspective*. Penguin, Harmondsworth.

Moore, S.F. and Myerhoff, B.G. (1977) Introduction in *Secular Ritual*, S.F. Moore and B.G. Myerhoff (eds.). Van Gorcum & Co. B.V., Assen.

Morrice, K.W. (1979) 'Basic Concepts: A Critical Review', in *Therapeutic Communities, Reflections and Progress*, R.D. Hinshelwood and N. Manning (eds.). Routledge & Kegan Paul, London.

Myerhoff, B.G. (1977) 'We Don't Wrap Herring in a Printed Page: Fusion Fictions and Continuity in Secular Ritual', in Moore and Myerhoff.

Rapoport, R.N. (1960) *Community as Doctor*. Tavistock, London.

Sugarman, B. (1984) 'Towards a New, Common Model of the Therapeutic Community's Components, Learning Processes and Outcomes'. *International Journal of Therapeutic Communities*. Vol. 5, No. 2.

Turnbull, C. (1985) *The Human Cycle*. Paladin, London.

Turner, V.W. (1969) *The Ritual Process*. Penguin, Harmondsworth.

Turner, V.W. (1974) *Dramas, Fields and Metaphors*. Cornell University Press, Ithaca, NY.

Turner, V.W. (1977) 'Variations on a Theme of Liminality', in Moore and Myerhoff.

Van Gennep, A. (1960) *The Rites of Passage*. Routledge & Kegan Paul, London.

Weiss, J. (1977) 'Folk Psychology of the Javanese of Ponorogo'. Unpublished Ph.D thesis, Yale University.

Chapter four

Coming of age among Jews: Bar Mitzvah and Bat Mitzvah ceremonies

Leonard Mars

This chapter examines an example of ritual innovation among Jews, namely the ceremony of *Bat Mitzvah* for Jewish girls aged about twelve, and demonstrates that in order to comprehend its emergence and continuing development we need to consider not only the internal structure of Jewish society, but also how Jews have responded to influences from the wider, non-Jewish world, especially notions about gender equality. The Bat Mitzvah is intended to balance and to complement the far older ceremony for boys, the *Bar Mitzvah*, which takes place when the boy is thirteen, with which both Jews and non-Jews are acquainted.[1] The girls' ceremony is a less well-known development in Britain, coming from the USA after 1945.

I shall discuss both ceremonies and demonstrate how these rituals express ideas about Jewish life, Jewish values, the roles of men and women in society, about the family and the local and wider Jewish community. In the first part of the chapter I present an ethnographic description of the two ceremonies with minimal commentary and in the second part I comment on and discuss their anthropological significance. One clarification needs to be made at the outset, namely that I am dealing with Orthodox and not Reform Judaism.[2] Reform Judaism has been more radical than Orthodox Judaism since its Bat Mitzvah ceremony requires the girl to read from the *Torah* on the Sabbath, and to wear a *tallith* and permits women to become rabbis. In short, Reform Judaism acknowledges no distinction between male and female in the service of the synagogue.

I have referred to the development of the Bat Mitzvah as recent, but in fact the Bar Mitzvah is also a latecomer given that the fifteenth century is new in terms of the long history of the Jewish religion. There is no mention of Bar Mitzvah in the *Torah*, the Jewish Bible, nor in the Code of Jewish Law (the *Shulchan Aruch*) of the seventeenth century. Both ceremonies, then, represent examples of religious innovation even if one, the Bar Mitzvah, has become institutionalised and formalised, whilst the other, the Bat Mitzvah, is still in the process of crystallisation.[3] Intriguing questions arise as to why the Bar Mitzvah developed in the late Middle Ages but I am not enough of a historian to answer them. However, in the case of the Bat Mitzvah I shall argue that the secularisation of Jewish life, especially for girls in the USA after 1945, and also ideas about sexual equality, prompted the creation of this ceremony.

Literally, Bar Mitzvah means 'son of a commandment', that is, a person who is obliged to fulfil the religious duties incumbent on a Jewish adult male – it marks the transition from boyhood to manhood in so far as the initiate is religiously responsible for his actions. Full adulthood is not bestowed upon him because he is not of an age to marry and assume the responsibilities of a householder (*ba'al ha bayit*) or to have dependants. Importantly, however, he can now count as a member of a *minyan*, the quorum of ten males necessary in Orthodox Judaism for a congregation to say the full range of prayers, and he can be called upon in public to read from the Torah, the Pentateuch.

Bat Mitzvah means 'daughter of a commandment' – and the ceremony that such a girl and others of her group undergo does not mark such a significant transition for her as the Bar Mitzvah does for her brother. The alternative term for the girls' ceremony is *Bat Chayil* (daughter of valour or of worth) and would seem to derive from the biblical passage, 'Who can find a woman of worth for her price is far above rubies?' (Proverbs 31:10). The choice of the term Bat Chayil represents an attempt by Orthodox Judaism to distance the ceremony from that of the Bar Mitzvah and to emphasise that it is a quite different occasion.

The ceremonies

Preparation and instruction

About a year before his Bar Mitzvah a boy will begin instruction on the chanting of the portion of the Law that he is to recite on the Sabbath[4] of his Bar Mitzvah – this reading of the Law consists of the last three verses of that Sabbath's reading from the Pentateuch, known in Hebrew as the *maftir*. In addition the boy will chant the portion of the Bible that follows the reading of the Law; this piece is known as the *haftorah*.

In addition to such instruction he will learn how to put on *tephillin* (phyllacteries), two little leather boxes, one of which goes on the head, and one on the arm, which contain extracts from the Pentateuch. These, if he is religiously orthodox, he will don every morning in prayer except on the Sabbath and on festivals. His father or grandfather will purchase a pair of tephillin and the boy's religious teacher will instruct him in the wearing of them. The acquisition of tephillin also marks his transition from a religious minor to a religiously responsible adult. A few days before the Bar Mitzvah he will receive from his father or grandfather a prayer shawl, tallith, which he will wear for the first time in public on the day of the ceremony.[5]

In Judaism prayer is less an individual question of faith and private utterance and more a public affirmation of community – hence the minyan: the reading of the Law is conducted in public; the phyllacteries may be donned in the privacy of one's home but preferably should be worn of a morning in the synagogue; the prayer shawl is mainly worn in public at services but can also be worn at home every morning of the year except *Tisha B'Av* (a fast day commemorating the destruction of the Temple).

All the boy's instruction then prepares the way for his performance in the public, religious domain of Jewish society. The girl's instruction pertains not to the public domain but to the domestic realm of the home. Nowadays she will attend *cheder* with her brother, but she is not taught to read from the Law. The year prior to her Bat Mitzvah, she and the group of girls who will be initiated together will commence instruction under the guidance of senior women in the domestic arts and crafts.

First and foremost they are taught the principles of *kashruth* (what is edible) – they will learn the rules, or criteria, for what is edible in livestock, poultry and fish. Then they will be taught how to prepare *kosher* meat, by soaking and salting for the table – rules about the separation of dairy and meat foods. Such instruction will be carried out in the homes of one or more women of the community. They will proceed to bake biscuits and Jewish delicacies; either the same or other women will instruct them in embroidery, often skullcaps for their fathers and brothers, or tablecloths and napkins for the Sabbath table – such embroidery will bear Jewish emblems. Thereafter instruction will take place in the lighting of the Sabbath candles and the associated benedictions.

It is immediately apparent that the girl's Jewish education is preparing for her future as a married woman with a family, confined to the domestic sphere, whereas in the secular school which she attends teaching is more or less the same as for her brother, and likewise at university where she may pursue the same studies as her male peers. However, religious rituals, even those recently created, tend to be traditional and to emphasise a past experience albeit one related to and affected by the modern world. The fact that a Jewish mother or wife may be a professional woman does not in religious terms exclude her from responsibility for running the home and responsibility for children (even if she employs *au pair* or domestic staff).

Age of initiate

A boy's Bar Mitzvah is celebrated on the Sabbath following his thirteenth birthday according to the Hebrew calendar – this is a day that is fixed and usually invariable. For the girl it is customary for the Bat Mitzvah to be held some time after the twelfth birthday. However, because the Bat Mitzvah is rarely an individual event and more often includes a group of girls numbering between two and ten, the age of the celebrant may range from twelve to fourteen, and the date of the ceremony may be subject to alteration. Fixity of the boy's celebration and fluidity of the girl's are in marked contrast to each other. If, for some reason, a boy has not experienced a Bar Mitzvah at the age of thirteen, he can at a later age, even as a grandparent, undergo the Bar Mitzvah ritual.

Day of ceremony

The day of the ceremony also varies for boys and girls; the Bar Mitzvah is held on the Sabbath whilst, in synagogues affiliated in the United Synagogue Organisation, the Bat Mitzvah is celebrated on a Sunday, and quite often not in the synagogue at all. The Chief Rabbi of Great Britain, Dr Immanuel Jakobovits, in a short note on the Bat Mitzvah, cites an American rabbi who, after considerable deliberation, gave his approval to this new ceremony but noted: 'the author nevertheless objects to holding such functions in synagogues. They should be celebrated at home or in a congregational hall' (Jacobovits 1967: 256). The Sabbath, as a holy day, separate from the rest of the week, which special status is marked by its name,[6] clearly signifies the importance of the Bar Mitzvah compared with the Bat Mitzvah which takes place on a day which in religious terms for a Jew is a weekday, a secular day.

Task of the initiate

The Bar Mitzvah boy's main task is to chant in Hebrew both concluding parts of the portion of the Law (Torah) for that particular Sabbath and also the reading of the Prophets (haftorah). Depending on the boy's ability he may do less than the customary amount. If he does not have a pleasant singing voice he may recite rather than sing his piece.[7] The boy will have been thoroughly prepared for this occasion by his teacher but to perform it in public before a large congregation composed of family, friends and congregants amounts to an ordeal for most boys.

In Europe before 1939 a boy might have been expected to deliver a learned disquisition on a religious theme.[8] Nowadays the boy's speech is delivered at the meal held for family and friends after the ceremony.

The task of the girl on her Bat Mitzvah is still uncertain in terms of content, since the ceremony is so recent and has yet to be institutionalised. Among Reform Jews the Bat Mitzvah approximates the Bar Mitzvah since the girl is called up on the Sabbath to read from the Law but in Central Orthodox congregations her assignment is not an integral part of the service. If it is held on the Sabbath, and most are not, the ceremony takes place as a postscript to the service when her task will be to say a few words about the study project she has prepared.[9] As individuals or as a group, girls may recite various Psalms.

Boys recite a Bar Mitzvah prayer in English and in Hebrew when they are called up to the Torah, though they may also recite it after an address from the rabbi, whereas girls recite, in English only, a much shorter prayer. The prayer is a relatively recent addition[10] to the Bar Mitzvah ceremonies but links into Jewish tradition by invoking the ancient patriarchs. It clearly announces the boy's transition from boyhood to manhood and refers to his circumcision which conferred upon him membership of the Jewish people and religion, in which ceremony he was a passive participant since he was only eight days old. On his Bar Mitzvah he actively reaffirms his membership of the Jewish people and religion and concludes with the Jewish affirmation that represents the assertion of positive membership of the faith, and which is traditionally associated with Jewish martyrs.

The Bat Mitzvah prayer is not yet recognised by inclusion in the *Authorized Prayer Book*. It seems to have been modelled on the boy's prayer though considerably abridged. Congregations individually have devised a form of words that acknowledges the termination of childhood but the phraseology lacks reference to other Jewish symbols such as the patriarchs, the Torah, the affirmation.[11] Furthermore its recitation in English only and not in both English and Hebrew denotes its secular as opposed to religious status.

Public address by rabbi

The Bar Mitzvah boy is addressed by the rabbi from the pulpit. His remarks are about the role of the Jewish man in general in the modern world but also refer to the individuality of the boy as a person, usually through reference to his particular family background. An instructive, eloquent and moving example of such an address is that delivered by Chief Rabbi Immanuel Jakobovits on his first son's Bar Mitzvah when he spoke primarily as a father but also as the rabbi of a congregation (Jakobovits 1967: 282–6). In it he referred to the patriarch Jacob and his son Joseph; the heritage that the boy had received from both the paternal and maternal sides of the family, but especially his paternal grandfather after whom the boy was named; the importance of studying the Torah and the performance of good deeds; the hope that God would bless the boy with righteous children who would learn the Torah; the sacrifice involved in being an observant Jew in the modern world which precludes certain occupations because of the need to observe the Sabbath as a day of rest; the need to donate one's earnings to religious and charitable causes rather than to spend them on luxuries; urging the boy, 'Whatever the choice of your career, be it a doctor, a lawyer, a cobbler, or even a rabbi, remain a *Bar Mitzvah*, a practising Jew, and become a *Ben Torah*, a learned Jew' (Jakobovits 1967: 286).

The address to the Bat Mitzvah girl, since she is one of a group, concentrates on the role of Jewish women in general and ignores the individuality of the girl. In a typical address given in an English city, the minister of the congregation urged the girls to attend synagogue regularly; to maintain the religious aspects of family life; to observe the Sabbath; to instruct children in the laws of *Kashruth*; to remain members of the faith. In addition he urged parents to retain an interest in their daughters' Jewish education.

Presentation of a gift by the synagogue

The address by the rabbi concludes with a presentation to the boy or girl of a prayer book which bears an inscription signed by officers of the synagogue, usually the wardens and the chairman. This inscription records the date of the ceremony and offers the congregation's good wishes to the initiate.

A recent development in the ceremonies is the presentation of a certificate by the congregation to the boy or girl. This document is formal in style, and resembles a certificate from the wider society such as a certificate of proficiency in music or a degree from a university, and signifies that the recipient has achieved a satisfactory standard in the course of instruction leading up to the Bar Mitzvah or Bat Mitzvah. In the case of the Bat Mitzvah girls the idea that they have earned a scholastic accolade is indicated by describing them as 'graduates' who should be treated with respect.[12] To my knowledge this term is not accorded to boys on completion of their Bar Mitzvah.

After the conclusion of morning prayers on the Sabbath, the parents of the Bar Mitzvah boy invite, through a public announcement by the Warden, all members of the congregation to a *kiddush* (food and drink) in the synagogue hall.

The chairman of the congregation presides at the kiddush and remarks about the parents, their commitment to Judaism and to the congregation, and about the boy's achievement on the successful completion of his Bar Mitzvah, expressing the hope that he will continue with his Jewish studies. He then calls on the boy's father to say a few words.

The boy's father refers to the changed status of his son in progressing from boyhood to manhood and in achieving equality with his father in religious terms. The father draws attention to Jewish experience in general but also to his son as an individual with a specific genealogy, as illustrated in the address by Rabbi Jakobovits mentioned earlier but also by less exalted fathers. For example, in one address delivered in a Welsh synagogue the father referred to the boy's descent in the maternal Hungarian and paternal English lines; the child's birth in Israel; his former residence in England; his education in Wales; and noted that his son was 'the living embodiment of the wandering Jew'. Where the new practice of the 'twinning' of the British boy with a named, Russian Jewish child who is not permitted to celebrate a Bar Mitzvah occurs, the father takes the opportunity to link the local celebration to the wider Jewish world and to draw attention to the nature of British society which allows freedom of worship, and contrasts it with the harsh life of Soviet Jews. Moving from the international scene to the local, the father concludes his speech by thanking local officers of the congregation, the cheder teachers, and the Ladies Guild for preparing the kiddush.

Although it has now become rare for the Bar Mitzvah boy to deliver a learned discourse on a talmudic topic,[13] he is still expected to speak either at the kiddush after the service or when a meal is served to invited guests. It is customary for the boy to thank his parents for rearing him and preparing him for the occasion of his Bar Mitzvah; to record his appreciation of his grand-parents; to mention his brothers and sisters, if any; to pay homage to his Hebrew teachers; to acknowledge his guests and their gifts; to promise to serve the Jewish people now that he is responsible for his actions. In one socialist Israeli village where I conducted anthropological research,[14] the boy had a modest, traditional, religious ceremony in the wooden hut that served as a synagogue, and a lavish party in a large hall in Tel Aviv to which four hundred guests had been invited. In his speech to this large audience a few months after the Six Days War, the lad made the customary remarks but added that he would not reach full manhood until he had served in the Israeli Army.

Girls may deliver a few words on their research project but they are not expected to deliver a speech at their Bat Mitzvah ceremony.

Commentary and observations

The initiation ceremonies of Bar Mitzvah and Bat Mitzvah enable the anthropologist to document changes in Jewish beliefs, values and social organisation over a period of time. Although the Bar Mitzvah is a far older yet not ancient ceremony and has become institutionalised, its significance has changed as the social experience of Jews has changed. The Bat Mitzvah, which is a recent socio-religious innovation, reflects the changed position of women in general and Jewish women in particular. The two ceremonies assert and express ideas about Jewish identity as it concerns individuals, the family, the local community and the national and international Jewish world.

The individual

The boy's Jewish identity is bound up with the world of men and with the social roles he plays in public, especially in the synagogue. His male identity is marked, literally, by his circumcision at the age of eight days, a ritual in which he is a passive participant. The Bar Mitzvah allows him a more active role in his social development but his degree of choice is limited since he is still a child subject to parental authority and is obliged to undergo the experience, mapped out for him since attendance at Hebrew classes.

The notion that a boy of thirteen has become a man is clearly at odds with the reality of his social position in the secular world where he still attends school and is dependent on his parents. Even in the religious field he remains less than adult since he is not married. Nevertheless he is no longer a child, he is able to participate in prayer as a member of a minyan; he is responsible in religious terms for his own sins; he will observe the religious laws more fully than before;[15] in terms of Jewish study he is expected to progress beyond the elementary level of children though, in fact, for most Jewish children both Bar Mitzvah and Bat Mitzvah signify the culmination of their Jewish education.[16]

The Bar Mitzvah boy has been removed from the domestic domain, predominantly a female domain which extends to boys and girls, and moved towards the male domain into which he will be fully incorporated at marriage. The Bar Mitzvah ceremony marks yet another stage in the development of the Jewish male; it terminates his religious minority and anticipates his eventual majority which will be attained under the marriage canopy (*chupah*).

For the girl there is no suggestion in the ceremony that she has been transformed from a girl into a woman, unlike the case of her brother who is considered to have made the transition from boy to man. Until the recent introduction of the Bat Mitzvah ceremony no transition was deemed to have occurred; the onset of the menses was not a public matter and no puberty rituals were held to mark this physical change. Even with the Bat Mitzvah ceremony the girl assumes no public duties and has no rights and duties conferred on her since she remains in the domestic realm of the home and the family symbolised in her preparation classes by the theory and practice of kosher cooking and of needlework.

In traditional and orthodox Judaism[17] the synagogue constitutes a male domain with no scope for female participation in prayer and ritual. Changes in the identity of boys and of men are marked by increasing involvement and participation in communal prayer, and since women and girls are excluded from this realm there is no need to signify anything since nothing has changed for them. The individuality of the boy, but not the girl, is permitted expression by the opportunity to elaborate on the basic ritual by performing an expanded or truncated reading of the Law, by the chance to shine in his speech. This individual glory or failure reflects not only on him but also on his family.

The family

Although the main focus is on the individual initiate in the Bar Mitzvah and on a group of girls in the Bat Mitzvah, the other members of the family are involved in and affected by these ceremonies and certain family relationships are altered.

In the case of the Bar Mitzvah the relationship between father and son is transformed in the religious sphere from inequality to equality. This transformation is manifest in two ways: the boy wears for the first time in public his tallith and he reads in public for the first time from the Torah. The changed relationship is expressed in the paternal blessing that the father utters in the synagogue, 'Blessed is he who has freed me from the responsibility of this child.' While the blessing indicates that the boy is now responsible to God for his actions, however, the father still retains responsibility for his son as the latter remains economically and socially dependent on him.

The relationship between mother and son is also altered since the boy is removed from the women's world and the realm of the mother into the men's world and the realm of the father. In some synagogues this modification of the mother–son relationship is marked by the practice of the mother and other women showering sweets from the women's gallery to the floor below where the boy is seated with the men. Another sign of this changed relationship occurs when the boy is urged by the rabbi after reciting his portion of the Torah to ascend to the gallery to greet his mother – the last occasion on which he will venture into that area.[18]

The grandfathers, whether alive or dead, feature in the Bar Mitzvah. If the grandfathers are alive it is highly likely that they will be called to read from the Torah, and if dead their memory will be invoked at the kiddush or at the meal after the ceremony. If a grandfather dies before the Bar Mitzvah boy is born, then the latter is likely to inherit his name and be identified with him.[19] Sharing the same name indicates the identification of grandparent and grandchild and hints at continuity after death of the grandfather and also of his forebears. When the grandfather is present to celebrate his grandson's Bar Mitzvah then once again equality in religious terms is achieved.

The Bar Mitzvah boy's elder brothers may also be called up, not usually to read from the Torah, but to pronounce a blessing, and depending on the size of the family so, too, may his uncles and male cousins. The celebration of the Bar Mitzvah is a family activity and family honour is at stake.[20]

In the case of the girl and her Bat Mitzvah, negligible change takes place in her relationship with her father or mother. No paternal blessing is said by the father releasing him from the responsibility for the child, in contrast with his son's case, since precisely no change has occurred as he remains responsible for her until she marries. Her position as a dependant, subject to paternal authority, persists until she passes out of his hands into those of her husband. Her relationship with her mother continues, as before, to be concerned with domestic matters such as cooking and sewing as demonstrated in the instruction preceding her Bat Mitzvah ceremony.

A girl may be named after her grandparent if the latter dies prior to the birth of the girl, but her identification with her grandmother is not as strong as that of her brother with his grandfather if only because religious roles in Orthodox synagogues are confined to males, and active and equal membership in religious services is what the Bar Mitzvah celebrates, whereas for Bat Mitzvah girls no such religious role is assumed. Similarly as girls in Orthodox synagogues are precluded from reading the Torah, so there is no opportunity for her brothers, let alone her sisters, to be in the number called to read.

Whereas family members will, and do, travel from abroad and from long distances within a country for a Bar Mitzvah, they are less likely to do so for a Bat Mitzvah, which remains more of a local affair and therefore does not bring the extended family together so much in a geographically mobile society.

The local community

The celebration of a Bar Mitzvah or Bat Mitzvah requires most parents to turn to the local synagogue and its officers for assistance in holding the ceremony.

Even if the father is capable of preparing his son for the Bar Mitzvah it is not customary for him to do so. The child's preparation and instruction are entrusted to the congregation and its agents. In most cases the family will already be members of the synagogue, and indeed will have joined it in order to be able to invoke the synagogue's resources and personnel for the ceremony.[21] Occasionally, however, the parents may not have joined the synagogue, either out of choice or because they have been debarred from membership,[22] yet still choose to send their children to Hebrew classes so that they can have a Bar Mitzvah ceremony. One of the rights accruing to parents of membership of a synagogue is that their child will receive instruction and usually there is no problem in exercising that right. However, the synagogue may on occasions withhold that right or observe it in an attenuated and even humiliating manner.[23]

When a Bar Mitzvah is celebrated, attendance in the synagogue is usually much larger than for a regular Sabbath service. The larger than usual congregation stems partly from the presence of members of the extended family, often from out of town, but also, depending on the status of the parents in the local community,[24] many congregants feel an obligation to support the family of the boy. In the case of the Bat Mitzvah ceremonies held on a Sunday local congregants also feel an obligation to attend.

Those among the congregation who would rarely, if ever, attend a synagogue will be the non-Jewish associates of the parents of the child. Sometimes non-Jewish teachers from the secular school will be invited but it is rare for non-Jewish school friends to be present since it is the parents rather than the initiate who invite the guests. In this manner, the incorporation of the Jewish community in a multi-religious, multi-ethnic society is signified.

Whereas Bar Mitzvah ceremonies attract members of the local Jewish community and also Jews from out of town and even from abroad, the Bat Mitzvah ceremony tends to attract mainly local people and a few persons from out of town. It appears that the sense of obligation to attend a Bat Mitzvah ceremony is not as strong as for a Bar Mitzvah – perhaps because of the relative novelty of the former and its ambiguous position in Central Orthodoxy in Britain.

The national and international Jewish world

We have noted a difference between the more parochial nature of the Bat Mitzvah and the more cosmopolitan aspect of the Bar Mitzvah. This difference is also highlighted by the announcement made by the parents of the boy, together with the grandparents, of the child's forthcoming Bar Mitzvah in the columns of the *Jewish Chronicle*.[25] To my knowledge no such announcement is made of a Bat Mitzvah ceremony. However, the *Jewish Chronicle* does publish photographs of both boys and girls after the ceremonies, and the name of the synagogue as well as those of the children and the officiants are also featured.

Though one ceremony may be more localised than the other in terms of family attendance each invokes aspects of Jewish history, culture and religion beyond the immediate family, neighbourhood and town. For example, as already mentioned, a recent custom has developed whereby the child is 'twinned' with a named, Jewish coeval from another part of the world where Jews have restrictions placed on the observance of their religion. In this way Jewish solidarity is affirmed and the child and the whole congregation are made aware of their good fortune to enjoy freedom of worship.

Since the Six Days War of June 1967, which resulted in the reunification of the city of Jerusalem and restored the Western Wall to Jews as a place of worship, it has become the practice for some diaspora Jews as well as Israeli Jews to hold Bar Mitzvah ceremonies at this shrine.[26] This pilgrimage serves to link diaspora Jewry with Israel, reinforces the strong sense of history that Jews have and also affirms the importance of Jerusalem in both the actual and the cognitive geography of Jews.

The choice of research topics by girls for their projects links them to Jewish scriptures through such matriarchs as Sarah, Rebecca and Rachel and to other women in the Bible such as Deborah, Esther and Ruth. Some of these figures stress the traditional role of the mother, others of resourceful, courageous women. More recent, female, Jewish role models such as Golda Meir, Anne Frank, and Hannah Szenes[27] move away from the stress on maternal values to themes of heroism, self-sacrifice, political activism and personal independence, values which do not square with the exclusion of women from the administrative affairs of synagogues and their confinement to the culinary activities of the congregation.

Whilst the ceremonies stress Jewish identity, values and culture they do not ignore the national and cultural values of the countries of which the celebrants are citizens. For example in Britain the services include prayers for the queen and her family and references are made to the quality of life in Britain; in the USA the American state is lauded, and in both these cases contrasts are made with states in which Jews suffer oppression. The emphasis in Britain and the USA is on the hyphenated Jewish-British, Jewish-American identity and within these overall identities further specification as to the Welsh, Scottish and English Jewry, or New York and Californian Jewry.

Dramatic performance

Apart from the structural aspects of Bar Mitzvah and Bat Mitzvah that link the initiate to the family, the local Jewish community and the wider Jewish world, the ceremonies also have what Beattie (1980: 35), in discussing sacrifice, calls a 'functional' significance, namely the sense in which these rituals constitute a dramatic performance for the various participants in the event. The star role is reserved for the boy and the girls who wear new clothes, and secondary parts are played out by their parents and kinsfolk as well as the officials of the congregation and the clergy, and finally the witnesses of these events who constitute an audience that ritually applauds the initiates by shouting out *'Mazaltov!'* ('Congratulations', literally 'Good luck') and *'She'Koach!'* (literally 'May you have strength' and idiomatically 'Well done!').

Apart from the sense of social obligation experienced by kinsfolk and members of the congregation to attend these ceremonies, the element of drama also enhances the size of the congregation since they, too, have an active part in the performance, more so than in the ordinary Sabbath service.[28]

For the individual initiates the dramatic ritual marks their transition to increasing adulthood, whereas for the congregation it brings together a group of persons who may be differentiated in economic, political and kinship interests but who are united in their religious and ethnic affiliations. The occasion reconfirms and reconstitutes their collective identity.

Conclusion

Both Bar Mitzvah and Bat Mitzvah ceremonies are occasions on which the Jewish identity of the adolescent is publicly stated and defined and where faithfulness to Judaism and the Jewish people is formally and ceremonially declared. This need to reaffirm adherence to the faith and the people would not be necessary were they not jeopardised by the high rate of assimilation, especially through intermarriage,[29] and the low birthrate of Central Orthodox and non-Orthodox British Jews (Waterman and Kosmin, 1986: 12).

Whereas intermarriage between Jews and non-Jews had previously involved mainly Jewish grooms and non-Jewish brides, from the 1960s onwards there has been an increase in marriages between Jewish brides and non-Jewish grooms.[30] It would seem no coincidence that both in the USA and in Britain when Jewish society saw itself threatened increasingly by secularisation and loss of members, it has turned to ritual as a protective, reassuring response. Both the Bar Mitzvah and Bat Mitzvah ceremonies contain exhortations to the adolescents to maintain their ethnic and religious identity, and both anticipate and refer to the celebration of marriage within the faith. The social reality, however, is that many of the celebrants will not in fact marry endogamously but will 'marry out'.

In recognition of this possibility, the rite of passage at twelve or thirteen may be the last public occasion on which parents may celebrate and may define the Jewish identity of their children and it may come to resemble a wedding. In fact the lavish celebrations and conspicuous consumption that characterise these rituals are often compared by guests to those that mark Jewish weddings, the clear implication being that a Bar Mitzvah or Bat Mitzvah should be on a lesser scale. If the adolescent rituals should be the final passage then it becomes a wedding *manqué*.

The Bat Mitzvah ceremony represents an attempt to provide a ceremony for girls that approximates the Bar Mitzvah ceremony for their brothers. In Reform synagogues the Bar Mitzvah rituals in their totality have been applied to girls and no distinction is made between boys and girls in the performance of the celebrations. Ultra-Orthodox synagogues will have no truck with ritual innovations such as *Bat Mitzvah* (Poll, 1962: 42)[31] and because they restrict their links with the wider, largely secular and non-Jewish society they are more resistant to general societal pressures which push for change involving women and girls.

Between Reform Jews and the ultra-Orthodox Hasidim are to be found the majority of Jews, 'middle of the road Jews' as they call themselves, for whom Reform Judaism represents too great a break with Jewish tradition and for whom Hasidism in most forms is incompatible with modern life since it represents a return to the ghetto and cuts itself off, as far as possible, from interaction with the non-Jewish world and also from the world of secularised Jews.[32] For 'middle of the road Jews', termed 'Conservative' in the USA,[33] and affiliated to the United Synagogue Movement in Britain, the introduction of the Bat Mitzvah represented an attempt to reconcile traditional Jewish customs with trends to increasing equality between the sexes in the wider society.

The Bat Mitzvah, as practised in Central Orthodox synagogues, acknowledges that girls have been ritually deprived at puberty and that such deprivation has to be rectified. Increasing equality in the secular world where girls and women interact and compete with boys and men, more or less as equals, has produced a demand to recognise that some change be instituted in the ritual sphere so that a change in their status is publicly acknowledged and validated. The demand emanates from the wider, non-Jewish, secular world and is taken up by Jewish teachers and parents and clergy. The way in which this demand is met is to create a ritual, reminiscent of the Bar Mitzvah but qualitatively different. This ritual, the Bat Mitzvah, is a gesture to balance the ritual passage of boys; it acknowledges girls as a category rather than as individuals. But in traditional religious terms it is unnecessary since women and girls cannot be counted as members of a minyan, cannot read from the Torah, and, even in the routine and non-religious administrative affairs of most synagogues of the United Synagogue Movement, are not full or 'privileged' members, that is they have no voting rights and cannot stand for office.

Whereas the ceremony of Bar Mitzvah bestows on the boy an adult ritual status which entitles him as an individual to participate actively as a full congregant in the religious sense, taking him outside of his family into the male domain of the congregation and the local Jewish community, the Bat Mitzvah in contrast fails to mark any transition in ritual status for the groups of girls who undergo the ceremony. What it does is to identify them with the world of Jewish women in general, whose role in synagogue affairs is confined to preparing the food for communal occasions. For girls the Bat Mitzvah constitutes a ritual but not a rite of passage – no change in status will occur until they marry when they pass from dependence on a father to dependence on a husband.

The Bat Mitzvah represents a compromise between the demands of a secular society that are felt by Jews as members of that society and the values of traditional Judaism that have a limited place for women in the prayers and affairs of the synagogue. For Orthodox Jews, I conclude that the Bat Mitzvah ceremony represents a gesture to balance the ritual position of girls *vis-à-vis* their brothers. It is simultaneously both conservative and innovative; it acknowledges the ritual deprivation of girls at puberty and endeavours to rectify that situation but that is as far as Central Orthodox Jews will go for the present. Not for them the adamant, traditional stance of the ultra-Orthodox with the strict distinction between men and women in the religious domain, nor the radical abolition of that distinction by Reform Judaism, hence this example of innovative conservatism.

Acknowledgements

This chapter is based on a research project partly funded by the Memorial Foundation for Jewish Culture, New York.

I am pleased also to acknowledge the contributions of the following to an earlier version of this chapter: M. Chazan, J. Hutson, R. Jenkins, A.J. Parker and G. Mars.

I am grateful to Carol Cook for all her secretarial skills at various stages in the preparation of this chapter.

Glossary

Bar Mitzvah   Boy's initiation ceremony, introduced in the fifteenth
century; also practising Jew.

Bat Mitzvah   Girl's initiation ceremony, introduced mid twentieth century.
Also known as *Bat Chayil*.

Ben Torah A learned Jew.

Cheder   Classes for children to learn the rudiments of Hebrew, organised
by the synagogue.

Chupah   Marriage canopy.

Haftorah   Portion of the Bible that follows the Sabbath reading of the
portion of the Pentateuch.

Halacha   Jewish religious Law.

Kashruth   Rules for the edibility and preparation of food in Jewish Law.

Kiddush   Literally sanctification, refers to food and drink served to a
congregation on a special occasion.

Kosher   Edible according to Jewish Law.

Maftir   Last three verses of a Sabbath's reading of the Law from the
Pentateuch.

Minyan	Quorum of ten men necessary to congregate for a full range of prayers.
Shema	The Jewish affirmation of faith. From Deuteronomy 6: 4. 'Hear, O Israel! The Lord is our God, the Lord is One.'
Tallith	Prayer shawl.
Tephillin	Extracts from the Pentateuch in little leather boxes worn on the head and on the arm in morning prayer.
Tisha B'Av	A fast day commemorating the destruction of the Temple.
Torah	The Pentateuch, also the whole body of Jewish practice and Law.

Notes

1. From various British and American films, e.g. *Sunday Bloody Sunday, Thoroughly Modern Millie, The Jolson Story, The Jazz Singer*, and in Britain from Jack Rosenthal's television drama *The Bar Mitzvah Boy*.
2. A recent study on male synagogue membership in the UK in 1983 gives the following distributions by religious grouping: Right Wing Orthodox 4.4%, Central Orthodox 70.5%, Sephardi 2.7%, Reform 15.5%, Liberal 7.3% (Waterman and Kosmin 1986: 28). My study is concerned with what Waterman and Kosmin term the Central Orthodox, basically the United Synagogue whose head is the Chief Rabbi of Great Britain.
3. An interesting indicator of the newness of the Bat Mitzvah can be detected by consulting Jewish encyclopaedias published this century. The *Encyclopaedia Judaica* (Jerusalem 1972) contains an article by Zvi Kaplan on Bar Mitzvah to which is tacked on a final paragraph devoted to Bat Mitzvah. The *Jewish Encylopaedia* (1901) has no mention of Bat Mitzvah. Marshall Sklare states that the Bat Mitzvah was developed by Mordecai M. Kaplan (1881–1983), the founder of the Reconstructionist Movement (Sklare 1972: 155). Efron and Rubin contend that the ceremony of the Bat Mitzvah developed in the 1920s in the USA but that it took some time to become accepted (1977: 12). An indicator of the time taken for acceptance of the Bat Mitzvah, even by the authors themselves, is that the first edition of their book, published in 1963, and entitled *Your Bar Mitzvah*, confined itself to the boys' ceremony.
4. Though not necessarily on the Sabbath in Orthodox Judaism, where the Bar Mitzvah boy may be called up on Monday or Thursday morning, if his Bar Mitzvah date coincides with one of these days.
5. On death a Jew is buried in his tallith and this may well be the one he received on his Bar Mitzvah.
6. In the Jewish calendar the days of the week do not have names. They are called First Day, Second Day and so on. Only the Sabbath has a name.
7. One concerned mother whose son's voice was not too melodious, but was more so than that of his elder brother who had recited his Bar Mitzvah, asked the rabbi whether he could sing his portion and was wryly told that he could, even though he was no Caruso.
8. Shmarya Levin, in the first volume of his autobiography, *Childhood in Exile,* wrote that his 'Bar Mitzvah address was a complicated and involved treatise on a Talmudic point' (Levin, 1939: 270). Tamara Deutscher, in an introduction to a collection of her husband's essays, notes that Isaac Deutscher in 1920 delivered a learned discourse for two hours on whether the saliva of a mythical bird, the Kikiyon, was kosher or not, that is whether it was edible according to Jewish ritual

(Deutscher 1968: 4).

9. These projects may involve research into biblical characters, for example the matriarchs Sarah, Rebecca and Rachel, or Esther and Deborah are popular topics. Recent historical figures such as Golda Meir, Anne Frank and Hannah Szenes are frequently chosen. Sometimes topics as diverse as *Kashruth*, marriage, the Hebrew University, the Sabbath and Jerusalem are selected. These projects, often beautifully illustrated and written, will be exhibited on a table for perusal by the congregation.

10. J. Hertz, formerly Chief Rabbi of Great Britain and the British Empire, observes that it was composed by Chacham Altom (1835–79) who was head of the London Sephardi community, and was incorporated in the *Authorized Prayer Book* in 1923 (1948: 1043)

11. The affirmation (*shema*), however, is often recited as one of the readings that the girls perform and it seems likely to be a permanent feature in any subsequent formalisation of Bat Mitzvah ceremonies.

12. For example in the published programme of one synagogue the following request was made: 'Congregants are requested to remain seated until the Officiates and graduates have left the synagogue.'

13. So rare in fact, even among ultra-Orthodox Jews, that Poll (1962: 144) reports an advertisement in the American Yiddish Press by a professional speech writer, 'If you need a *Bar Mitzvah* speech in the old familiar style, call Ulster 5–6028.'

14. Mars (1980: 147–53).

15. After Bar Mitzvah he will observe the various fast days in the Jewish calendar from which as a child he was previously exempt.

16. Sklare and Greenblum (1979: 295) for the USA and Rayner and Hooker (1978: 106) for Britain.

17. In Reform Judaism equality of the sexes is manifest by the Bat Mitzvah girl being called up to read from the Torah, her wearing of a skull-cap and tallith and by the fact that the rabbi who officiates may well be a woman.

18. In Woolf (1983: 42) the author recalls his Bar Mitzvah that took place in 1913 in Cardiff.

19. Among Ashkenazi Jews it is the custom to name the children after deceased, rather than living, relatives.

20. Woolf (1983: 41), Rosenthal (1986).

21. c.f. Sklare and Greenblum (1979: 85–91) who cite parenthood and imminent Bar Mitzvah celebrations as a major consideration for people to join the synagogue in an American city that they call Lakeville.

22. They may be precluded from membership by certain local rules that debar a Jewish person who has married a gentile. Though the parents may be debarred membership, the children, if Jewish according to *halacha* (Jewish religious Law), may be entitled to receive, for a fee, instruction at the synagogue's Hebrew classes.

23. For example, one synagogue in the London area did not allow the Bar Mitzvah boy to have any member of his family on the *bimah* whilst he read his *maftir* and *haftorah*, did not hold a *kiddush* and withheld the rabbi's blessing from him. This synagogue was subsequently condemned by a Jewish religious court (see the *Jewish Chronicle*, 6, 13, 20, 27 March, 24 April 1987).

24. See Mars (1980) for a discussion of how the status of the family affects attendance at rites of passage.

25. The *Jewish Chronicle*, a weekly newspaper founded in 1841, is the major organ of British Jewry.

26. The Western Wall, known to many non-Jews as the Wailing Wall, is the last remnant of the Temple destroyed in AD 70. For its significance in modern Judaism and Zionism see Liebman and Dan-Yehiya (1983: 158–9).

27. Hannah Szenes was a Hungarian Jewish woman who was parachuted by the British into Nazi-occupied Europe during the 1939–45 war and who was captured and killed by the Germans.
28. Aslow observes: 'A sense of compassionate participation grips the audience' (1982: 195).
29. Waterman and Kosmin (1986).
30. Ellman (1987: 7) and Mayer (1985: 103).
31. 'They [the Hasidim of Williamsburg, USA, who originated from Hungary] saw with great disgust that even the more religious in America may make a Bat Mitzvah for a girl who becomes twelve or thirteen years old. They could not conceive of such a formal rite being conducted for a girl whose initiation is not required by traditional law' (Poll 1962: 41–2). Traditional Law, it should be emphasised, does not require a Bar Mitzvah. The institutionalisation of the Bar Mitzvah is so entrenched that it has the semblance of requirement and what was an innovation is now a tradition.
32. An exception to this generalisation is the Lubavitch Hasidic group which encourages non-Orthodox Jews to practise traditional Judaism.
33. Sklare (1972).

References

Aslow, Jacob A. (1982) 'A Psychiatric Study of a Religious Initiation Rite: Bar Mitzvah' in Ostow, M. (ed.), *Judaism and Psychoanalysis*, Ktav, New York (first published in 1951).
Beattie, John H.M. (1980) 'On Understanding Sacrifice', in M.F.C. Bourdillon and M. Fortes (eds), *Sacrifice*, Academic Press, London.
Deutscher, Isaac (1968) *The Non-Jewish Jew and Other Essays*, Oxford University Press, London.
Efron, Benjamin and Rubin, Alvin D. (1977) *Coming of Age: Your Bar/Bat Mitzvah*, Union of American Hebrew Congregations, New York.
Ellman, Yisrael (1987) 'Intermarriage in the United States: A Comparative Study of Jews and Other Ethnic and Religious Groups', *Jewish Social Studies*, vol. XLIX, no.1, pp.1–26.
Encyclopaedia Judaica (1972) Vol.4, Jerusalem.
Hertz, Joseph H. (1948) *The Authorized Daily Prayer Book*, Bloch, New York.
Jakobovits, Immanuel (1967) *Journal of a Rabbi*, W.H. Allen, London.
Jewish Chronicle (1987) London.
Levin, Shmarya (1939) *Childhood in Exile*, Routledge & Kegan Paul, London.
Liebman, Charles, C and Dan-Yehiya, E. (1983) *Civil Religion in Israel*, University of California Press, London.
Mars, Leonard (1980) *The Village and the State*, Gower, Aldershot.
Mayer, Egon (1985) *Marriage Between Jews and Christians*, Plenum, New York.
Poll, Solomon (1962) *The Hasidic Community of Williamsburg*, Free Press, New York.
Rayner, John D. and Hooker, Bernard (1978) *Judaism for Today*, Union of Liberal Progressive Synagogues, London.
Rosenthal, Jack (1986) *Bar Mitzvah Boy and Other Television Plays*, Penguin, Harmondsworth (first published 1973).
Singer, Simeon (1962) *The Authorized Daily Prayerbook*, Eyre & Spottiswoode, London (first edition 1890).
Sklare, Marshall (1972) *Conservative Judaism: An American Religious Movement*, Schocken, New York (first published 1955).
Sklare, Marshall and Greenblum, Joseph (1979) *Jewish Identity on the Suburban Frontier*, Chicago University Press, Chicago (first edition 1967).

Waterman, S. and Kosmin, B. (1986) *British Jewry in the Eighties*, Board of Deputies of British Jews, London.

Woolf, I.B. (1983) 'The Day I Became a Man', *CAJEX*, vol.XXXIII, no. 2, June, 41–3.

Zborowski, Mark and Herzog, Elizabeth (1962) *Life is with People*, Schocken, New York (first published 1952).

Chapter five

Interpreting life texts and negotiating life courses: youth, ethnicity and culture

Paul Yates

There is a way of thinking about ethnic minority youth in Britain which sees them as between two cultures, like the Anglo-Indians, neither comfortably Anglo nor acceptably Indian. Through the imposition of schooling there is an inevitable participation in English cultural life while home, for many, retains the features of a foreign parental culture. Thus minority youth are not between cultures in some liminal trans-cultural reserve, but they are ambiguously within. This chapter investigates the nature of this cultural plurality amongst a small group of Muslim girls, sixth formers at a comprehensive school in a prosperous town in the south-east of England which I refer to as Broadmere.

Recent decades have seen the end of the 'orthodox consensus' in social science (Giddens 1984), and along with this the rise of post-empirical philosophies of science (Ricoeur 1974, Taylor 1985a, 1985b). In these developments within phenomenology, hermeneutics and the broad applications of structuralism, the influence of linguistics has been critical. Within literary studies what has come to be known as critical theory (which confusingly in social science normally refers to the Frankfurt School) is a series of developments out of European structuralism that have been popularised in Britain, especially by Eagleton (1983) along with Culler (1975, 1981, 1983) and Belsey (1980).

Part of this debate, which is shared with the human sciences, is the question of the relationship between language, the individual and society. Within literary studies it is the nature of the individual as a receiver of language and a producer of texts that forms a corresponding area of interest with the social sciences. In short the shared ground is this: is it the case that our subjective experience of authorship of being in sole control of constructing our own language/texts merely disguises the superordinate quality of language itself? Are we merely vehicles of language, instances of its being, parroting its conventions? There is a middle ground within hermeneutics that gives primacy to language while focusing on its relation with the world (Klemm 1983, Reagan 1979, Van Leeuwen 1981). Current literary theory is centrally concerned with the regulation of the transition from the structure of the text to the world of the text, which in the case of living dialogue is the identification of cultural discourses and their realisation in the language of the subjects. It is within this framework that I look at the language of a group of adolescent girls and discuss the sources of their self identity.

The chapter is in two parts following the introduction. First, the ethnographic description taken from a series of interviews given to me during the autumn of 1987. The interviewees included boys as well as girls but the boys are here present only implicitly in that they informed my understanding of English Islam and the way in which women were understood within it. Although I had an interview schedule I rarely used it and encouraged the girls to set the ethnographic agenda. The first group of girls I discuss offer a general insight into modes of cultural negotiation. The second group represent specific problems and strategies concerned with being radical, being conservative and being in love. The second part of the chapter is a brief discussion of the utility of the person/text analysis.

Within two cultures

The life worlds of the girls are constantly reconstructed by a series of cross-illuminations from one arena to another, bringing their understanding of their ethnicity to bear on some aspect of English culture and vice versa. With immense energy the girls would constantly switch and mix codes, creating and participating in their own plural culture. For indigenous youth, consciousness of ethnicity, of the existence of alternative cultural strategies, is minimal. Identity is achieved without the tiresome necessity of monitoring self-development. Unlike Muslim youth they are not subject to racial abuse. As a majority population whose self-perception is constantly reinforced, the whites have no conception of their own ethnicity. The Asian minority only become known as individuals when they have adopted the codes and manners of the local culture, and are thus understood and incorporated largely within existing local meanings.

Two important differences existed in the patterning of age statuses within the majority and minority communities. First, between an active and passive understanding of ethnicity in relation to identity. Secondly, through the necessity of strategies for self-perception in a plural culture where self was not simply given. The future was almost literally unthinkable for the Muslim girls but largely predictable for the indigenous whites.

Being a girl in Broadmere: Farida, Ayesha and Lakshmi

Sex cultures have a high profile amongst all adolescent groups. They are highly visible; both indigenous English and Muslim boys and girls tend to stick together. Mixed sex groups in school or in the street are comparatively rare and virtually non-existent among the Muslim girls. The local youth are mainly upper-working/lower-middle class and spend large amounts of money on designer clothes, especially the more expensive Italian labels. There is a great deal of competitive dressing within school and elsewhere. Some of the Muslim boys in their late teens and with access to sufficient cash through working were aware of the fashion codes and operated within them, otherwise the boys dressed casually from department stores. The physical presentation and patterns of conversation were those of the local working-class culture. They displayed expansive, aggressive movement, shoulders carried straight and very high with an exaggerated oscillation when walking. They tended to drop into, rather than sit down on, chairs, with legs uncrossed and wide apart. Vigorous gum chewing was also a part of the macho display of the boys.

Muslim girls were more likely to wear school uniform, pleated skirts, jumper and sensible shoes. This was a good compromise strategy. It avoided the stigma of conservatism that went with what was variously described as 'traditional dress', 'Asian clothes' or 'our uniform'. It also avoided the possible imputation of unchastity levelled at those girls who wore the more sexually oriented dress of some indigenous white girls.

The semiotics of dress were important. A girl might consent to wear school uniform but have as part of it a pencil skirt with a slit which pointed towards English modes of sexual identity. For the Muslim community, maintaining the girls' reputations and marriage chances could be signified through dress, though I suspected a class element in this. Large families with relatively low incomes would be more liable to enforce traditional forms of female dress and behaviour than small households with an urban or middle-class background.

Resistance to 'traditional' dress ranged from nil to total with a range of intermediate strategies. Those girls who wore traditionally patterned trousers constantly were seen as oppressed by both themselves and their peers, who unanimously identified the source of oppression not in Islam but in men. The girls as a group subscribed to the notion of male oppression, borrowed perhaps from fashionable moralities but distinctly serviceable in understanding the active cultural constraints on their sexual identity and its expression. The girls, however, would negotiate with their families to maximise what they saw as freedom. In the area of dress, this would be done to minimise the sites and occasions when they would have to be the uniformed bearers of culture. Thus, school uniform would be traded for formal dress at home, or for the freer girls, fashionable clothes would give way on family occasions where cultural solidarity was at a premium, and action took place within the framework of conscious ethnicity.

Unlike the local Hindus, both boys and girls would constantly fuse culture and religion because of the high moral content of Islam and its use among male Muslim adolescents as the legitimation of cultural conformity. The communities were also distinguished by the degree of conservative attitudes towards women. Among the young men there was sometimes an obsessive anxiety in regard to the loss of male domination as though it were a crucial source of cultural integrity in a hostile non-Muslim environment.

Mothers were constantly cited by the girls as the surrogate agents of male domination. Sibling rivalry for mother's approval could be encoded in conformity to approved expressions of ethnicity. Farida, who had been born in Broadmere, the third youngest of five boys and three girls, lived with her mother, brother and elder sister, her father having died. Her family had come from Malawi and had no contacts that she knew of in Pakistan which, unusually, she had never visited. As a wearer of fashion-influenced, school-influenced school uniform she was in the predominantly middle group of orientation to indigenous English dress. Within the family she found herself in conflict with her mother, and finding no solace in her sister relied upon her brother for emotional support. The sister, Fatima, was described as 'really prim and proper', which mainly consisted in being very religious, which Farida was not. Fatima had read the whole of the Koran in Arabic, prayed, never wore skirts and hardly ever went out. Freedom of movement was a clear concern of most of the girls. Farida again occupied a middle ground. She was not entirely housebound but every month or so would go to local Asian gatherings chaperoned by her brother, who would keep her under constant surveillance; the wearing of traditional dress was a condition of these outings.

The girls were very conscious of being Muslim because it impinged on so many aspects of adolescent life. As a child Farida 'didn't like being a Muslim, preferred more being English'. English was her first language, which she spoke at home and to relatives who

> find it hard to cope, they think I've forgotten all the Muslim ways, but I haven't ... there's so much to do as a Muslim but here you have to go to school and do work ... there's always arguments about me not being religious. Mum says I'm growing up, I should keep my head covered, talk more politely – no slang.

The rigid sexual segregation was universally denounced by the girls as unnecessary and irksome. Rural cultural policing through gossip had translated perfectly to the insulated Islamic community. 'If I say hello to a boy in the street my mother finds out and then it's twenty questions on when and where I met him, what day of the month....'

Farida's friend Ayesha found her family 'over protective, they want to know every move I do'. Apart from going to school and family outings she was confined to the house. She found the lack of freedom especially irksome as she had recently visited Pakistan where her peers were surprised at the lack of basic freedoms allowed to girls in Britain. She thought her mother's constant suspicion and her lack of access to boys was positively disabling. 'I'm not used to talking to boys – I can't mix in now.'

Farida and Ayesha's Hindu schoolfriend Lakshmi admitted no such problems of constant and oppressive surveillance. Lakshmi was seventeen, and was allowed out with a known English girlfriend in the evening, and although she realised that she did not have the licence of English girls, the rigid segregation of the Muslims did not exist for her. She could 'go round talking to boys – but it's just friendship – she [her mother] doesn't mind that'. This mild licence by comparative standards allowed Lakshmi to pass in public as indistinguishable from the majority community. While there was no actual sexual access to boys any more than for the Muslims, the absence of utterly foreign restrictions enabled a satisfactory compromise to be made between available models of relations between the sexes. Lakshmi always wore English dress, though she knew some families were 'strict' and girls had 'to wear their costumes to school'. Ayesha wore traditional school uniform to school but had to change when she got home, 'before my dad gets in'.

English schooling inevitably developed in the girls a sense of individuality and pertinently of social and emotional desires, the fulfilment of which was frustrated by their ethnic and cultural location.

Every girl I spoke to had experienced racial harassment as a pupil in English schools. Lakshmi had been persistently abused by an English boy in her street, until finally, 'I couldn't take it. I hit him one.' This caused some upset and so 'my dad went round and sorted it out'. In general it was agreed that the early teens were the most likely time to experience racial abuse, although Lakshmi's thirteen year old sister had never suffered in this way, 'never been called nuffink, but she looks English, gotta fair skin'.

Farida reported repeated vandalism on moving to a predominantly English area in town; they had been burgled and their front and back doors smashed. Even in an area of high employment Farida thought that 'they' saw Asians as taking their jobs, 'I've seen it on telly'. But for her, 'Muslims work hard to get what they want – if they don't want us to take their jobs they should work hard'.

The freedom attributed to English girls was not seen as resulting in unalloyed happiness. Lakshmi thought that there were 'some sixteen year olds, going out everyday until 4 o'clock [a.m.], don't know how to cook, they don't know how to iron a skirt – they expect their parents to do everything, but you're not going to live with them for the rest of your life ... we have an advantage'.

Farida made even less favourable comparisons: 'they go out, but then they get into more trouble; you see it in the papers, English people robbing banks, raping, murdering – the English twist around and blame Indians, you never read about Asians doing that'.

The next section deals with the development of the girls' narrative selves. That is the way in which they make their own story through participating in the major discourses that shape their identity. I present them as individuals, but the themes they address are not only personal but also social and political. Kristeva (1980) argued that texts cannot be read or written in isolation, but that every text functions in terms of others. Each individual can be seen as constituting a voice that is dialectically linked to the institutions of society. These institutions both inform and are informed by the girls actively constructing their own narrative text.

Radicalism, conservatism and love: Yasmin, Mumtaz and Shobana

Shobana and Mumtaz were friends, Yasmin was more of a loner. Shobana, in designer jeans and with short hair, was very much concerned with what she saw as the restrictions of her position, more especially as she had a romantic attachment to a boy. Mumtaz, in full traditional dress and anorak, with long plait intact, was capable of critical analysis of her position, but saw less chance of personal control. Yasmin wore her hair short, makeup and a fashionable long blue wool coat with sleeves turned back to reveal the pin-stripe lining. Shobana had been born in Britain, Mumtaz had come when she was three years old and Yasmin at eighteen months. Like the other girls they had all spent time in their respective home villages. Shobana had been for three spells of eight weeks, Mumtaz for one summer holiday, and Yasmin had been sent back to boarding school at the age of eleven.

In our conversations, the girls themselves very largely determined the agendas, I merely began by asking them what it was like living in Broadmere and they generally took it from there. These agendas were remarkably uniform. The major problem was constructing an identity that could be lived out within two cultural milieux with the minimum stress. The relation with the parental generation, the personifications of expatriate culture, and the place of women in Muslim society (as compared to English) were major concerns.

Freedom and expectations: Yasmin

Yasmin's parents were separated, 'they were close, but they drifted apart', and her father had returned home to Pakistan. 'I still love my dad a lot, but I'm not very close to him.' Yasmin blamed him for sending her away from her mother to boarding school. 'He actually did that on purpose.' She had elder brothers in the subcontinent and in Europe and one remained unmarried at home with her mother and filled the affective elements of the pater role for Yasmin, though she thought his bachelorhood odd: 'If you're not married they think there's something wrong with you.'

Yasmin had a somewhat isolated position within her family. She was the youngest sibling, the only girl and the only one to have spent most of her life in Europe. She was affectionately critical of her family's rural origins but applied a distinctly western analysis to the position of women, 'My country's about two hundred years backward with primitive attitudes to women.'

> Important men get together, start talking, women bring the tea and go off again. Women aren't capable of talking – all they've got to do is cook food and bear children. If they read the Koran properly it says women are equal, but they mould it their own way. I don't know where they get it from – it's society rather than our religion.

Yasmin made a clear separation between Islam which was 'quite perfect in a sense', and its appropriation by men as a tool of female oppression.

> Men make it how they want to see ... you never get women priests. Women need to place an argument against it – say 'you're wrong, it doesn't mean that', and if women don't do that they're always going to be so called inferior to them. If you say something's wrong you've gotta fight for it. I feel strongly but some of my people, they don't, they just accept it.

Yasmin accepted herself as culturally distinct from her family. Speaking of a brother who had refused to come to Britain, she said, 'I don't blame him, you can relate yourself to those people, they're your people, I don't feel that way – not that much anyway – this is my country.'

The girls all had a sympathetic understanding of the lack of manoeuvre open to their mothers' generation. Yasmin saw her mother as trapped by her position, 'She couldn't talk back, she had all the children and was totally dependent on the men in the village ... my mum she realises what she's been through – she thinks it's wrong.' For Yasmin, already an outsider, avoidance of male domination meant isolation for there was no other way of achieving independence and preserving her family's good name. She had no close girl friends in the Muslim community. 'I know them but I don't actually go with them – I'd like to have some Asian friends but it's not possible ... I'm the odd one out.' Yasmin had English friends and occasionally went out unchaperoned in the evenings with her mother's consent. She saw this as following the pattern of her father who had English friends also, 'but he's always got that Asian bit, it doesn't go'.

Within the Muslim community Yasmin was cited by other girls as the personification of liberation. Her mother had problems in dealing with Yasmin's determined individual sense of self and with the family's standing in the community. Yasmin was aware of this and took care to protect her mother.

> I don't go around telling people, advertising that I've been to a pub – that'd be totally bad – but they [parents] use respect to their advantage, if you speak up you're not respecting your parents – my dad's modern, he listens to you – I express myself all the time.

Yasmin saw her peers as essentially faint-hearted, 'girls don't try hard enough – they won't pay the price for independence, they can get out – they won't'. Yasmin's goal was financial independence and she planned to go on to vocational higher education, away from home, and to enter a profession. Other girls she knew had gone on to higher education, but only by way of an accomplishment before being married. In Yasmin's view this was a waste of time. 'What's the point of all that education if you've just got to obey your father's rules – adults can do what they want.'

Yasmin could not only conceive of her future but looked forward to it with relish. She saw herself unmarried, living in a flat in London, 'that's more central' (than Broadmere), and 'being myself, or trying to be myself'. Yasmin did have friends amongst the few Afro-Caribbean girls in the school,

> they're much freer, their culture is more related to ours than English....
> It's funny they do witchcraft over there and my gran does it as well – she
> has all those herbs and she cured my tonsils – if you believe in it anything
> works.

Yasmin wanted children, but not a husband, and so had fantasised about
adoption. 'I want a black little boy, I love them, they're so cute, and a white
little girl three or four years old – I wouldn't have to change any nappies then
– I hate all that.'

It was Yasmin's recognition not of her individual needs but of the position
of her sex within Islamic culture which formed the framework for her self understanding.

> I think my religion holds back women ... it was written such a long time
> ago when they weren't supposed to do the things we're doing now. I won't
> be married and having a few children and obeying a husband, maybe in
> their eyes I'll be just a rebel.... It takes a long time to change, they're not
> gonna change just 'cos I want them to, but maybe my attitude will help
> and other women's attitudes as well.

A sense of oppression: Mumtaz

Mumtaz was warm and intelligent; she had a clear vision of herself and her
society. She bore an uncongenial present and anticipated an unappetising future with a stoic recognition of the inevitable feebleness of the individual
faced with indomitable social systems. She lived with her parents and six siblings, five of them boys. Mumtaz was second eldest and as the eldest was a boy,
and the only other girl a toddler, she found herself domestically heavily bur-
dened. The demands made on Mumtaz were all legitimated by appeals to Islamic culture and community pressure. Apart from going to school Mumtaz
had hardly left the house since she was thirteen. 'I used to go out and play, then
mum said people will say, "Why's she going out? She's old enough to do
work", so I stay at home and do the housework.'

Even when her mother went visiting other women in the neighbourhood
Mumtaz had to stay behind and look after the remaining children. When I had
first spoken to Mumtaz, I had asked about the differences between Pakistan
and England and she had immediately cited the freedom of girls in Britain as
the crucial difference, 'We can go out by ourselves but there they never let
them – it's really strict there.' However, this not only misrepresented not only
Mumtaz's personal life, but also her actual impressions of life in Pakistan.
Later she described herself as 'just trapped at home all the time, there is no
freedom really'. School only provided a limited freedom and she was brought
to account for any lateness in arriving home. If she were late she would

pretend to have had a detention, 'but then she goes, "you shoulda phoned me"'.

Mumtaz had recently seen a home video from Pakistan of a family gathering, and had noticed the girls wearing their hair short, using makeup and mixing freely with boys. When she pointed this out to her mother, her reaction had been to ask if Mumtaz thought she should behave in that way, inviting the inevitable negative response. Mumtaz's friend Shobana was in no doubt that life was freer in Pakistan. 'Here they say don't shave your legs and all that, down there they're doing waxing and everything. Eight year old boys are going round pinching girls' bottoms.'

Mumtaz recalled with embarrassment going shopping with her aunt in Pakistan, 'it was only me and my aunt with things on our heads – I felt really old fashioned'. Like most girls, Mumtaz was aware of the double standards operating within the Muslim community in regard to sexual fidelity. She knew her father had a girlfriend when he came to England, her mother had shown her a photograph and told her of her suspicions, 'but dad doesn't know we know'. Mumtaz accepted her position but felt put upon, every reference to her parents involved some form of control over her.

Doing well at school was thought to be a matter of conformity rather than any sort of ability and failure was associated with idleness or lack of commitment to study. 'My dad has a go at me if I do badly, he says the only reason we come to this country is to do well in exams and go back to start a business of our own.'

Some girls and most boys did some part time work in the busy local shopping centre, but Mumtaz's father had not allowed her to, 'he never lets me, he says Muslim girls don't work'.

Parental control was extended to her only respite, in school, by her elder brother. 'If he sees me talking to a boy at school he says "don't do that again" and then he says he'll tell our dad.' This made the sense of surveillance almost complete for Mumtaz and made the solace she found in her controversial friend, Shobana, all the more valuable; as she said of her brother, he 'takes after my dad, he thinks a girl's place is in the home'.

Mumtaz saw marriage arrangement as inevitable. There had been a case in her near family of a cousin marrying an English girl and she retailed with evident sadness how the family had conspired against the lovematch, despite there being a child and had finally persuaded the man to leave and divorce his wife. For herself she saw it as 'really bad, getting married to a complete stranger, having to live with him and you don't know what to say to him'. She thought communication would be further hampered by English being her first language as she naturally assumed her husband would come from Pakistan.

Mumtaz suffered constantly from being invidiously compared to domestic paragons by her mother, 'she bugs me'. Both Mumtaz and Shobana rejected the local islamic model of women. Shobana was afraid she would be sent back to Pakistan and married off. 'I'm not going down there, I don't really like it, it's all right for holidays, but you're not used to it, if you do something wrong, they say, "Oh she's not very good."'

Shobana rejected her religion and the fatalistic concept of destiny that her mother offered her as the solution to earthly ills. 'Just my luck! There's no such thing as luck – it's just what we make.' The comparative lack of freedom of movement was bitterly resented by both girls, especially Shobana.

It really gets me down, locked in the house all the time – I was born here, I feel like everyone else. They just think God! Our culture isn't like this, we don't allow you to go out with boys – they live in a different community – inside I just say she'll never know how I feel – Mum says, 'You can talk to me, I'm your friend, I'm your sister.' She doesn't understand, she's a Muslim mum, she can never be my friend.

Shobana's father had had an affair, 'I think it's common in Asian people, my mum didn't mind', and although this was clearly tolerable it was also seen as unjust. 'No one ever says anyfink about my dad, he's smoking and drinking and having a bit on the side, but if it was my mum – that'd be it.' Boys in general were seen to have advantages summed up in more freedom. They were also judged by different standards, for example, more readily imputed with intelligence. 'Girls are not really clever, boys are clever.' The moral distinction between the English and the Muslim community was clear in Shobana's depiction of boys' tolerated access to girls.

If a boy's going out with a black girl he won't get anyfink done to him – if he's going out with a white girl, nothing's going on. They think white girls are slags, they say, 'don't go around with anybody who's going out with a boy': but everyone's talking about boys.

On being in love: Shobana

Shobana was small, nervous, noisy and vivacious. Having a boyfriend was presented as the central fact of her existence and was clearly the source of all her joy and sorrow. Not only was she attached to a boy, difficult enough in itself, but one in the most problematic social category, not an invisible white but a Hindu. Both sets of parents were aware of the liaison, both disapproved, 'his mum found out about me, and he got it really good'. The significance of religious difference was not lost on Shobana. 'Moslems and Hindus are absolutely enemies – that's centuries ago, but it really goes through the blood all the time.'

Shobana's parents were aware but pretty much chose to publicly deny their knowledge of the attachment. Apart from relying on the efficiency of communal surveillance, they had strategically attempted to end the liaison, but as both she and her boyfriend, Dilip, adopted a position of outright denial, it was proving a difficult task. 'I told her it was all rumours ... I dunno what she'd do

... she believes in me. She keeps saying to me, "If I find out you're going out with a boy, I'll send you to Pakistan and get you married off."' Shobana's father had proposed a similar but less drastic alternative. 'My dad says, "Don't stab me in the back, if you want to marry someone tell me and I'll get you married off to them."' In other words, that he would marry her to a *mutually* acceptable candidate.

Shobana's mother had also attempted to use the ethnic divide. 'My mum says he's a Hindu, he hates all girls – he'll just blackmail you. She knows there's something going on and she's trying to scare me.' Shobana was made sufficiently anxious however to present this notion to Dilip who naturally denied it.

There was no support for Shobana from the majority of her female peers amongst whom were the originators of her parents' intelligence of her love affair. 'All the black girls here are bitches – they're real jealous – "How come she's going out [with a boy] we're not." Mumtaz is the only girl I can trust.'

Shobana felt powerless to control the network of gossip and rumour, 'it's hard to keep people's mouth shut'. The power of the community and her responsibility for maintaining her parents' position within it were accepted by Shobana, but supporting this aim was incompatible with satisfying her emotional needs.

> Mum says, 'don't let me down' an' all that, they're more careful of their pride than they are for me, they care about what other people say, not about what we feel. I know I disobey them but I can't face up to them and say, 'Well, what are you going to do about it.' I don't want to hurt them but I want to have something for myself as well.

Shobana had a strong sense of isolation from her immediate community, having been betrayed was a painful experience. 'I know what it is to be grassed up – you go through mental torture – your mum and dad don't talk to you – you can't eat, you just sit in your room.'

Dilip had a day job and a night job which combined with the other restrictions on their movements made meeting a difficult and perilous undertaking only possible at interstitial points of the day. They met at lunchtime and before and after school whenever possible. This hardly allowed them much scope for developing their relationship, indeed sometimes they would simply 'sit together and think about what excuses we'll give'. On days when they couldn't meet, Shobana was desolate. 'I get uptight and my mum says, "Why you upset?" and I can't say, "Oh, I didn't see him today", you can't say that to your mum.' Dilip and Shobana wanted to marry but couldn't see how it could be effected. Shobana couldn't walk out on her parents, 'after I'd gone they would have shame on them', and so they simply planned to wait in the hope that time would establish the rightness of their cause through the demonstration of their fidelity.

Shobana's English girlfriends were sympathetic, 'they're happy for you, they'll never know how you feel, but they try their best to help us'. The distance she felt her parents at, however, remained total. 'You can't say, "I'm happy, we feel relaxed with one another, I love him" .' Dilip and Shobana's fondest wish was simple acceptance. 'Wouldn't it be good if we could walk hand in hand across town with all the black people looking and they wouldn't say a thing.'

Social structure and frontier culture

Giddens's (1984) notion of structuration provides a model of social action within which I set my final remarks. For Giddens, individuals act out of their own knowledge resources within institutional boundaries. Social structure is presented as dual in nature. 'The structural properties of social systems are both medium and outcome of the practices they recursively organise ... Structure is not to be equated with constraint but is always both constraining and enabling' (Giddens 1984: 25).

I earlier remarked upon the comparative ease with which indigenous white youths construct and maintain their identities. They are able to live with a comfortable sense of a relatively predictable future, accommodating their sense of self within the dominant themes of their culture. Sexual identity, for example, can be largely trusted to conform to consensus expectations, and to be supported by everyday interactions.

By contrast, the Islamic girls were living in a frontier culture of contested meanings. They had, in a sense, to work harder at achieving identity because the range of consensus understanding, upon which they could unreflectively draw, was relatively narrow. Religion, sexuality and sexual identity, family relationships and future expectations were all areas of potential instability and shifting meanings.

It was not admiration for English culture that made the Muslim girls engage with it. It was its unavoidable reality in their experience and the necessity of its accommodation into a tenable life story.

It may be the grinding of the tectonic plates of cultural systems that produces a discourse which we might recognise as English Islam, but the dynamic is subjectively worked out by the girls not simply bearing, but actively transforming, their culture and their selves. The meaning of being young in England is achieved through the mediation of the myth and metaphors of the component cultures of their life into a subjective narrative. This narrative is partly constructed by ordering the past, through the stories of the parental generation. The mythologies of current cultures are generated in the culturally transforming narrative of the girls' lives.

The girls live within a duality of cultural experience. There are felt and expressed contradictions between indigenous English culture and English Islamic culture, and again between Pakistan and the parental generation's mythologising of a cultural golden age and place which serves to legitimise aspects of their social control. In Willis's (1977) ethnography of working-class boys, he speaks of penetrations and limitations. Penetrations are the points at which the structures of the system that oppresses them are perceived. Limitations are the ways in which the necessity of cultural production and reproduction lead to accommodation of that oppression, which though partially understood is also connived at.

The stories of the Muslim girls are of penetrations into the falsification of their authenticity by the mythologies of male dominated cultural discourses. Accommodation is the price of recovering authenticity, but crucially the further from their limitations they live, the more firmly they are engaged in transformation, actual cultural production. In Ricoeur's terms the girls are framed in human time, between the public time of their languages and the private time of their own mortality (Klemm 1983).

© 1990 Paul Yates

References

Belsey, C. (1980) *Critical Practice*, London: Methuen.

Culler, J. (1975) *Structuralist Poetics*, London: Routledge & Kegan Paul.

Culler, J. (1981) *The Pursuit of Signs*, London: Routledge & Kegan Paul.

Culler, J. (1983) *On Deconstruction: Theory and Criticism after Structuralism*, London: Routledge and Kegan Paul.

Eagleton, T. (1983) *Literary Theory: an Introduction*, Oxford: Blackwell.

Giddens, A. (1984) *The Constitution of Society*, Oxford: Blackwell.

Klemm, D.E. (1983) *The Hermeneutical Theory of Paul Ricoeur*, Lewisberg: Bucknell University Press.

Kristeva, J. (1980) *Desire in Language*, Oxford: Blackwell.

Reagan, C.E. (ed.) (1979) *Studies in the Philosophy of Paul Ricoeur*, Athens, Ohio: Ohio University Press.

Ricoeur, P. (1974) *The Conflict of Interpretations: Essays in Hermeneutics* (ed. D.Idhe), Northwestern University Press, Evanston, Ill.

Taylor, C. (1985a) *Human Agency and Language. Philosophical Papers 1*, Cambridge: Cambridge University Press.

Taylor, C. (1985b) *Philosophy and the Human Sciences. Philosophical Papers 2*, Cambridge: Cambridge University Press.

Van Leeuwen, T.M. (1981) *The Surplus of Meaning: Ontology and Eschatology in the Philosophy of Paul Ricoeur*, Amsterdam: Rodopi.

Willis, P. (1977) *Learning to Labour: How Working Class Kids get Working Class Jobs*, Teakfield: Saxon House.

Chapter six

The notion of adulthood in rural Soviet Georgian society

Tamara Dragadze

An attempt to comprehend the notion of adulthood in rural Soviet Georgian society leads one into an interesting sphere of the social construction of maturation processes. Concepts related to adulthood touch at the heart of the villagers' own moral philosophy and their precepts of indigenous psychology. In this chapter I shall relate how the notion of adulthood is linked with that of personal responsibility. This reveals particular ideas about people's psychological and physical development and about their place in society, especially according to domestic status within the context of a village community within the Soviet Union.

My definition of 'adulthood' in its ethnographic context is developed throughout, but as a starting point the term will imply that a person is deemed to be responsible for his or her acts and to have self-control over moods and physical powers and to have opinions that display an adequate amount of sound judgement, as measured by village opinion.

The ethnographic context

My fieldwork data were collected in a village in Ratcha Province, in the North-West of Soviet Georgia, in the foothills of the Great Caucasian Mountain Range.[1] Of the 78 households I counted in Abari Village, 51 were Lobjanidzes of peasant origin (surnames are bestowed patrilineally), and 18 had the surnames of men who had married Lobjanidze women who had been only children (usually brides go to live with their husbands). There were 9 other households who were all Japaridzes, descendants of a nineteenth-century priest of gentry origin. Although the Japaridzes and Lobjanidzes did not intermarry, the Japaridzes since the Khrushchev era have been frequently chosen as godparents for Lobjanidzes which creates a special bond of kinship (Dragadze 1988b). The economy was mixed, with some villagers engaged in agriculture, some in a mining and chemical industry in the next village and some in the tertiary services. The village was some 18km from the regional capital Ambrolauri, which was about 317km distant from the capital Tbilisi.

In many ways, my work was a case study of a regional enclave of traditional culture which had retained its character despite the impact of Soviet rule. The extent to which Abari Village is representative of the rest of rural Georgia is debatable. Parts of what I shall describe are common to society in the Soviet Georgian republic as a whole. I have discussed elsewhere the reasons for the tenacity of Georgian culture and the way in which the villagers maintained traditional structures in response to the distinctive conditions of Soviet life (Dragadze 1988b). I shall only repeat these here when they seem indispensable for understanding the notion of adulthood.

Growing up

Increasing interest in anthropological approaches to cognitive development is revealed in a recent collection of papers on childhood (Jahoda and Lewis 1988). However, unless one is a psychologist as well as an ethnographer, many general principles are difficult to extrapolate on the basis of fieldwork data. It so happened, however, that I was able to take note of some issues concerning the principles labelled and discussed currently under the rubric of 'indigenous psychology'.[2]

Villagers consider that a child is born with no knowledge at all and that everything has to be taught, with patience and persuasion. For example, although babies are breast-fed on demand, mothers are told to coax them to suckle. Under the age of 7 a child is rarely punished and is not thought to be responsible for his or her actions (Dragadze 1988a). Their misdemeanours are usually seen by adults to be amusing. They spend most of their time in the villages, among their kin. At the age of 7 they start school and encounter the outside world. Earlier, however, children begin to be taught in a confident way about their traditional roles and in a more ambivalent way about how to behave as citizens of the State (Dragadze 1988a). Commenting on my data, Jahoda and Lewis noticed how 'There is a sharp contrast between the actually collectivist village world of shared solidarity and the official collectivist state world where actual survival depends on guarded individual opportunism' (Jahoda and Lewis 1988).

After the age of 7 approximately, families will be anxious that their children should display appropriate behaviour. Families are considered solely responsible for the way children behave, although the limits of what can be taught to children are acknowledged. It is only around the age of 15 or so that children are expected to answer for their own standards of behaviour in any way. On the grounds that they are too young and are innocent through lack of knowledge, this indulgence towards them continues for another couple of decades.

'Correct' behaviour demanded of children is complex, and becomes even more so as they progress into adolescence. It involves the use of correct verbal forms and deportment towards adults and those considered their superiors (even those who have not yet reached 'adulthood'). More important, however, is the way they conform to expectation according to gender. Most villagers think that people, although endowed with no knowledge at birth, are nevertheless born with some innate qualities: fair or dark skin, for example, or a lively or passive temperament. Also, each girl or boy at birth is thought to be endowed with immutably different attributes, gender-linked, which are physical, emotional and spiritual. Male and female qualities have to be developed and channelled in the right direction through correct teaching. These gender-linked qualities are believed to have their own essence with a momentum of their own. Sex roles are thus relatively easy to teach, unlike polite behaviour, for example, which has to be created *ab initio* (Dragadze 1988a, 1988b). Those who do not manifest acceptable gender qualities in their sex roles despite being physically and mentally developed are perplexing to others. When villagers meet such a person within Ratcha Province or more frequently in the world beyond, he or she may be pitied but is unlikely to be *fully* accepted as a fellow human being. Such an attitude, based on views very fundamental in their conceptions, contributes to the general disinclination to embrace ideas of 'official' Soviet collectivisim and fusion with Soviet society (Dragadze 1988b).

In adolescence, a child is expected to begin helping with domestic and agricultural tasks. Yet reluctance to do so will still be met with indulgence, despite the disappointment that other people will not praise the family for their industrious child. Between the ages of 15 and 25, however, a person is expected gradually to become fully socialised, when he or she will require increasingly less advice on how to behave in varying circumstances and less reminding about appropriate deportment. People of that age will also be expected to be full participants in domestic tasks, according to gender. However, they will not yet be expected to be in full control of emotional impulses, such as anger. Neither will their judgement be considered mature. When their point of view is thought to be correct then they are said to be 'clever' for their age and admired. Punishment for misdemeanours, meted out by senior members of the family, is severe at least in the angry invective expressed. It is seen to be an important way of teaching people of this age. The range of decisions they take alone is limited, for example on how to spend the money they earn, and they are unlikely to voice opinions that might be considered immature.

By the time a person of either sex is 25 years old, he or she is deemed to have reached sexual maturity and is likely also to have married and to have become a parent. Yet 'adulthood' still eludes that person, from the point of view of the villagers.

Adulthood

Adulthood is an example of a concept that is understood as clearly by the native informant as by the British anthropologist. Discussion needed no prodding on my part during fieldwork. Yet there is no precise, exclusive term for it in Georgian. Vocabulary translated into English as 'fullness of years' (*srultslovanoba*) or being 'mature' (*mtsip'e*) are ambiguous because the words only partially convey the sense. *Srultslovanoba*, for example, also doubles up as a legal term in the Soviet code of law, where at the age of 18 a person becomes an 'adult'. The very contrast between the legal Soviet concept of adulthood of which the villagers are aware, where those over 18 years old are considered totally responsible for their actions and even old enough for the death penalty on the one hand, and, on the other, the villagers' notions of adulthood, where someone of 18 is little more than a child, embodies the tension between village and State. It is considered quite legitimate, for example, to hide young criminals from law enforcers if at all possible, not simply because they are members of their community, but because it would be inhumane to deliver to the law those who are 'young' and clearly not responsible for their actions. The law, which does not recognise this, has to be resisted. In my own fieldwork I did not come across a case when a youth was caught and charged with a severe crime, but in 1981 I saw on Georgian State Television a documentary report of a village in another province debating whether or not the parents and whole family of a youth found guilty of robbery and murder should be made to leave the village. One of the arguments used was that someone of only 20 years could not be responsible, as an individual, for his acts and so his family should bear the punishment for not having brought him up and controlled him in a better way.

For reaching adulthood there is no ceremony either, no initiation to mark the passing from one state to another. It is a gradual process, almost intangible, lasting between 10 and 15 years or so when the surveillance and intervention of senior members of the family and the excusing of 'bad behaviour' – whether serious crime or simply the use of inappropriate language – on the grounds of youth gradually diminish.

I have used the English word 'adulthood' advisedly, despite methodological drawbacks since it is not a translation from the Georgian in the way I use it here. On the other hand, it best conveys the expectation among Georgians of a person that this term in English also reflects. I shall consider now the broad outline of the life course for women and men that is spanned in these important years.

Gender, domestic status and adulthood

Towards the end of adolescence, earlier for girls than boys, a person is expected to reach sexual maturity. Girls are expected to retain their virginity before marriage and Soviet law permits girls in the Transcaucasian republics to marry a year earlier than is legal elsewhere, i.e. at 17 years. Boys are presumed to have have had some sexual peccadilloes while serving in the Army outside the Georgian territory from which they return around the age of 21.

Arranged marriages were, at the time of fieldwork at least, the norm, with the family of the boy seeking out a suitable bride among the Ratchuelians (Dragadze 1988b). An accidental meeting is arranged between the potential partners and unless there is some violent dislike on the part of one of them, which his or her family feel would be impossible to dispel, a marriage is negotiated. Occasionally it is the youths themselves who decide to marry and have the task of persuading their families to negotiate on their behalf. Occasionally too the girl is abducted (*motats'eba*) or a mutually agreed 'elopement' (*gap'areba*) is contrived to appear as an 'abduction'. If a girl is known to have spent a night with a boy, she is considered *de facto* married to him (Dragadze 1988b). Such activity needs the acquiescence of older family members on the boy's side, although they often plead ignorance and blame the abduction on the hot-headedness of youth, which has therefore to be excused. Marriages are usually hastily arranged whatever the circumstances, and are not accompanied by noticeable exchanges of wealth, although they are celebrated with a large banquet with several hundred guests on occasion.

Usually a bride will have been trained in a skill before marriage, unless she marries exceptionally early. The nature of her job is taken into consideration when judging her suitability as a bride since families like to strike a balance in allocating members to the different sectors of the domestic economy (Dragadze 1988b). Almost invariably, the bride goes to live in her husband's home, where she comes under the tutelage of her parents-in-law. Visits from members of her family and anxiety to retain a good reputation within the village usually ensure that she is humoured and well treated. Great emphasis is put on her youth and her general lack of knowledge of domestic and village affairs. When she has her firstborn child she will nurse it constantly but most decisions about clothing and feeding, for example, and most tasks such as bathing the child will be accomplished by her mother-in-law. As a female, the young bride and mother will be expected to display those qualities associated with her sex, such as modesty, a good deal of control over emotions of anger and desire and so on (Dragadze 1988a, 1988b) and over her hands, one aspect of which is good handwriting. She will chat and consort with her husband's unmarried sisters who in turn are expected to have a protective attitude towards her, even if she may be older by a few years or so. She will assist in cooking family meals and will do light domestic and agricultural tasks: heavy work is thought to impair her fertility. When she works outside the home, she will perhaps command respect, but people will be aware of her youth and she is likely to be forgiven for mistakes. It varies as to whether this work starts immediately after marriage or is delayed until the first child is over a year old, according to individual circumstances. Only as her children grow older, and she takes over more domestic responsibilities from her mother-in-law, is she deemed to have accumulated knowledge of social affairs and to have acquired sound judgement, and ultimately to be capable of taking over the custody of the family's economic wealth.

A 'senior woman' will include her daughters-in-law increasingly in the collective decision-making as they get older. Imperceptibly, women acquire the status not yet of 'senior women' but of what could be called, for the sake of simplicity, 'adulthood'. This incorporates the notion of acting and speaking in one's own right and being personally responsible for one's actions – all within the framework of family membership in a society where personal identity is so closely linked to that of the family. Thus adult women will voice opinions and be attentively listened to. However, they will also incur the full of force of opprobrium in the case of misbehaviour, without the mitigation of being 'still too young'. An example of this is quarrelsomeness, which is seen as threatening in a village society that tries as far as possible not to call in outside intervention in settling internal disputes. There comes a stage in a woman's life where behaviour deemed to be 'quarrelsome' is no longer considered somewhat amusing in view of her 'youth'. She is expected to understand the full consequences of her attitude, say, towards her affinal kin, and to have reached an age where she can fully control the display of her emotions when necessary. In the cases I came across, a few well-placed words in the circuit of village gossip were sufficient to stop both parties in a dispute from displaying their animosity – overtly, and so 'immaturely' – both among men and women.

A woman's graduation to 'adult status' is linked to her married and maternal status. An unmarried woman (or man) or one not yet a parent is thought to be less than a 'full' or a 'real human being' (Dragadze 1988b). Once she has children, however, and as they grow, so her own physical strength visibly increases. She is no longer fearful of impairing her fertility and can now undertake heavier physical tasks. As far as chronological age is concerned, it is usually around her early or mid thirties that the transition takes place, depending on her age at marriage.

A boy's life course in relation to domestic status follows much the same pattern as for girls in so far as it is marriage and parenthood that endow him with the rudiments of those qualities he will bring to maturity with the fullness of time. In contrast to girls, boys and men in general are considered, implicitly and to a lesser extent explicitly, to be prone in temperament to unruly feelings of violent temper or jealousy.

In order to understand what is meant more fully, a small diversion into a discussion of gender identity is unavoidable (Dragadze 1988a, 1988b). All females are the potential sources and bearers of life and it is thought that all essential female characteristics derive from that. Features such as constancy, the capacity of endurance, stability and so on are supposed to be strongly developed in women, and weakly in men by comparison. Historically, however, men were the warriors of Georgia, women the keepers of the village and the home. Men went out into the world and into the wild. Men had to learn to be brave and fearless and develop their physical strength. Women had to keep order in the home and village and develop their innate qualities of cool-headedness and calm. Georgians both in the villages and in the towns are much inclined towards historical explanation and this kind of interpretation of gender difference is heard everywhere. Men are thought still to be more capable than women of fighting adversity in the outside world, whether administrative difficulties or hazardous travel.

Men, whatever their age, are considered less able to control displays of emotion. Women, by contrast, are dependable; they nurture and also are considered to be the agents of social control and the maintenance of order. They are also traditionally the 'guardians of literacy' whose responsibility it is to teach children, especially daughters, the art of good handwriting and, in past times, knowledge of such poetry as the twelfth-century epic *Knight in the Panther's Skin* (Dragadze 1988b). The significance of female literacy can be explained first because women are, in a sense, the guardians of 'civilisation', having the main role in the socialisation of the young and in maintaining village society while the men come and go (in a sense this is a reverse of any Lévi-Straussian assertion that woman is to man as nature is to society: Ortner 1974, Strathern and Macormack 1980). Secondly, a female attribute is thought to be the capacity to control her movements more effectively than a man can, especially those of the fingers.

Men in Ratcha traditionally were famous as silversmiths and carvers. This ability, however, allegedly came with age and effort. Today, boys still have to work harder and longer than women to achieve self-control to master the qualities expected of a full adult: to be well-spoken, both for offering toasts and to petition bureaucrats *inter alia*, and to control their temper. Finally, they must learn to use their physical strength diligently, under control and thus in a superior way to younger males who may be stronger but who do not know how to use their limbs and muscle movements to best advantage.

Decisions concerning a young man are taken collectively, with his grandparents having the last word over most expenditure, for example, or travel or choice of work (and in their absence, his parents). Ideally all married brothers should spend their lives living together in the same compound. By convention, the eldest brother should have authority over the younger ones, although in practice this does not always happen, because the older brother will often migrate to the towns either seasonally or permanently. In their old age, parents are likely to live with the youngest son. After marriage, a young man is likely to spend less time drinking with his peers and to prefer being at home with his wife and, later, with his children. This is the first step in combating the excesses to which men of his age are prone, it is thought. As in the case of women, a man's maturity comes at a time when his children are usually well past infancy, his own parents are beginning to age but are still 'in command of their senses' (a loose translation from the Georgian), and he is considered capable of self-control in the sense described above. Again, depending on the age of marriage in particular, this state appears to be reached in a man's mid or late thirties.

For both sexes domestic status is important. It should be noted here that, although much child-rearing is done by the grandparents and no decision is taken without their participation, children are nominally under the authority of their parents rather than grandparents. When they are around 18 years old, however, decisions concerning them devolve on the grandparents as the male and female heads of the household. This formal transition does not mark a recognition of adulthood in the full sense of the term I have defined above, but it does mark their role in contributing towards the collective wealth of the household. Significantly, the size of this contribution is not seen in itself to be a criterion of adulthood.[3]

Adulthood and seniority

The main asset for a household when a person finally becomes an 'adult' is that he or she is trusted to act as a protagonist for the family's reputation and to represent its interests in the outside world. A young person would never be expected, or indeed be allowed, to petition a bureaucrat for a 'permission' (to study or work in a particular place, for example). An older family member or an 'adult' kinsperson would do so on the younger person's behalf, or someone of the 'senior generation' if it is a matter of extreme importance requiring their presence. If for some reason a young person has become responsible as virtual head of household before reaching the age for 'adulthood', the person is still considered vulnerable and 'young', whatever the domestic status. Members of the senior generation among kin and villagers will act as 'protectors' and 'advisors' in such a situation.

The contrast between a member of the 'senior generation' (*uprosi*) and someone who is an adult is a complex matter. The difficulty of discussing many of the relevant nuances lies in the nature of the ethnographic data: I encountered a lot of variety in these distinctions, based often on the personality of various protagonists. Adulthood is a state which, once achieved, continues until death, although senility is a modifying factor which will be discussed later. The time one is just an adult and no more, that is without additional status in the community in virtue of one's greater age, generally spans approximately the ages from early to mid thirties till around the early fifties. After that, having most likely become a grandparent, one is not only an adult but additionally a 'senior' person, even a head of household, male or female. Whereas the notion of 'seniority' denotes a hierarchical position of authority within the family and village society, the notion of 'adulthood' is more of an 'inner state'. One could almost venture an ethnocentric description, which would nevertheless be apt, by seeing adulthood as a 'state of mind'.

The elders (*uprosebi*) have particular importance in the family. As heads of household they acquire authority in decision-making at every level. There are several reasons why, by and large, the eldest generation commands this respect. The male head of household is bearer of what can be called 'moral authority' for the family and his ultimate decisions are usually considered binding.

However, it is the female head of the household who as custodian of the family assets is given the wages of household members (Dragadze 1988a, 1988b; Charachidze 1968: 40 for the nineteenth century). It is she who has custody of the family purse, runs day to day domestic affairs and acts as go-between for the members of the domestic group. It is only in very advanced old age that she will hand over the task to the wife of the eldest son.

One 'technique' used by the senior generation for their authority to be recognised is that they rarely attempt to intervene, so that when they speak everyone will listen! With advancing age they are thought to be endowed with strong powers of observation, accumulated wisdom and a sense of 'spirituality' (having more time than the younger adults for religious contemplation). The best demonstration of these qualities is seen to be the judicious use of their authority and their word.

A villager is deemed to achieve his or her prime well into adulthood, both physically through careful control, and mentally. Only after the age of 60, approximately, when physical strength begins to diminish, are people no longer considered to be in their prime. By 'prime' I mean simply that someone is in a 'state of greatest perfection' (*Oxford English Dictionary*).

Indigenous psychology links mental capacities, by and large, with physical ones. When people in old age still retain good eyesight, hearing and health they are likely to retain their full authority despite delegating a considerable amount of decision-making to younger people – a sign of wisdom anyway.

Diminishing strength, however, accompanies advancing age. Old people, in order to retain some measure of 'respect', will avoid risking a rebuff from their juniors. They tend to anticipate this increasing loss of powers by participating even less in the day to day running of the home. They spend, for example, more time at the private plots than before on tasks such as weeding that are considered light but boring. They do similar work on the collective farm.

In advanced old age people are expected to be quiet and discreet, bringing ridicule among themselves if they should make a display by shouting and being overbearing. Instead they should not forget to serve others in their household and village with their last strength. Such an effort of self-effacement is thought to prepare them well to meet the departed souls who preceded them into the next world where they themselves will soon go. Other members of the family are gentle and affectionate with the aged: young people and children are often seen stroking the head or back of an old great-grandparent or grandparent. The old people's foibles are treated with humour, and if completely senile they are constantly watched to ensure they are sensibly clothed and do nothing to lose the 'respect' shown towards them. A blind eye for absenteeism at work is usual when the reason is known to be the temporary distress of an elderly family member. It is considered 'bad luck' to neglect the old; one should not court the risk of a bad end in one's own old age, at least.

97

Underlying conceptual themes

My approach embodies Neugarten's processual, seasonal view of the life course as 'a changing constellation of roles and perspectives associated with appropriate behaviour at each stage' (Neugarten and Datan 1973).

Visitors to Georgia, and Ratcha Province in particular, have often been impressed by the relatively late age at which people are still treated as 'young', and, for example, are expected to stand when spoken to formally by someone of the older generation. In comparison with some other societies, it seems that 'adulthood' is a state which, in formal age at least, is achieved relatively late. The age of achieving adulthood might perhaps have increased with 'modernisation' brought by Soviet rule, and it is possible even to speculate that in past centuries in Georgia the status of young warriors might have been different with more prestige given to sheer physical strength than at present. Certainly today the male experience in the Red Army does not mark a young man with particular status in his growth towards maturity.

Yet it seems reasonable to assume that the current view would have been appropriate for at least the previous two centuries for which considerable Georgian data are available, if not necessarily earlier medieval times. One may note that the twelfth-century epic poem, *Knight in the Panther's Skin*, incorporates essential precepts of Georgian morality as still aspired to today. One of the young heroes, Avtandil, proves he is a better huntsman than his sovereign, King Rostevan, who is also the father of his beloved. The younger man has to go through a whole series of adventures in which he develops his various abilities other than mere physical strength before returning to take his place in adult society, marrying the princess in whose favour Rostevan abdicates.

Adulthood as I have described it does not correspond to any particular term, and it is not preceded and followed by signs of life crisis or by particular rites. It is a notion that is clearly recognised in the local society and used as a principle in the evaluation of correct behaviour and in the elaboration of village organisation. It reflects many aspects of Georgian village social thought, of relations between the sexes and peers, for example. It also embodies ideas associated with national identity. Importance is attached to the capacity to be vigilant, prudent and self-controlled which reflects, in a broad sense, the concern of Georgians to survive as a people, surrounded by belligerent neighbours in the past and by encroachments today of Sovietisation or Russification which they see as a threat: in brief, many aspects of the notion of adulthood reflect the Georgian's kind of 'siege mentality'.

There are three themes in the notion of adulthood among villagers in Ratcha Province which seem to lead one into further fields of ideas.

The nature of knowledge

The family teaches a person all he or she knows, from the time of birth. Knowledge is not acquired spiritually, so to speak, through communion with God or the saints. It is, in brief, acquired through lengthy practice over many years of observing the world around with care. This learning process can only be successful if it goes hand in hand with learning to control impulses which lead to ill-judged behaviour: being hot-tempered, indiscreet and so on. By giving people time, well into their thirties, to achieve this measure of self-control and to accumulate knowledge through observation is probably one way of ensuring that the chances of succeeding are increased.

The philosophical implications of this interpretation of knowledge, revealed through a study of the notion of adulthood, would be most interesting to pursue, both within the context of the particular community I studied and in a comparative way demonstrating the wide potential of studying age.

Responsibility

The essential *social* characteristic of adulthood, in this particular community, is that people become responsible for their actions. This opinion has to be qualified in several respects. The word *bedi* is used for 'luck' and for 'destiny'. It is generally supposed to be controlled by God, in His unknowable wisdom. Humans themselves cannot control it. Like the weather, it blesses or afflicts good and bad people alike. A person's aim must be to rise to the occasion. In that sense once you are an adult, what you make of your 'destiny', the events that beset you or gladden you, is your own responsibility.

Social identity is closely linked to that of one's family and this has several consequences. On the one hand, it is bestowed through birth and residence and not through one's own effort, so to speak. On the other hand, in a village community such as the one I studied, a person's own actions and personality contribute to the family's reputation which then reflect back on the person. Eventually, when adulthood is attained, the excuses stop and one is answerable for one's actions.

Generally speaking, adults aim for what they consider to be a comfortable material standard through judiciously allocating members of the same household to different sectors of the economy. This also necessitates careful and swift purchasing of goods in an economic system where the distribution of commodities and produce is irregular. Adulthood implies that one will act shrewdly and fast in such matters! Senior members of the household, in consultation with the younger members, take most far-reaching decisions, and these have to be obeyed so as not to incur criticism from the community at large. Yet again, what is important is what one makes of those decisions and whether they are used to advance the welfare of the family or not. This devolves on the wise use of responsibility by each adult within the confines of overall control by the oldest members of the family.

Adulthood and the State

In Soviet economic and administrative conditions in rural Georgia it is difficult to become independent of one's family, which alone provides residence, social networks and the benefits of the collective income of several adults. Some of the youth among Party activists for well over half a century have often had political power and control over various resources, but this has not as yet caused most villagers to reconsider their views on age and maturity, at least for the time being. When villagers encounter administrators in positions of power who are themselves still visibly 'young', it arouses a certain amount of unease. In such a case, the idiom of national sentiment is often used to create the common bond necessary before making a petition (Dragadze 1988b). Bureaucrats anyway present themselves as 'merely obeying orders', although as a great favour, they say, they bend the rules for you personally! If it is a case where the bureaucrat is young, such kind consideration is appreciated and considered 'lucky' by villagers privately, because such a young person could only guess at what the right course of action was. When it is someone who is considered an adult, however, then the person is praised genuinely for his or her good sense.

I have written elsewhere about the sense of powerlessness that villagers feel towards the State which, like the weather, cannot be controlled (so informants told me) and brings both good and bad (Dragadze 1988b). With decrees changing frequently, with the threat, whether real or not today, of severe repression and with local officials confirming and most people experiencing that decisions concerning the community and individuals are all taken elsewhere, in the capitals of Tbilisi and, ultimately, Moscow, it is not surprising that no sense of participation would be felt. Yet once again, perhaps through optimism, the notion of adulthood fosters the idea of a 'zone of autonomy' in a world where people feel generally that they have little power of decision-making in their lives. Moreover, as noted earlier, there is a contrast between the collectivist solidarity of the village and the officially encouraged collectivist State world. This contrast is reflected in the resistance of local culture to assimilative tendencies and in the idea that, because a person who is an adult is able to be the responsible for his or her acts, the resistance is reinforced.

General conclusion

To sum up, there are ideas of indigenous psychology, on gender and infancy, for example, that are revealed in the concept of adulthood. The capacity to be responsible for one's acts once a person has reached adulthood (but not before) is indeed a notion rich with possibilities, because of the close way it combines moral and psychological ideas, and even a few political speculations.

©1990 Tamara Dragadze

Notes

1. Fieldwork was carried out mostly from June 1970 to the end of 1972, with return visits in 1975, 1976, 1978 and 1981.
2. I must acknowledge here my debt to Charlotte Hardman for drawing my attention to the subject some time ago now.
3. This is in contrast, for example, to Lydia Sciama's field data from Venice (oral communication).

References

Charachidze, G., 1968, *Le Systeme religieux de la Georgie paienne; analyse structurale d'une civilisation*. Paris: François Maspero.

Dragadze, T., 1988a, 'State roles and sex roles; infant socialisation in rural Soviet Georgia', in Jahoda and Lewis.

—— 1988b, *Rural Families in Soviet Georgia.*, London: Routledge and Kegan Paul.

Fortes M., 1949, 'Time and social structure; an Ashanti case study', in Fortes, M. (ed.), *Social Structure: Studies Presented to A R Radcliffe-Brown*, Oxford: Clarendon Press.

Jahoda, G. and Lewis, I.M. (eds), 1988, *Acquiring Culture*, London: Croom Helm.

Neugarten, B.L. and N. Datan, 1973, 'Sociological perspectives on the life cycle', in Baltes, P.B. and K.W. Schaie (eds), *Life-span Development Psychology*, New York: Academic Press.

Ortner, S. B., 1974, 'Is female to male as nature is to culture?', in Rosaldo, M. A. and L. Lamphere (eds), *Women, Culture and Society*, Stanford: Stanford University Press.

Strathern, M. and C.P. Macormack, 1980, *Nature, Culture and Gender*, Cambridge: Cambridge University Press.

Chapter seven

Metaphors the Chinese age by

Stuart Thompson

Writing in the 1930s, the essayist Lin Yutang had the following to say about how Chinese cultural conceptions of ageing are antonymic to those he had become acquainted with in the West:

> In my efforts to compare and contrast Eastern and Western life, I have found no differences that are absolute except in this matter of the attitude towards age, which is sharp and clearcut and permits of no intermediate positions ... the East and the West take exactly opposite points of view.
>
> (Lin Yutang, 1937: 194)

Half a century later, in the very different ambience of my fieldwork village in western Taiwan, informants held very similar notions about how their respect for, and care of, the elderly contrasted with Westerners' thoughtless neglect. These adamant feelings concerning the high value accorded and courtesy attached to the elderly in Chinese society, as compared with the 'abandonment of the elderly' in 'America', were intensified by awareness that Westerners simply 'forget about their ancestors'. Working in northern Taiwan, Stevan Harrell likewise encountered 'a common Taiwanese stereotype of Americans ... that they consign their parents to old folks' homes' (1981: 199).

Andrea Sankar has suggested that 'if one ever wishes to present an example of a culture where old age is venerated, it is probably China that first comes to mind ...' (1984: 271). We might be wary of such recourse to what comes first to mind, being mindful of the trappings of 'Orientalist' representations (Said, 1978), but Sankar's suggestion is one with which most Chinese would readily concur. Indeed, an argument could be proposed that the cultural emphasis given to the veneration of the aged in Chinese society is, in part measure, sustained by their 'Occidentalist' representations of a counter process of ageing in the West. In such representations, America is portrayed as 'paradise for the young, and hell for the old' (to borrow the theme of an article in the Taiwanese magazine *Ren Jian* (2 June 1986)).

The extent to which such cultural representations actually inform and become reflected in practice is a complex issue. In the 'youth-centred' societies of the West, where the predominant image of the elderly seems to be that of decrepitude and redundancy, gerontologists have found that 'realities of aging simply do not fit the stereotypes' (Hendricks and Hendricks, 1977: 140): how the elderly regard being old differs markedly from the cultural image foisted upon them, whilst in Chinese society, despite proclamations of respect, state or collective provision for the elderly is scant, and this allows little alternative to reliance on family support.

The role of metaphor

Age meanings, like the sexual meanings discussed by Ortner and Whitehead, 'do not simply reflect or elaborate upon biological "givens", but are largely products of social and cultural processes' (1981: 1). We are thus dealing not with 'intrinsic ineluctable "facts of life" ... [but] ... on the contrary, [with] "facts of culture"' (La Fontaine, 1978: 2). 'Ageing' does not inexorably encapsulate *a priori* specifiable social entailments. The process of ageing can only be seen through metaphor-lensed spectacles, for it is through a culture's metaphors that ageing is given social shape.

Metaphor, the transfer of meaning from one domain to another, is much more than mere aesthetic embellishment. Bolinger has argued that 'the world is a vast elaborated metaphor' (1980: 141), for metaphor allows us to map and signpost what would otherwise be *terra incognita*. Often these metaphors we map by cannot be paraphrased in 'literal' language. Lakoff and Johnson argue that 'the essence of metaphor is understanding and experiencing one kind of thing in terms of another' (1980: 5). In their view, metaphor is a ubiquitous, not a fringe, feature in everyday life: 'the way we think, what we experience, and what we do every day is very much a matter of metaphor' (1980: 3). Metaphor is not just expressive, but can also be constitutive and, indeed, generative of how reality is experienced and perceived, perceived and experienced. Metaphors infiltrate 'common sense' views of reality as well as the more systematized postulations of philosophical, ritual and mythico-ideological discourses.

For the purposes of the present discussion I wish to highlight four aspects of metaphorization. Firstly, metaphors can generate divergent ways of seeing the world. In so doing, they can provide paradigms by means of which complex, abstract or unformulated experience of reality (such as of ageing) can be grasped. They enable people to 'get a handle on' (Lakoff and Johnson, 1980: 60) what James Joyce calls the 'whorled without aimed' of that reality. However, as metaphors cast spotlights on certain senses of reality they simultaneously banish other perspectives to the shadows. When metaphorical usage has gained an acceptance it acquires a pre-emptiveness: 'its power to provide, or to thwart, understanding' (Cooper, 1986: 18).

Secondly, Lakoff and Johnson suggest that there is a 'directionality in metaphor' such that 'we tend to structure the less concrete and inherently vaguer concepts ... in terms of more concrete concepts, which are more clearly delineated in our experience' (1980: 112). There is a circularity in this notion that metaphor is grounded in concrete experience, for the perception of concrete experience is itself irreducibly metaphorical. The 'concrete experience' of ageing is most intensely stimulated and generated by rituals which dramatize culturally vital metaphors. Ritual 'may link the celebrants to their very selves, through the stages of the life cycle, making individual history into a continuum, a single phenomenological reality' (Myerhoff, 1984: 305), thereby making 'ageing' into a 'concrete experience'. So the process of metaphorization is not unidirectional. Rather, there is a dialectical reverberation between metaphor and experiential basis; an alteration in the one can entail a change in the other.

Thirdly, metaphors that fit with the fundamental concepts of a society find readiest acceptance. Furthermore, the adoption or rejection of a new metaphorical concept relates to the deployment of power. As Lakoff and Johnson recognize, 'people in power get to impose their metaphors' (1980: 157). By foisting their root metaphors on the wider society and specifying the appropriate or admissible interpretations of already conventional metaphors, reality is defined 'their way'. The intrinsic variety of the metaphorical concept is denied, thereby limiting its interpretation and concealing its arbitrariness, 'so as to give [it] the finality of incontestable pronouncement' (Aspin, 1984: 34).

This leads to my fourth point about metaphor, the notion of a 'dead metaphor'. Max Black (1979: 26) and others suggest that a 'so-called dead metaphor is not a metaphor at all', for such metaphors are used in ignorance of the plurality of meaning which gives metaphors their *vitality*. Dead metaphors are no longer evocative. In this view a metaphor's life course can be measured on what Cooper suggests we call a 'geriatric scale' (1986: 119). The metaphor's freshness and resonance – hence its vitality – wanes as it ages. But from the vantage point of the powerful it can be argued that the only good metaphor is a dead metaphor! For, from a sociological rather than an aesthetic perspective, metaphors are at their most effective when they 'are so deeply embedded ... that they are used automatically rather than consciously' (Lawton, 1984: 80). The metaphors we live or age by shape perceptions and actions most when, through a process of routinization, they become unproblematically accepted as literal truth. In this respect the notion of 'dead metaphor' is more apposite when we see death through Chinese eyes, with the deceased, though buried, continuing to exercise (for better or for worse, as ancestors or as ghosts) a weighty influence over the living. Dead metaphors can maintain a grip over, can get a handle on, the living.

Metaphors of ageing in traditional Chinese society

Chu Xi (AD 1130–1200) is the intellectual most associated with the founding of Neo-Confucianism, the state-promulgated doctrinal orthodoxy till 1905. Knowledge of Chu Xi's writings was a prerequisite for successful candidature in the civil service examinations. Bearing in mind the claim that 'people in power get to impose their metaphors' (Lakoff and Johnson, 1980: 157), and given the apparent effectiveness with which the literati exercised hegemony over subordinate classes, it should be instructive to investigate the extent to which metaphorical precepts which undergird Chu Xi's philosophical writings feature in the less structured discursive practices which partly constitute peasants' 'common sense' appreciations of reality. To this end, I am fortunate in being able to draw on Donald Munro's perceptive analyses (1985; 1988) of Chu Xi's structural imagery. In particular I examine those metaphors which relate to ageing, seeking to indicate their hegemonic impact. This approach is less oblique than might appear, for a central strand of Neo-Confucian thought is concerned with the question of authentic human ageing, the process of becoming human.

Neo-Confucianism incorporated features of Daoism and Buddhism in addition to revivifying Confucianism. All major traditions of Chinese thought presuppose a symbiotic conjunction between humanity and the universe. Humans are seen not as separate from but as immersed in nature. Traditional Chinese views of the world are non-Cartesian, and in this respect Neo-Confucianism is no exception. The root metaphor is of the cosmos not as machine but as organism, the 'organic philosophy of nature' in Joseph Needham's (1979: 247) terminology. The universe is conceptualized as a complex system of interaction characterized by recurrent rhythmic change. It seems unsurprising that a predominantly agrarian society should metaphorically conceptualize the cosmos by reference to processes and cycles familiar to those who live on and by the soil.

Chu Xi retains the conceptualization that *qi* ('vitalizing energy') courses through all things and beings, human and otherwise, and through the universe itself, substantializing everything as it circulates. There is no radical disjuncture between the natural and human worlds, for both are products of the same vital stuff (*qi*). The *qi* of each species or entity is shaped by its immanent organizing principle (*li*) of growth and change, a principle homologous with the *li* of the cosmos as a whole. *Li* orders *qi* which 'on its own is just pure being', while *qi* animates *li* (Feuchtwang, 1974: 49). Cognate to *li*, is the concept of *dao* ('the way') which signifies the ultimate reality, the essential process which generates the continual impermanence in which the cosmos as organism is implicated. At a more specific level, each entity or species has its own *dao*, its natural way of growing and changing. *Rendao* is the 'proper' way of becoming human, of realizing one's humanity, through conforming to one's *li*, and is perhaps the central concern of Neo-Confucian philosophy.

We would expect views of ageing to align with a culture's metaphorical concepts of time. Joseph Needham (1979) in dismantling the myth of the 'timeless orient' illustrates that the Chinese have long had well-developed concepts of both linear and cyclical time. Indeed both notions of time seem neatly expressed in the well-worn Chinese saying that 'time is like an arrow, days and months like a weaver's shuttle'. In cosmological thinking 'cyclicity' is emphasized. The characteristic motion of nature is cyclical, the *dao* viewed as a ceaseless rhythm of 'beginning and return', such that change is a constancy of the cosmos. Such movement – the circulation of *qi* – is generated by the dialectical interplay of complementary, yet inseparable, opposites signified by *yin* and *yang*, which themselves engender more complex phasings.

Elaborated correlative thinking is the preserve of geomancers and other specialists, but the system's general logic – especially with regard to *yin* and *yang*, and the significance of correspondences between human rhythms and natural time cycles – is something with which villagers have an acquaintance. In the relative absence of a concern for salvation (see Cohen, 1988) life itself is much prized. 'Better linger on earth than lie in it' in the words of one proverb. Longevity (*shou*) *per se* is culturally valued, and living to a ripe old age is a source of pride. Symbols expressive of wished-for longevity abound. Authentic ageing – of which longevity is one aspect – is achieved by living in conformity with the *li* or *dao* of one's (human) nature, by maintaining an existential rapport with the rhythm of the universe. 'The continual rhythm of "beginning and returning" is both the macrocosmic life of the Tao in nature and the microcosmic true life of man' (Girardot, 1983: 49). The human body has *qi* flowing through its meridians, the ebb and flow of which should be in harmony with the pulsations of cosmic *qi*. To be out of phase with Nature is harmful to the realization of one's telic potential. Villagers are aware of a veritable array of techniques for 'nourishing life' (*yangsheng*) ranging from herbal potions and dietetics to yoga-like breathing exercises and *coitus reservatus*, means of conserving and harmonizing the *qi* with which one was endowed at birth. Dissipation of *qi* results in death, but the process can be decelerated by such practices.

Villagers in western Taiwan talk about the ageing process in various ways which make the term 'life cycle' more appropriate than the more linear 'life course' view. They perceive life in terms of various cycles, echoing the more systematized conceptions of cosmological sophisticates. At one level, there is the prevalent, if inchoate, notion of reincarnation, that after an unspecified sojourn in the *yin* world, life will start anew. A further cyclical correlation involves the sexagenary cycle (the sixty year period engendered by associating the twelve Animal Years with the Five Phases). Whilst on the linear reckoning reaching one's sixtieth year is a status marker for old age, from the cyclical perspective it marks the beginning of a second childhood (*fanlao huantong*), though not meant as such in a derisory sense. The human life cycle is also metaphorically tallied with the daily cycle and the annual seasonal cycle. One's early (*zao*: morning), middle (*zhong*: noon) and late (*wan*: evening) years correlate with the three mealtimes which partition the day. Similarly in village talk correlations are made linking spring with birth and childhood, through to an identification of winter with old age and death.

This latter correlation is reminiscent of the theory expressed in some medical classics and other systematized writings by which a concomitance is established between the passing of the four seasons and the growth pattern of crops, on the one hand, and the *qi* (vital energy) of the human body on the other. Thus, spring is associated with 'coming to life'; summer with 'growing up'; autumn with 'gathering in'; and winter with 'storing away' (after Graham, 1986: 61). The close bonding of crop growth and human society is sustained by the annual cycle of festivals. Marcel Granet (1975: 46), writing of early peasant religion, claims that 'the dead season was established by a festival of old age, just as spring had been by the festivals of youth'. The linking of human affairs and plant growth stages in such a fashion is complicit with the Daoist notion that 'the whole of Nature ... [can] be analogized with the life cycles of living organisms' (Needham, 1979: 227).

Chu Xi incorporated this idea into Neo-Confucianism. He specifically proposed that 'the four-season growth process of plants characterizes all the myriad things that exist in the universe: all things must pass through the stages of sprouting, development, fruition, and death and preparation for renewal, in a never-ending cycle' (Munro, 1985: 277). As Munro (1988: 113) indicates, Chu Xi developed plant growth as the explanatory image from which his 'general theory of movement' stemmed. For Chu Xi, authentic human ageing – that is, in accordance with the *li* or *dao* of being human – was conceived as a four-season growth cycle coterminous with that of plants. Chu Xi's particular focus was upon the 'mind' (*xin*) – metonymic of the person – and its proper maturation, involving the phased acquisition of *ren* (humaneness, benevolence) 'in sequence, so that going through all stages constitutes completion (*ch'eng*)' (Munro, 1988: 116). The mind is seen as a seed that requires continuous cultivation – and protection from injurious weeds – if integrity (i.e. 'completion') is to be realized. 'Although associated with all four stages, humaneness ... as the principle of life, whether conceived cosmically or in man's mind, is identified specifically with *yuan* (originating growth), or spring, the beginning of life and the first stage in the process' (Munro: 1988: 122). The state-espoused orthodoxy, then, metaphorically identified ageing with plant growth (birth, development, decline and death) and stressed the significance of 'the root', of origins. What is 'death' for the individual plant, though, yields a growth potential for the next 'generation': future harvests spring from buried seed, the plant after a sojourn in the *yin* world is 'reincarnated'. Likewise, from the viewpoint of individual time, death is, as it were, a fact of life; from the viewpoint of family time, though, '*ch'i* [*qi*] endures even though individuals die' (Munro, 1988: 116).

Such systematic exposition is the preserve of the intelligentsia. At village level neither Chu Xi nor the examination system loomed large. None the less the metaphoric equationing of people and plants is manifest in a variety of utterances on ageing, in myth and ritual as well as everyday parlance in 'popular culture'. To start at what I suppose is a beginning, mothers-to-be are thought to be linked to a coexistent plant in the *yin* world. Red flowers on the maternal plant betoken male children that the woman will bear, while white blossoms betoken female children. In cases where a woman fails to conceive, a shaman or spirit medium may 'ascertain that a woman's "plant" needs attention, a ritual watering, or fertilization' (Topley, 1974: 239; see, also, Ahern, 1973: 234–40). The character for 'birth' (*sheng*) betrays its etymological sense of the earth producing a plant. Switching tack a little, the word *zi* connotes both sons and seeds, and, particularly in wedding ritual, much play is made of this coincidence to express hoped-for fertility. Infants are sometimes regarded as akin to seedlings, in need of nurturance. The term *miao*, meaning 'sprouts' or 'shoots', is also used to refer to human offspring. A common metaphor for ageing suggests that the human life pattern is the same as that of grass and trees (*caomu*), passing through correlative stages of growth toward decay (*renyu caomu tongxiu*), an expression that parallels Chu Xi's four-phase growth pattern. The plant metaphor can entail interconnection between the generations, as conveyed in the saying that 'trees are for shade, children for old age', or the injunction to 'grow rice in case of famine, rear children for old age'.

The linking of human and plant growth is further evident in the myth of the impetuous farmer Wang Ji, a story with which many villagers are familiar. Wang Ji worked diligently at growing his rice, ploughing and transplanting at the appropriate times. But, fretting because of the time the rice was taking to grow, he attempted to accelerate the natural process by pulling each shoot up higher. Consequently, the next morning, to his dismay, he found that his premature action had caused the rice plants to wilt. One moral of this tale is that the growth process of humans, like that of the rice, should not be forced. In his efforts to cultivate rice the farmer betrayed his own lack of self-cultivation.

A well-known Chinese aphorism tells that 'falling leaves settle on their roots' (*yeluo guigen*), usually said in connection with a migrant's aspiration to return to his roots, his home, for death. The renowned Chinese anthropologist, Fei Xiaotong, in discussing Chinese peasants' attachment to the land, resorts to the plant metaphor, and refers to this aphorism when he suggests that

> men ... are like plants that take their nourishment from the land. But when the spring-time of their growth is past and they come to the fall of life, they must return to the land, just as leaves of a plant fall and come in time to nourish its roots.

> (Fei, 1953: 129)

Here we have a popular notion of 'returning to the roots' (the movement of the *dao*), with the implication that decay (of the leaves) enhances the fertility of the plant. This notion of endurance beyond the 'death' of an individual, the conjunction of the themes of decay and regeneration, is implicit in the *yin–yang* circulation of *qi*, the oscillation between activity and stillness, life and death being part of a totalized unity. Death and putrescence is part of, indeed a prerequisite for, the regeneratory cycle, the continual rhythm of beginning and return. Granet (1975: 50), in similar vein, points out that in ancient China 'the Yellow Springs, retreat of the dead and reservoir of life, were the place from which there emanated the principle of the fecund humours which endowed human beings with creative power', whilst more contemporaneously Aijmer (1979: 76) claims that 'the grave is treated as a rice nursery'.

Rice is the paradigmatic plant. It is the Oriental Staff of Life, and a symbol of fertility (see Thompson, 1988). It is also a metaphor for livelihood, as in the well-worn expression 'iron rice-bowl' for a job that has security of tenure. Rice is, further, a symbol of life itself, for death is ratified by the smashing of a rice bowl. Rice, I would suggest, is a metaphor for *qi*, the vital energy which circulates in a person's body and which, to achieve longevity, has to be replenished and recycled since its dissipation and diminution result ultimately in death. The written character for *qi* significantly betrays its original conception as 'the vapour of rice'. A *dou*, a cylindrical container for the standard 'bushel' measure of rice, represents the measure of life that fate has apportioned to an individual, his *shoushu*. The *dou* bucket can also stand for the fate of the family generally and, at special community rituals, for the wider community. The term *dou* also refers to the constellation Ursa Major, said to be the residence of the gods of fate. The *dou* thus conjoins individual, family, community and cosmos. It is a core symbol, omnipresent on the more important ritual occasions. At funerals, the heir (i.e. replacement) to the deceased carries the rice bucket, containing symbols of fertility, to the grave. The ceramic pot used for secondary burial of bones, and, indeed, the womb, are also termed *dou* (see Thompson, 1988). So the standard measure for rice, the 'life-food' of the (southern) Chinese, seems to be a metaphor for the *qi* that is transferred from one generation to the next. As Shiga points out (1978: 123) of father and son, 'the life that pulsates through them is identical. Every man's life is nothing other than an extension of the breath he received from his father'. At funerals the transfer of *qi* to male offspring is marked by the distribution of rice from the *dou*. The Yellow Tails myth (see Ahern, 1973, for other versions and another interpretation of the myth) makes enhanced sense when interpreted in the light of the plant metaphor. The gist of the tale, told to me by an elderly neighbour, is as follows:

> In earlier days men used to have tails, and when the tail went yellow it meant they were about to die, and their sons would kill them to eat their flesh. But one time a man hid and his flesh rotted and the descendants couldn't eat it, so they buried him.

Goran Aijmer's (1984: 27) suggestive hunch is that 'the tail that turns yellow could be seen as ripening rice. The killing is the harvest. The killing provides food (rice) which is the flesh of the dead forefathers'. The rice has to 'die' and be 'buried' for the next 'generation' to continue. The most unfilial act of all, according to Mencius, was not to have posterity, not to continue one's patriline, to deny the prospect of further harvests. Rice symbolizes the cosubstantiality of ancestors and descendants, engendering what I am tempted to refer to as a relationship of patrilineal 'riceiprocity'.

The plant metaphor stems from the conception that everything in the universe *grows* in homologous patterns. Another prevalent conception is that everything *flows*: that is, the *qi* that courses through all things and beings is analogized with water. The circulation of *qi* around the human body mirrors the circulation of *qi* around the meridian points of a landscape. The life course (*mingtu*) on this metaphorical basis can be seen as a stream. Fei Xiaotong (1953: 129), for instance, writes that 'the stream of life of which everyone is a part flows parallel with the life of the earth, which has its own life'. A proper flow of *qi* should result in the indefinite extension of the patriline. Conceived of as the flow of water, this metaphor, like the plant metaphor, seems grounded in agricultural processes. The flow of *qi*, or life's stream, like irrigation channels, is subject to blockage, or too precipitous a flow. Illness thereby results, to be remedied by measures that regulate the flow of vital energy. Acupuncture is one method for unclogging the *qi* channels. It might seem that the life-stream metaphor contradicts the plant-rooted metaphor of the life cycle, but the flow of water is not to be imagined as a finite course. A hydrological metaphor encompasses the finite flow from spring to sea, so that, by precipitation, water is carried to springs again and the cycle is regenerated. A common saying that 'rivers have sources, trees have roots' suggests a fruitful analogy between roots and (water) sources. The importance of roots to the growth potential of a plant has already been discussed. Granet's discussion of the Yellow Springs gives an indication of the generative potential of springs. In Chu Xi's writings, 'the portrait is of principle [*li*] as the pure water from a spring source that flows through and penetrates all things' (Munro, 1988: 57). Following Mencius, the Neo-Confucians put great stress on the innate goodness of the human child. Conforming to the *li* of becoming human means, for them, retrieving the 'heart' (*xin*) of a child, recovering the purity and potential of one's root. The flow of water provided Chu Xi with an analogy for such endeavour, sustaining belief in human perfectability, for 'water can be purified by removal of sediment, and light gradually reappears as water reverts to its sourcelike purity' (Munro, 1988: 74). One's muddied *qi* can, by dint of self-cultivation, be cleansed to facilitate the assertion of one's pure humanity.

The notion of the *dao* as a way is best understood not in terms of a human-constructed road but in the sense of the undulating, meandering flow of a stream, a water-way. The downward flow of a stream is inexorable, but its trajectory takes into account the nature of the terrain, rather than constructing a straight roadway to a pre-set destination. It is – to mix metaphors – going with rather than against the grain. '*Li* is the pattern of behavior which comes about when one is in accord with the Tao, the watercourse [as Alan Watts calls it] of nature' (Watts, 1979: 15). Michael Young depicts the modern attitude toward the river of time as akin to making measurements from the bank with a view to establishing control, like some irrigation engineer (1988: 244). The Daoist view involves immersion in the watery course, flowing with the currents – a concurrence with Nature. From the Neo-Confucian perspective, the metaphor of 'being "on the way" ... [represented as] the continuous flow of ... water ... symbolizes a ceaseless process of self-realization ... the Way [is] ... inseparable from the person who pursues it, [and] is never perceived as an external path' (Tu Weiming, 1979: 36).

At village level the anthropologist Huang Shumin (1981: 185) reckons that 'a man's life is considered a time stream'. He shows that the Taiwanese villagers with whom he worked operate with two concepts of time, natural time and a personal time. The natural time stream is 'the stream of life of which everyone is a part' (to use Fei's phrase), and involves flows of a patterned and ongoing sort, with a regularity which allows geomancers and others familiar with 'time-picking' techniques to decide the 'timeliness' or inauspiciousness of a particular date for a particular enterprise or endeavour – for instance, starting up a business, or conducting a funeral. Almanacs were the most published books in traditional China, and most village households keep a copy. They record whether an activity would be 'in phase' or 'out of phase' with the flow of natural time, and warn of unfavourable conjunctures, or 'time spots'. 'Just as one cannot grow certain crops at certain seasons, one cannot do certain things in a particular time spot' (Huang, 1981: 189). As Huang goes on to say, 'the natural time stream and natural time spots are given. People who live through them cannot avoid or manipulate them, but must endure and obey the rules' (1981: 190). Individuals, though, have their own time rhythms, which operate in a theoretically predictable fashion, determinable from one's *ba zi*, eight characters which indicate one's time of birth, and from which the flow of one's life stream can be calculated.

In theory a fortune-teller can calculate favourable and unfavourable time spots by gearing one's personal time to the flow of natural time. The trajectory is predictable, and so too are blockage points which 'form when a man's character meets unfavourably with the character of natural time' (Huang, 1981: 191). When with hindsight or, preferably, with foresight a ritual specialist determines a susceptibility to such blockage, attempts can be made to realign the flow, for one's fate, to an extent, can be modified. Villagers know, for instance, that they are susceptible to unfavourable time spots especially when they are twenty-nine years of age (half a sexagenary cycle) and take ritual precautions to deflect their anticipated bad luck. Prior to marriage, the eight characters of the intending couple are checked for compatibility – incompatibility being an excuse to withdraw from negotiations. If compatible, an auspicious date is chosen for the wedding ceremony. Deflecting one's luck is one thing; altering the course of one's 'original fate' is much more difficult, wellnigh impossible. McCreery, though, describes a fascinating ritual for 'reforming original fate'. The 'patient's' affliction was duly diagnosed in terms of constriction of the flow of *qi*, and to unblock the flow involved the ritual substitution of rice for the patient, with 'uncooked rice ... used to construct a life-size figure of a naked man' (McCreery, 1973: 150), a substitution which adds weight to my suggestion that rice is metaphor for *qi*.

Before dealing with the implications of these metaphors of ageing I want, first, to introduce one further direction of the plant metaphor. As Tu Weiming says, in the

> Confucian perspective ... from childhood to old age the learning to be human never ceases.... Adulthood [is] ... a process of becoming ... without self-cultivation as a continuous effort to realize one's humanity, biological growth becomes meaningless. Adulthood, then, is 'to become a person'.
>
> (Tu Weiming, 1979: 35)

Commitment to learning, and to self-cultivation, are essential to the process of authentic ageing, of properly becoming a person. The effort is life-long and unceasing. Education, nourishment of the mind, was thus rated very highly in Neo-Confucian thought. This sort of authentic maturation was portrayed as a 'ripening' process. The word for being born, *sheng*, also means 'raw' or 'unripe' or 'uncooked', and so 'ripening' is a natural metaphor. But the word for 'ripe', *shu*, has other definite connotations. *Sheng-fan* is the term for an uncivilized barbarian, whilst *shu-fan*, literally 'ripe' or 'cooked' barbarian, is used for barbarians who have adopted Chinese civilization. By this count, the process of maturation is coterminous with the acquisition of 'culture' (*wen*). The character *wen*, however, has as a constituent part of its meaning, an inextricable association with 'writing' on the one hand, and 'sinification' on the other. Thus, on this continuum of maturation, becoming 'older' (i.e. becoming more human, more a person) is associated with sinification, acculturation and literacy, all considered an ineluctable part of the process of humanization and self-cultivation. Education was supposed to facilitate the development of one's innate capacities, to cleanse one's muddy waters to retrieve the true self. Physiological ageing and the acquisition of this sort of knowledge did not necessarily coincide. The acquisition of this sort of knowledge enabled one to become old before one's time – or at least to be identified with the authority of seniors in advance of one's years. Hence, teachers, doctors, geomancers and other 'knowledgeable persons' are referred to *xian sheng* (literally 'born earlier') irrespective of chronological age.

On the other hand, the illiterate, or the uncultured, are seen as incomplete human beings, as relatively immature by this grammatocratic scale. Ageing should be a process of nearing 'completion', 'perfection'. The examination system accredited that successful candidates had acquired 'learning', and legitimated Mencius's view that 'those who work with their minds should rule over those who work with their hands'. There was much peasant acceptance of their own 'ignorance', as the 'ethical' knowledge of the rulers was privileged above pragmatic knowledge of the natural world. The knowledge of the elite vouchsafed their maturity and ratified their right to rule. The elite were granted agency, encapsulated in a further Confucian metaphor: 'when the wind blows, the grass bends'.

Implications

I wish at this stage to draw together some of the implications entailed by recourse to these metaphors of ageing – the implications extend to domains apparently separate from ageing.

One key conception underlying Chu Xi's imagery is the importance to be attached to 'origins' – roots for plants, springs for streams. From one angle, this fits into the idea that the motion of the *dao* is that of 'returning to the roots'. But it also connects with the strong sense of place, of attachment to the land – *topophilia*, Meyer (1988: 283) calls it – which has often been noted for the Chinese. This seems natural for a largely self-sufficient peasantry which 'acquires its means of life more through exchange with nature than in intercourse with society' (Marx, 1971: 230). A symbiosis is established between man and nature, seemingly. The peasant, his produce (rice) and his land are cosubstantial. In Fei's words (1953: 129), 'human life is not a process of exploiting the earth but only a link in the organic circulation'. Producer and product, life and livelihood, are merged such that, in Taussig's words, there is 'the embodiment of person in product' (1980: 28). However, the metaphor encourages a misrecognition of political reality, for it tends to naturalize the fixity of place, and the self-containedness of peasant agriculture, but ignores the existence and expropriations of the state.

Further, the metaphor, by emphasizing the inexorability of attachment between 'sources' and 'branches', underpins the notion of *xiao*, filial piety, the root virtue and relationship of Chinese society. It affirms a '"filialism" [that offers], no recognition of the independent existence of the individual; the individual was submerged into the familistic ethics' (King, 1985: 58). The senior generation, by virtue of its anteriority, is seen as the root from which following generations stem. Authority is vested in the roots, and, inasmuch as the organic metaphor incapacitates counter-perspectives, this is a state of affairs that is seen as 'natural', 'fixed' and unalterable. Likewise with the stream analogy, significance is attributed primarily to the source of the stream. The deterministic implications are similarly evident. The roots metaphor not only fixes peasants on a particular (ideally ancestral) tract of land, but also allocates an attachment to the 'head' (i.e. root) of the household. The state bolstered the position of the family head *vis-à-vis* the rest of the family, allowing him autonomy of decision-making in the domestic sphere. For peasants the metaphor implies knowing one's place, both by reference to one's roots in the landholding which constituted the ideological basis of the Chinese family, and knowing one's place in the family hierarchy. There was established an obligation and a moral and legal bond, which were considered as natural, toward the paterfamilias. Ideologically speaking, it was as futile to attempt to deny this bond

113

as to separate the flow of a river from its natural source. Filial piety, a particular kind of generalized reciprocity, was the pivotal relationship of the family, and the family, in turn, was metonymic of society in general. Family relationships provided the template for wider social relationships, in which the same acceptance of obligation and authority was extended up the societal ladder. Teachers, magistrates, and ultimately the emperor himself were seen as acting *in loco parentis*. Kinship itself served as an ideological metaphor.

A further implication extends from the idea that 'the relation between things like a root or a seed and buds, flowers, fruit, and leaves is an organic interconnection of things linked in a single life process' (Munro, 1985: 277). Life-long interdependence extends beyond death in the form of ancestor worship. The biological implication of the life cycle metaphor entails a sense of unalterable continuity through the generations. The metaphor of the line of descent exerts a powerful tug. 'The meaning, or value, of the individual's existence is defined by his being a link in the chain of social continuity which is concretely conceived in terms of descent' (Fei, 1983: 127). A vitally important part of one's 'becoming human' involves having posterity to continue that line. Not to do so is to be incomplete.

It should not be ignored that this very emphasis on the continuance of the patriline, the extension of intergenerational relationships and interdependence beyond the grave for men, involves marked discontinuities for women who are 'transplanted' at marriage. If men's life courses are metaphorically associable with rice plants, women are 'maggots in the rice' (to use the novelist Maxine Hong Kingston's vivid phrase) or 'useless eaters of rice' (Ikels, 1975: 31), or 'wild grain' as in the proverb 'wild grain does not go for grain taxes, a daughter does not support her mother'. Continuity marks the relationship between father and son, but not between mother and daughter. The latter, in her new marital abode, is of ambivalent status, and her menstruation, sign of her fertility, is at the same time liable to harm the rice crop. Uxorilocally married men are, similarly, depicted as *mingling*, an insect viewed as a rice parasite. Since a girl is eventually to be uprooted from her natal family, by the traumatic discontinuity of marriage, her brothers gain parental favouritism. 'Why tend someone else's crop?'

Metaphors are grounded in experience, but as experiences differ, so metaphors may atrophy or be less pertinent for some. Emily Martin proposes that, because of their radically different experiences, 'each gender has evolved a separate view of what life and death mean and how they interrelate' (1988: 168). The same point applies, equally, to the conceptualization of ageing, which, from a woman's vantage point, tallies much less appropriately with the dominant metaphors. Women's roles as daughters, then wives, then mothers, effectively partition their life courses into three distinct phases and there is little doubt that marriage causes the greatest disjuncture.

Social change and rival metaphors

The efficacy of these metaphors is grounded in the experiences of farmers familiar with the diurnal and seasonal cycles of agriculture. As people move to occupational niches which separate them from direct involvement with agriculture and the rhythms of nature, we might expect these key metaphors of ageing in traditional Chinese society to lose ground to alternative depictions of time and ageing.

The population of Taiwan, the rural sector included, are no longer peasants who live symbiotically in accord with nature. The pattern of decentralized industrial growth has led to an abrupt swing of resources – land, labour and capital – away from agriculture to off-farm and non-farming enterprises and activities (see Thompson, 1984). While the younger generation of the workforce 'sell their youth to the company' (Gates, 1979: 396) – usually in the cities and often with a view to setting up their own family-based enterprise in the future – there has been a marked senescization of the agricultural workforce. The young are reluctant to farm. 'There's no money in agriculture' is an often voiced complaint of older villagers, the exception being the commercial farming of various cash crops – agribusiness rather than agriculture. In the last thirty years, especially, occupational heterogeneity has replaced the occupational homogeneity typical of villages in the past. Capitalist practices have 'colonized' Taiwan's villages. Rural Taiwan is a post-peasant society evidencing what we might refer to as 'capitalism with Taiwanese characteristics'. The most noticeable 'Taiwanese characteristic' in the encounter with capitalist forces has been the retention of the 'family' (albeit in modified and often federated form) as a key institution. Family *farms* have become family *firms*, with agriculture as only one component of a more diversified federal family economy.

Nisbet (1969: 6) has argued that 'revolutions in thought are quite often no more than the mutational replacement ... of one foundation metaphor by another in man's contemplation of universe, society, and self'. In line with the deep-seated changes I have sketched above there has been an incursion of an alternative and rival root metaphor. The new foundation metaphor is mechanical rather than organicist, reflecting the tendency of commodity production to fragment the organic unity between person, land and produce. The new and increasingly intrusive metaphor is premised on a perception of people as cogs in a great machine rather than as plants that grow as everything else in nature. It emphasizes the honing and fashioning of bodies over self-cultivation and growth, and the assembly line over the patriline. The customary perception of the ageing process has been challenged by a new gaze which focuses upon chronology – age metaphorized as number – and the increasingly precise cellularization of the life course enabling what Michael Young refers to as 'the bureaucratization of aging' (1988: 109), a key feature of which is the measurement and grading of the population according to their attainments plotted against chronological age.

This new *gaze* is a 'normalizing gaze, a surveillance that ... establishes over individuals a visibility through which one differentiates them and judges them' (Foucault, 1977: 184). The organic view of the way (*dao*) is, in this gaze, replaced by a series of road tests which, at set mileages, measure an individual's attainment, assessed and evaluated and graded in relation to normative criteria. This reiterated procedure of examination constitutes an apparatus of control by which a coercive discipline is imposed. The emphasis is upon end-products and being 'up to standard' – 'act your age' – rather than upon the process of individual development *per se*. In this respect the role of schooling is *vital* (in both senses of the term). The school is a disciplinary institution in which students are strictly '*class*ified' with others of the same chronological age, thereby facilitating the constant examination of individual attainment matched to age. 'The examination combines the techniques of an observing hierarchy and those of a normalizing judgement' (Foucault, 1977: 184). In a 'schooled society', schooling is a mechanism for rationing and authenticating the allocation of individuals to different slots in social and occupational hierarchies – scathingly referred to by Ronald Dore (1976) as 'the diploma disease'. The ramifications of this sieving and legitimating function of schooling are not confined to the period of childhood but reverberate throughout individuals' life courses, for school certification is a vital determinant of 'life chances', and, the more schooled a society is, the more predictive does schooling become for the rest of the life course. The implications of schooling resonate beyond the school walls. It is a peculiar but crucial feature of 'schooled societies' that, through the procedures of mass education, young people are literally and metaphorically 'marked for life'.

In the Taiwan context we can clearly discern that much of the logic of institutionalized schooling – at least from the vantage point of the state – is based on a metaphor of the school as a factory. Education is thereby conceptualized primarily in terms of investment in human capital. Children are seen as raw material to be honed and fashioned through the processes of schooling. The dependency of pupils is intensified by the vertical transmission of information from teacher to pupil. Pupils derive knowledge by means of making withdrawals from the deposits of knowledge for which teachers are gatekeepers. The curriculum is centrally controlled by the state, and there is a rigid stipulation as to the what, when and how of teaching. Literacy is seen as the key metonym of school-certified competence, the key criterion by which attainment is measured and evaluated. Maturity is, in school terms, assessed in terms of competence in literacy skills. Illiterates, in terms of the school's normative gaze, are regarded as incomplete human beings – as rejects. The central control of the curriculum by the state, and the stress laid on the attainment of literacy, were very much features of the traditional education system, but the extension of institutionalized educational provision to the mass of the population – and thereby subjecting the entire population to the normative gaze of schooling – is a new step. We can see, then, the deployment of what

Raymond Williams refers to as a 'selective tradition' (1977).

There is a pronounced 'Taylorism' about the whole process, most evident in the hidden curriculum of the inculcation of time-discipline and other disciplines appropriate to an industrial setting. As pupils are shunted along the conveyor-belt of schooling, they are subject to a rigid 'quality control' (cf. Taylor, 1984) through examination in terms of pre-defined objectives, a metaphor that corresponds to Foucault's assertions about 'normalizing judgements'. Though the textbooks give emphasis to traditional values – most notably filial piety – and stress 'the dynamic and natural process of moral growth' (Meyer, 1988: 278) – none the less young people are initiated into a world premised upon individual competitiveness and the constant measurement and evaluation of work from which they are thereby alienated. Herein lies a paradox. While parents are 'invited' to view their child's education – and, indeed, children themselves – as a kind of capital investment (so engendering an increased emphasis upon youth, and marginalization of the old), at the same time the processes of individuation implicit in the metaphor of the school as factory militate toward releasing children from the authority of their parents, and from an obligation to repay parental investment. Whilst the organicist metaphor of people as plants seems to have inscribed within it the idea of intergenerational connectedness and allegiance, the mechanistic metaphor of people being processed to be cogs in a societal machine separates producer not just from his or her product but also from his or her 'producers' (parents). The ideological state apparatuses (Althusser) of the school and the family seem to be pulling in different directions.

The implications of this new metaphor for the experiencing of ageing and the relationships between the generations are revolutionary. However it would be very misleading to suggest that the new metaphor has 'successfully' inculcated the *habitus* of rural Taiwanese villagers. The diploma disease is not (yet?) a contagion. To characterize Taiwanese society as a 'schooled society' is to ignore the issue of the extent to which the population have, as it were, learnt the lesson of schooling – the extent to which school-certification has become the single route to adult accreditation. Whilst those with jobs in bureaucratic contexts – for which educational qualifications *are* prerequisite – do 'at each stage in their careers ... calculate their progress in relation to all the other striving people around them' (Young, 1988: 114), the pivotal aspect is this very conception of life as a *career*. In Taiwan's capitalist society with its economic stress on family-based enterprises, there are alternative routes toward a successful life and livelihood, routes separate from the hegemonic track based on academic achievement certified through the educational process and the conception of life as a career. Though the experience of Taiwan's transformation from an agricultural society has somewhat undermined the aptness of organicist metaphorizations of the life cycle, this has not led to a ready acceptance of the rival mechanistic metaphor promoted most pertinently in the state's ideology of education. The hegemony of the latter does seem to be gaining ground, encroaching particularly upon the authority of the older generation – despite the promotion of filial piety in textbooks – through the accenting of the future, and the extension of the period of childhood by isolating children in schools and separating them from their parents. But even those who follow the career track often do so as part of a family strategy of diversifying 'resources', without individuation from the federated family being a necessary outcome. In many cases the perspective of the family proves stronger than the individuating perspective of the school. The 'educational script' does not have to be read in conformity with the state metaphor. Taiwanese villagers, though there are significant exceptions, tend to see education and the life course as a whole in a different light, one that does not accept the imposition of the state's normative gaze. In the words of one representative informant: 'If you have too much education you don't fit in with the world. Money is the important thing. It's no good if you have a lot of education but don't know how to earn money for your family.' This statement indicates that although the former organicist metaphor is losing its tenacity, this does not imply ready acceptance of the metaphor of the life course as conveyor-belted career subject to – but also validated by – constant inspection and 'quality control'.

© 1990 Stuart Thompson

Acknowledgements

I gratefully acknowledge my debt to the Department of Education for Northern Ireland and the University of London Central Research Fund for funding my field research, and to Professor Wen Cheng-i and members of the Institute of Ethnology, Academia Sinica, for their assistance and hospitality while I was in Taiwan. Chinese terms have been rendered in Modern Standard Chinese, using pinyin romanization.

References

Ahern, E., 1973, *The Cult of the Dead in a Chinese Village*, Stanford: Stanford University Press.
Aijmer, G., 1979, 'Ancestors in the spring', *Journal of the Hong Kong Branch of the Royal Asiatic Society*, Vol. 15.
Aijmer, G., 1984, 'Birth and death in China', *Ethnos*, Vols. 1–2.
Aspin, D., 1984, 'Metaphor and meaning in educational discourse', in Taylor (ed).
Black, Max, 1979, 'More about metaphor', in Ortony.
Bolinger, D., 1980, *Language: The Loaded Weapon*, London: Longman.
Cohen, M., 1988, 'Souls and salvation: conflicting themes in Chinese popular religion', in Watson and Rawski.
Cooper, D.E., 1986, *Metaphor*, Oxford: Basil Blackwell.
Dore, R., 1976, *The Diploma Disease: Education, Qualification and Development*, London: Allen & Unwin.

Fei Xiaotong (Fei Hsiao-tung), 1953, *China's Gentry*, Chicago: University of Chicago Press.

Fei Xiaotong, 1983 (1936), 'Peasant social life', in his *Chinese Village Close-Up*, Beijing: New World Press.

Feuchtwang, S., 1974, *An Anthropological Analysis of Chinese Geomancy*, Vientiane: Vithagna.

Foucault, M., 1977 (1975), *Discipline and Punish*, Harmondsworth: Penguin.

Gates, H., 1979, 'Dependency and the part-time proletariat in Taiwan', *Modern China*, Vol.5, No.3.

Girardot, N., 1983, *Myth and Meaning in Early Taoism*, Berkeley: University of California Press.

Graham, A.C., 1986, *Yin-Yang and the Nature of Correlative Thinking*, Singapore: Institute of East Asian Philosophies.

Granet, M., 1975 (1922), *The Religion of the Chinese People*, Oxford: Basil Blackwell.

Harrell, S., 1981, 'Growing old in rural Taiwan', in P. Amoss and S.Harrell (eds), *Other Ways of Growing Old*, Stanford: Stanford University Press.

Hendricks, J. and C. Hendricks, 1977, *Aging in Mass Society*, Cambridge, Mass.: Winthrop.

Huang Shumin, 1981, *Agricultural Degradation: Changing Community Systems in Rural Taiwan*, Washington: University Press of America.

Ikels, C., 1975, 'Old age in Hong Kong', *Gerontologist*, Vol.15, No.3.

Joyce, J., 1939, *Finnegan's Wake*, London: Faber & Faber.

Kertzer, D.I. and J. Keith (eds), 1984, *Age and Anthropological Theory*, London: Cornell University Press.

King, A.Y.C., 1985, 'The individual and group in Confucianism: a relational perspective', in Munro (ed).

La Fontaine, J.S. (ed), 1978, *Sex and Age as Principles of Social Differentiation*, London: Academic Press.

Lakoff, G. and M. Johnson, 1980, *Metaphors We Live By*, Chicago: University of Chicago Press.

Lawton, D., 1984, 'Metaphor and the curriculum', in Taylor (ed).

Lin Yutang, 1937, *The Importance of Living*, New York: The John Day Company.

McCreery, D., 1973, 'The symbolism of popular Taoist magic', Ph.D. Thesis, Cornell University.

Martin, E., 1988, 'Gender and ideological differences in representations of life and death', in Watson and Rawski.

Marx, K., 1971, 'Peasantry as a class', in T. Shanin (ed), *Peasants and Peasant Society*, Harmondsworth: Penguin.

Meyer, J.E., 1988, 'Teaching morality in Taiwan schools', *China Quarterly*, No.114.

Munro, D.J., 1985, 'The family network, the stream of water, and the plant: picturing persons in Sung Confucianism', in Munro (ed).

Munro, D.J. (ed), 1985, *Individualism and Holism: Studies in Confucian and Taoist Values*, Michigan: University of Michigan Press.

Munro, D.J., 1988, *Images of Human Nature: A Sung Portrait*, Princeton: Princeton University Press.

Myerhoff, B., 1984, 'Rites and signs of ripening: the intertwining of ritual, time and growing older', in Kertzer and Keith.

Needham, J., 1979 (1964), 'Time and eastern man', in his *The Grand Titration: Science and Society in East and West*, London: Allen & Unwin.

Nisbet, R., 1969, *Social Change and History*, New York: Oxford University Press.

Ortner, S.B. and H. Whitehead (eds), 1981, *Sexual Meanings: The Cultural Construction of Gender and Sexuality*, Cambridge: Cambridge University Press.

Ortony, A. (ed), 1979, *Metaphor and Thought*, Cambridge: Cambridge University Press.

Said, E., 1978, *Orientalism*, Harmondsworth: Penguin.

Sankar, A., 1984, "'It's just old age": old age as a diagnosis in American and Chinese medicine', in Kertzer and Keith.

Shiga, S., 1978, 'Family property and the law of inheritance in traditional China', in D. Buxbaum (ed), *Chinese Family Law and Social Change*, Seattle: University of Washington Press.

Taussig, M., 1980, *The Devil and Commodity Fetishism in South America*, Chapel Hill: University of North Carolina Press.

Taylor, W., 1984, 'Metaphors of educational discourse', in Taylor (ed).

Taylor, W. (ed), 1984, *Metaphors of Education*, London: Heinemann.

Thompson, S., 1984, 'Taiwan: rural society', *The China Quarterly*, No. 99.

Thompson, S., 1988, 'Death, food, and fertility', in Watson and Rawski.

Topley, M., 1974, 'Cosmic antagonisms: a mother–child syndrome', in A.P. Wolf (ed), *Religion and Ritual in Chinese Society*, Stanford: Stanford University Press.

Tu Weiming, 1979, *Humanity and Self-Cultivation: Essays in Confucian Thought*, Berkeley: Asian Humanities Press.

Watson, J.L. and E.S. Rawski (eds), 1988, *Death Ritual in Late Imperial and Modern China*, Berkeley: University of California Press.

Watts, A., 1979, *Tao, the Watercourse Way*, Harmondsworth: Penguin.

Williams, R., 1977, *Marxism and Literature*, Oxford: Oxford University Press.

Young, M., 1988, *The Metronomic Society: Natural Rhythms and Human Timetables*, London: Thames & Hudson.

Chapter eight

Growing old gracefully: physical, social and spiritual transformations in Venda society, 1956–66

John Blacking

The ageing of the anthropologist and the discovery of new meanings

This chapter is concerned with the ageing of social anthropologists and the methodological problems of analysing data many years after they were collected, and with particular data on ageing whose interpretation was affected by the passage of time. A discussion of problems related to the ageing of the author and the effects of life experience on his anthropological analysis, is followed by an ethnographic report on a conceptualization of life which saw spiritual and physical growth as inexorably interrelated.

The argument about the data is expressed chiefly in relation to a set of ideas about life, ageing, and death which were invoked on many different occasions both to explain particular actions and events, and as part of general speculation on the coherence of a world view which many Venda people shared. Since I do not have quantifiable data with which relationships between people's beliefs and convictions and their practice could be precisely evaluated, and in any case I would not trust such evidence even if I had it, the mode of discourse is reflective and exploratory rather than strictly empirical. It is the outcome of a double dialectic: between the researcher and different Venda opinions and events during a specific time period, and between the researcher and his own life experience over a much longer period of time.

The second, introspective, dialectic applies to all research, even if it is not openly declared. I doubt if it is possible to be wholly objective in any enterprise that involves human perceptions and calculations; but I am sure that it is impossible where matters of feeling and metaphysics are concerned, as in religious beliefs and practices, and concepts of life, ageing, and death. Anthropological fieldwork, in particular, is a rite of passage which can change the outlook of a researcher both during the periods of intense participation and during subsequent periods of reflection. Consequently, greater consciousness of subjectivity, and deliberate inclusion of the results of introspection, can usefully be built into models of cultural analysis or interpretation. This has, in effect, been a characteristic of much anthropological writing of the past fifteen years or so, but its personal dimensions have frequently been masked by scholarly references to non-anthropological writers, rather than dialogues with experience.

There is a sense in which anthropological training and fieldwork can leave a person 'scarred' for life, and incapable of living without 'anthropologizing' every social encounter. Life experiences are often measured against the yardstick of beliefs and patterns of action observed in the field, and analyses of data are validated or not by encounters with similar or contrasting social situations. Periods in the field become like a text or musical score whose meanings are changed by the intrusions of experience (see Wachsmann 1982), and whose 're-readings' can influence subsequent perceptions and decisions. A major problem is therefore posed by the fact that analysis and interpretation take place over a much longer period of time than fieldwork, and that when, as in my own case, it is impossible to re-visit one's friends in the field, there is no way of checking to what extent one's own life experiences have distorted or clarified the meanings of people's observations, actions, and explanations.

I am convinced that I now understand many of the things that were done and said to me in the field more clearly than I understood them at the time, and that this would not have been possible without many years of life experience and reflection. I am sure that there are and have been many social anthropologists who have not needed such a long apprenticeship, and that one does not have to be middle-aged in order to write about ageing! It is possible to have a powerful intuition and to be sensitive to other people's feelings and meanings at any stage of life. But at the time of my fieldwork in Venda, my understanding of many metaphysical matters was constrained by the behaviourist, positivist, and materialist premises which underpinned my research and my approach to life.

I was, for example, constantly looking out for sociological explanations of personal development, and it seemed to me that many Venda did likewise. They frequently explained personality and social action in terms of family characteristics, and especially of particular individual members, and they had a common saying which seemed to support the view that the self is a product of social interaction: *muthu ndi muthu nga vhañwe* means literally, 'a person (or human being) is a person through (association with) other persons'. This seemed to be further confirmed by many women's remarks when they visited and observed my second daughter, Jessica, who spent most of the first year of her life in the field. When they asked who she was like and predicted that she would soon be showing some family characteristics, it did not occur to me that they were not actually confirming my own view that personality traits of my wife and myself would be built into her by close association. Only some years later did I realize that they were talking not about her social person (*muthu*), but about her spiritual being (*mudzimu*). The social self was indeed considered to be the product of social interaction; but there was another self 'inside' babies from at least the time of quickening.

When I first described the rites that followed childbirth in traditional

Venda homes (Blacking 1964: 17–25), I understood that the birth of a baby was regarded as the reentry into the world of the spirit of someone who had died, but I misunderstood the status and strength of that spirit. I thought that people regarded the baby as not yet fully human in a negative sense, and saw 'its' proneness to infant death as a consequence of its spiritual and social fragility as well as its physical weakness. This seemed to me to be confirmed by the use of the words like *lushie* and *lutshetshe*, for infants in the first year of life, rather than *ñwana*. The former belonged to a nounclass (14) that was generally reserved for thin objects, while the latter belonged to the nounclass (1) to which 'human being' (*muthu*) and all kinship terms belonged. The explanations of terminology and ritual that were given, and the ways in which people spoke about birth and infant deaths, all seemed to point to the notion that babies began life as 'things', as sub-human but with the potential to become fully human as a result of social interaction. People said that the ability to speak a language, for example, was a defining characteristic of humanity, but one that could only be developed through sociability.

Babies as spiritual beings, and the problem of socialisation

Nearly thirty years passed before the 'affecting presence' (see Armstrong 1971) of a baby in my home helped me to understand what several Venda men and women had been trying to explain to me. I had already enjoyed and appreciated the infancy of several babies, but I had not before realized that babies are indeed neither human nor sub-human: they are *super*human! They cannot properly be described as junior adults, because they are in many ways essentially different from older children and adults. For many Venda they *were* spiritual beings, and that is why rituals of infancy were carried out by old ladies and little girls, who were closest to the purity of the spiritual world and whose ritual colour was black.

Babies were very precious and much loved, not only for their own 'angelic' qualities, but also because they provided people with a glimpse of and direct contact with the world of the spirit, which for many Venda was not a fantastic reality but a frequently noted bodily experience that could both be cultivated and take people by surprise. For them all matter was a manifestation of spirit: the presence of babies, performances of certain songs and dances and rites, and especially those concerned with possession by ancestor spirits, were not escapes from reality but means to experiencing the 'real world', the world of spirit. The altered states of consciousness which people were expected to have were experimental proof that although the social self is a product of social interaction, there is another self that is a reification of the cycle of existence. Personal discovery of these hidden facts and of their essential meanings was an absorbing and major task for all human beings, but one for which comparatively little time was available because of numerous social obligations. Because of this, much of the time spent singing and dancing was not regarded as leisure time, as 'play' (*mutambo*): it was rather time for the most important work of all, spiritual work. The same values were held by those who belonged to the independent Christian churches: they devoted whole nights and whole days to 'the work of the spirit', which was considered essential for the health and wellbeing of the community and the world of nature.

Growing old was therefore a pleasure, not only because it could bring to people more power and influence in social and political life, but also because it could bestow deeper understanding and experience of the spiritual reality of the universe. For this reason, several young grandmothers, who were less than forty years old, liked to be called 'old lady' (*mukegulu*); and one friend of mine kept on reminding me that he was an 'old man' (*mukalaha*), even though he had no grey hairs. I spent very many hours with one old man, who was blind and a retired Master of Domba Initiation Schools, and he often alluded to the growing sense of peace and spiritual strength that he felt as time passed and the changing seasons touched his face.

Babies and very young children, then, at first lived in the closest contact with the spiritual reality of the universe, and that was why their behaviour often seemed strange. As their physical bodies grew and they became increasingly socialized and involved in the natural processes of production and re-production, they became distanced from the 'real world' of the spirit. Consequently rituals, including music and dance, became increasingly important as ways of maintaining close links with the spiritual world. Thus, experience of the 'real worlds' of time spent at initiation schools was often more highly valued than the immediate material advantages that came from having attended them. Again, because it gave experience of the spiritual qualities of infants, having children and grandchildren brought people close to a deep awareness of their beings.

The metaphor for human growth and reproduction was one of transformation, in which spiritual continuity transcended physical discontinuity. That is, fundamental and irreversible changes of the body and eventual physical decay, contrasted with the course of spiritual growth, which progressed steadily and was not marked by specific rites except at puberty and death, when individuals were separated respectively from their spiritual forebears and their physical bodies. I did not hear human growth described in terms borrowed from the cycle of horticultural production: from seed to maize shoot, to plant and ripe cob, and back to seed again. Rather, the growth of maize was defined as a series of transformations based on the human model of growth. Stages of human growth were marked by rituals, which will be discussed in the next section.

The traditional Venda religious system

There were, broadly speaking, three contrasting ideologies and corresponding life-styles which provided guidelines for Venda-speaking people as they grew up physically, developed their sense of personal, social, and cultural identity, and negotiated successive crises of life. They were the traditional religious system, centring on beliefs and rites related to the presence and action of the spirits of departed ancestors; Christianity as it had been taught, practised, and organized by various missionaries from Europe and North America since 1872; and Christianity as developed by independent black church communities, prophets, and priests in Southern Africa.

This chapter is concerned with the conceptualization of physical and spiritual growth by those who suscribed primarily to the first of these three systems. In the districts of Magidi, Thengwe, Lufule, Miluwani, and Gaba, where I carried out most of my fieldwork between 1956 and 1958, the proportion of traditionalists varied according to area from 35 per cent to over 70 per cent of the population. Several of these also subscribed to independent Christian churches and a few had, or had had, connections with European churches, if only during periods spent at modern schools.

Similarly many active members of the European churches were not as sceptical of traditional beliefs as they were supposed to be; and although they did not themselves pray openly to the spirits of departed ancestors in the traditional way, they participated in rites that involved non-Christian members of their families. Leaders of independent Venda Christian churches, whose work I studied both in rural Venda and in the urban township of Chiawelo between 1960 and 1966, proselytized vigorously among the traditionalists. But their Christian interpretation of the spiritual basis of life was often closer to traditional Venda ideas than to those of European Christians (see Blacking 1981), and many members participated in traditional rites, though they abstained from the alcoholic beer that was sometimes drunk at them.

It was impossible to obtain precise information on the range or extent of individuals' commitment to religious beliefs and practices, because this varied from comparative indifference but general assent, to deep conviction and assiduous practice. Furthermore, although public evidence of people's devotion tended to vary greatly according to the degree of their involvement in different social institutions, this could not be taken as a measure of their private feelings and attitudes. I had no reason to doubt people's sincerity in expressing their beliefs and feelings and explaining their actions; but I found it difficult to evaluate the strength of remarks that particular individuals made in the course of general conversations, in comparison with their responses to events such as: the sudden death from heart attack in his late forties of a much loved traditional healer who was the oldest son of the local ruler; the death of a sixteen-year-old Christian girl who was the daughter of the Chief Clerk at the District Office; the unsuccessful suicide attempt of an illiterate young woman, whose friends persuaded her to desist; and the tragically successful suicides of two young Christian teachers who were able to leave letters – one an unmarried man and the other a mother of two children.

Those who observed or assented to traditional Venda religion saw spiritual and physical growth in the context of a world of human beings who must live in harmony with vegetable and animal species, and above all with the spirits of departed ancestors, who were guardians of the land and its prosperity. Nobody owned land, but the hereditary rulers of *mashango* (large areas incorporating several districts and occupied by members of many different clans) were its custodians on behalf of the living and dead. They were responsible, through hereditary district heads, for allocating land fairly for house-building and gardens, as well as ensuring that certain areas, such as ancestral graves, were protected and that there was plenty of land for pasture. The rulers and district heads were paid tribute in kind, in order that they might devote time to settling disputes and have a surplus of food for ritual connected with the ancestral spirits, especially the annual sacrifices of *thevhula*, which was necessary for the wellbeing of people and crops. This surplus of food could also be redistributed to people in areas where crops failed or there was family misfortune.

Although rulers were sometimes surrounded with ritual and public honour that suggested great personal power, they were expected to act on the advice of their councillors and the unanimous will of their people, expressed in the public council, which every head of household was entitled to attend. The trappings of supreme authority reflected not the personal power of rulers but the sacred nature of their custodianship of the land and their communication with the spirits of departed ancestors.

By 1956, many aspects of the system had broken down because of a period of colonial administration and white domination, the conversion of many families and individuals to Christianity, and the migration of men and women to farms and urban areas. Restrictions on people's movement, which had been a way of protesting against unsatisfactory government, together with the colonialists' expropriation of previously available land and their support of rulers as agents of their alien government, encouraged autocratic and undemocratic action; and the introduction of money allowed rulers to hoard tribute which formerly had to be redistributed because it was perishable.

Physical, social and spiritual growth

Nevertheless, the traditional idea of an essentially spiritual world, and of the proper relations between human beings, land, rulers, and ancestors spirits, remained strong in the minds and actions of many people. It was publicly expressed in performances of music, dance, and rituals which had survived the onslaught of missionary disapproval and the influence of European-style schooling. In particular, the girls' initiation cycle of *vhusha-tshikanda-domba* (Blacking 1969) was very popular. It was also politically, as well as aesthetically, attractive: it entrenched the power of women in a strongly patrilineal system and, although sponsored by rulers, it was largely a tradition of commoner clans.

Although mission Christianity and schooling claimed to liberate women, many felt that the traditional system gave them more security as younger women and more power as they grew older. The worship of lineage ancestral spirits was conducted by *makhadzi*, the father's sister, who in royal families was a person of influence and responsible for naming the heir. Girls and old women were essential for all sacred rites, as mentioned above, and menstruating women (associated with the colour red) were responsible for spiritual regeneration by giving birth to babies. The importance of their work was expressed in the large number of terms referring to their growth. Male and female terms are compared below:

mudzimu – lushie (lutshetshe) – mwana (ñwana) – mutukana – mutuka (mu-thannga) – muvhera – munna – (mubebi) – mukalaha – mudzimu

(spirit – very small infant – child – boy – youth (lad) – young married man – married man – (parent) – old man – spirit)

mudzimu – lushie (lutshetshe) – mwana (ñwana) – musidzana – thungama-mu – khomba – muselwa – muthu wa Thovhela – mudzadze – mubvana – musadzi – (mubebi) – mukegulu – mudzimu

(spirit – very small infant – child – girl – girl just reaching puberty – girl of marriageable age – young wife – pregnant woman (called after Thovhela, a legendary hero and a title given to a ruler) – woman recently confined – woman with one child – married woman – (parent) – old woman – spirit)

These physical and social transformations were accompanied by spiritual growth, as a well-known saying made clear: *a hu aluwi muthu: hu aluwa mbilu*, 'it is not the person who grows up, but the heart', the 'core', the 'soul'. *U aluwa* referred chiefly to biological maturation, but it was also used to refer to spiritual growth. The point of the saying is that the acquisition of social status was an expected, more or less 'natural', consequence of maturation, and of less importance than spiritual growth. When someone died, people said a *hu tshee na muthu* (lit. there is no longer a person), but at the same time they hoped that there was *mudzimu*, an ancestral spirit.

The physical death of every 'identifiable', socially fulfilled person marked the birth of a new ancestral spirit, just as the physical birth of every baby marked the return of an ancestral spirit in human form. Every human being began life as a reincarnation of a deceased person, who at first maintained his/her autonomy as an ancestral spirit, and could eventually become an autonomous ancestral spirit in his/her own right. If an infant survived the first, physically dangerous year of life, it seemed that the innate characteristics of the deceased ancestral spirit lodged in the child's body would then gradually be modified by the different social experiences of the new person, who could eventually develop a strong and independent 'soul' (*mbilu*). It was the independent 'soul' who became *mudzimu* at the end of an individual's physical life.

Ideally, a person was supposed to pass through all the recognized stages of physical and social growth. Spiritual 'grace' developed fully in old age, whose onset was generally marked by the birth of a grandchild, even though the 'old' person might still be in his/her late thirties. This did not mean that people who died prematurely had no spiritual existence after physical death; but nor did it mean that the spirit world was a replica of the observed physical world. I was, for example, puzzled about the spiritual status of babies and children who had died, because people said that they were too young to have become *midzimu*. They were not considered nonentities simply because they had not developed strong social personalities (*muthu*); but when I asked people if there were child, as well as adult, ancestral spirits, I was reminded that an ancestral spirit was not an ordinary person (*muthu*), and that therefore spirits could not be described either as children or as adults. Ancestral spirits were ageless; and though they were not bound by time, they were apparently restricted to local space: for example, people could not be possessed by the spirits of their ancestors when they danced away from the ancestral home (see Blacking 1985b: 67). When at last I realized that babies were superhuman, I understood better what had been said to me: babies and children who died were too young to become 'new' *midzimu*, and their 'guardian' spirits had returned to the places from where they had come.

Although a baby's spirit was 'fully grown', as it were, when the baby was physically born, it could have as much difficulty in adjusting to an imperfect world as did the newborn baby. For example, the baby's father's father's sister, the priestess of the baby's lineage, could fail to identify the returning ancestral spirit correctly when naming the baby. The sense of alienation experienced by the spirit could make the baby physically sick until it was given a new and more appropriate name. Several rituals and available medical treatments were used during the first two years of a child's life (Blacking 1964: 17–24), in order to strengthen the child's physical body as a vehicle for its guardian ancestral spirit.

At puberty, however, the physical body was considered strong but the spiritual body weak. It was at this time that the development of an individual's independent 'soul' was enabled by rites of initiation. In 1956 the traditional rite of passage for boys (*vhutuka*, see Stayt 1931: 105–6) was almost entirely obsolete, and replaced by the *murundu* circumcision school, which had been brought to Western Venda in the nineteenth century (see Stayt 1931: 125 ff., and Blacking 1971: 205–6). Although one of the first Venda to be circumcised was Makhado, an heir to his father's kingdom round the mountain of Swunguzwi, north of Louis Trichardt, circumcision was resisted by the members of most other Venda royal families, who considered that a traditional ruler should not be circumcised. In 1956, many girls were attending the puberty rites of *vhusha* and the subsequent rite of *tshikanda*. Some youths joined them when they reached the third stage, of *domba*, in the *vhusha-tshikanda-domba* cycle. Traditionally, *domba* had been for both youths and girls.

These initiation schools were intended not only for formal education in the institution of parenthood, in the facts of childbirth, in local history, social etiquette, and so on. While participating in their rites, the novices were considered to be experiencing the 'real world' of the spirit which they had known intuitively as infants; but now they had to take on responsibility for their own spiritual growth. The music and dancing of *domba* portrayed symbolically the process of conception, foetal growth, and birth. But this was not merely a way of reinforcing the teaching about childbirth, as I implied in earlier publications (Blacking 1969; 1973: 78–88; 1985a). As the novices performed the music and dance night after night and day after day, they began to grow spiritually: their symbolic 'rebirth' at the conclusion of initiation marked a decisive phase in the independent growth of each one's 'soul', which would be expected to become an ancestor spirit at the time of physical death.

The rites of the last day and night of *domba*, at which each novice was symbolically born, were absolutely essential even though some of the earlier rites could be omitted by latecomers to *domba*. For example, the childlessness of some married women who had not been to *domba* was explained in spiritual terms: they were no longer protected by the ancestral spirits (*midzimu*) who had been with their bodies at birth, and their own individual spirits had not yet been born. Thus the growth of each one's social person (*muthu*), which included childbearing, could not be achieved without the successful growth of her 'soul' (*mbilu*).

It seems that the symbolic death and 'neuter' state of a novice at the beginning of the initiation cycle were the outward signs of the departure of the 'guardian' spirit and the conception of the person's independent 'soul'. Each novice was assigned a social guardian to accompany and assist her/him through the initiation. This ritual relationship was generally sustained throughout the lifetime of the pair.

The guardian spirit was not thereafter neglected. Like other ancestral spirits of the lineage, she/he was remembered at times of family prayer and at clan rituals (see, for instance, Stayt 1931: 242–59, and Ralushai 1977: *passim*). Specific ancestral spirits were also helped back to earth for a few days annually through the mediation of members of the possession cult (*ngoma dza midzimu*; Blacking 1985a), and sacrifices were made for all remembered ancestors of lineages at the annual 'harvest' rite of *thevhula*. Rulers' *thevhula* were accompanied by performances of *tshikona*, which I wrongly described in the 1960s as the Venda 'national dance', because it was played on state occasions and by migrant workers in urban areas, who also returned with dance teams at Easter and at Christmas. Professor Ralushai pointed out that its modern uses masked its meaning and significance in traditional Venda religion: it was a solemn, sacred dance of the ancestral spirits in which human beings participated, and whose profound effects on people were evidence of the

129

omnipresence of the spiritual world (see Blacking 1973: 50–2).

Participation in performances of *tshikona, domba, ngoma dza midzimu* and other rites provided individuals with different degrees of participation with the 'real world' of the spirit, as well as experiential proof of the power of the spirit and of the underlying continuity of all existence. They helped people to grow old gracefully, and with transformations of their physical bodies to achieve the desired end of spiritual growth.

© 1990 John Blacking

References

Armstrong, Robert P. (1971) *The Affecting Presence*. Urbana: University of Illinois Press.

Blacking, John (1964) *Black Background*. London and New York: Abelard Schuman.

Blacking, John (1969) Songs, dances, mimes and symbolism of Venda girls' initiation schools, parts 1–4. *African Studies* 28.

Blacking, John (1971) Music and the historical processess in Vendaland. In Klaus Wachsmann (ed.), *Essays on Music and History in Africa*. Evanston: Northwestern University Press, pp. 185–212.

Blacking, John (1973) *How Musical is Man?* Seattle: University of Washington Press.

Blacking, John (1981) Political and musical freedom in the music of some black South African churches. In Ladislav Holy and Milan Stuchlik (eds), *The Structure of Folk Models*, ASA Monographs Vol. 20. London: Academic Press, pp. 35–62.

Blacking, John (1985a) Movement, dance, music and the Venda girls' initiation cycle. In Paul Spencer (ed.), *Society and the Dance*. Cambridge: Cambridge University Press, pp. 64–91.

Blacking, John (1985b) The context of Venda possession music: reflections of the effectiveness of symbols. *1985 Yearbook for Traditional Music*, Vol. 17. New York: International Council for Traditional Music, pp. 64–87.

Ralushai, Victor Nkhumeleni (1977) Conflicting accounts of Venda history, with particular reference to the role of MUTUPO in social organization. Queen's University of Belfast: unpublished PhD dissertation.

Stayt, Hugh A. (1931) *The Bavenda*. London: Oxford University Press for the International African Institute.

Wachsmann, Klaus P. (1982) The changeability of musical experience. *Ethnomusicology* XXVI (2): 197–215.

Chapter nine

Dimensions of adulthood in Britain: long-term unemployment and mental handicap

Richard Jenkins

In this chapter I concentrate upon two particular age categories in contemporary British society – *youth* and *adulthood* – and the processes of transition between them. Within this area of enquiry my attention will be primarily focused upon the notion of adulthood, its meanings and the socially validated criteria which serve to mark it off as a distinct category or identity. Like most age categories it is diffuse and situationally defined in interaction and through social recognition. Unlike many other such categories, however, there are a number of precise, legally or administratively constituted thresholds which contribute to its definition. In order to explore the boundaries or outline of adulthood in contemporary Britain I shall briefly consider two situations in which it appears, for different reasons and in different ways, to be problematic: long-term unemployment and mental handicap.

Young people, families and unemployment

The sociology of youth developed as a response to the emergence of a distinct social category of youth in the post-war years, particularly from the 1950s onwards. Young people emerged as a significant independent sector of the population in western industrial societies, with money to spend and time to waste (Brake, 1980; Frith, 1984). Youth, as an interlude between childhood and adulthood, became the object of both adult envy and adult concern. The young were simultaneously celebrated and treated as a problem in studies of youth subcultures, delinquency and the transition from school to work.

The majority of these studies, however, concentrated upon problematic or deviant (and typically working-class, male) young people. In recognition of the limitations of these studies, a 'new sociology' of youth has developed, taking as its subject matter young women (Griffen, 1985; Lees, 1986; McRobbie and Nava, 1984) and/or 'ordinary kids' (Brown, 1987; Coffield *et al.*, 1986; Jenkins, 1982, 1983; Wallace, 1987c). In enlarging the scope of our concerns to include the boring, the mundane and the untroublesome alongside the more visible excesses of the subjects of earlier studies, young women alongside young men, the foundations have been laid for a more satisfactory understanding of 'youth' as a social category.

In addition, the rise of large-scale unemployment in the mid-1970s led to a shift away from research into the transition from school to work and towards an emphasis on the transition from youth to adulthood (see the studies by Coffield *et al.*, Jenkins, and Wallace referred to above). This transition is structured, among other things, by gender. Boys grow up to become men, girls grow up to become women. What is more, the routes to social majority are different for each.

For young men, the adult male wage appears to be central to the process of 'becoming a man' (Leonard, 1980, pp.71–5; Willis, 1977, p.150). By contrast, for young women it appears to be marriage and parenthood which are the most important criteria of adulthood (Griffin, 1985, p.50; Lees, 1986, pp.91–5; Leonard, 1980, pp.259–60). The two things are, of course, related: the adult wage is important for men because it means they can support a wife and family – important features of the adult male role – and, for women, marriage provides them with access to that wage during the extended period of child care responsibility which is their conventional adult lot.

If this depiction is generally accurate, then chronic levels of unemployment for the under-25s are likely to have 'knock-on' consequences for the move into adulthood of many young people.[1] Paul Willis, for example, has argued in an influential article that long-term unemployment consigns large numbers of young women and men to a state of 'suspended animation', a social and cultural limbo, permanently on hold, no longer kids but something less than adults (Willis, 1984). In this view he is supported by other researchers (Bostyn and Wight, 1987, p.142; Coffield, 1987).

Claire Wallace's ethnography of the young people of the Isle of Sheppey, in Kent (1986, 1987a, 1987b, 1987c), provides us with a more rounded view of these issues than Willis. For the young men, there is the possibility of finding a limited haven in the street-corner peer group, with its compensatory ideology of masculinity and shared adversity. By contrast, unemployed young women are likely to spend more time than they otherwise would in the family home, 'a form of extended adolescence' which is symbolised by their greater participation in domestic work (Wallace, 1986, p.109).

For the young women of Sheppey, there does appear, however, to be an alternative to dependency within their family of origin: a household of their own. Since actual marriage remains predicated upon the availability of at least one adult wage, this has tended to result in consensual unions, unmarried pregnancy and single parenthood. According to Beatrix Campbell (1984), who has also noted this trend and attributed it to the effects of recession, this is an escape strategy for young women from continued juvenile status in the parental home. There may be a resultant trend towards later marriage, or even its rejection altogether. The comparison with urban, underemployed black communities in the United States is suggestive, although one would not wish to push it too far (Aschenbrenner, 1975; Anderson, 1976; Hannerz, 1969;

Liebow, 1967; Rainwater, 1971; Stack, 1974). To return to Britain, however, it should be emphasised that other research, in Wolverhampton, for example, suggests that the situation is actually more complex than Campbell allows for (Youth Review Team, 1985, pp.110–13).

It was issues and topics such as these which informed a research project carried out by Susan Hutson and the author in Swansea and Port Talbot, South Wales, between 1985 and 1987 (Hutson and Jenkins, 1987a, 1987b, 1989).[2] Concerned in the main with young men and women between 18 and 25 years old who had been unemployed for more than six months, research was carried out in three locations: two working-class housing estates and an area of private housing. Altogether fifty-eight households were studied; thirty-seven young men, twenty-six young women, twenty-eight fathers and thirty-six mothers were formally interviewed. The smaller number of young women involved is a reflection of local labour-market conditions. Unemployment is more severe for young men than young women. Two of the project's central themes are relevant to this discussion. First, does the long-term unemployment of young people have implications for their courtship activities and marriage patterns? Second, is chronic unemployment preventing or obstructing the passage of young people into adulthood? I shall discuss each in turn.

The starting point for answering the first question must be Diana Leonard's classic study of courtship and marriage in Swansea in the late 1960s (Leonard, 1980), a fortunate point of comparison in both time and space. Leonard paints a very 'traditional' picture: young people lived with their parents prior to marriage, which typically took place in a young woman's late teens and a young man's early 20s. Pre-marital sex was strongly disapproved of and cohabitation was emphatically not publicly acceptable; it was almost unheard of, in fact. Expenditure on socialising and entertainment was very much the male responsibility; women 'invested' in their appearance and wardrobe. Engaged couples would ideally coordinate their expenditure, limit their socialising and save together for marriage; there is a clear indication in Leonard's material of the importance of the adult male wage to engagement and marriage strategies. Marriage was closely tied up with the assumption of adulthood; one did not usually marry before adulthood and marriage was the final criterion of adult status.

That was then. Now, nearly twenty years on, pre-marital sex is accepted, not only by the young people to whom we spoke, but also (albeit reluctantly perhaps) by the majority of their parents. Many young people leave home at one time or another prior to marriage, some for good. Cohabitation is a commonplace, if not yet a norm, and for some young women and men marriage may be deferred. In reflection of these changes, marriage may also have become less bound up with adulthood.

It is, of course, a moot point how much these changes are a consequence of unemployment. Causality is difficult to demonstrate at the best of times. There is likely to be some relationship between the two things. Other social changes must also be mentioned as contributing to the situation, however: the shift in women's consciousness and understanding of their role and identity, major changes in women's labour-market participation, readily available contraception and, more generally, 'new' attitudes to sexuality and its expression. National statistics illustrate a clear and long-term rise in cohabitation, a trend which probably has its own dynamic, recession or no (Central Statistical Office, 1986, p.13; Harris, 1983, pp.209–11).

Looking in more detail at our material on courtship, it is apparent how complex the relationship between these factors is. Although most of our respondents expressed the view that there should be equality between men and women with respect to who pays for 'going out', it is equally clear from our material that this rhetoric masks a reality in which it is expected that the young man should foot most of the bills. Thus it was agreed that young men needed more money than women. Comparative pay rates for men and women in the United Kingdom contribute to the continuance of this situation.

These expectations, however, lead to a problem in today's economic climate, particularly for the unemployed male. In the first place, he simply has less money than he would have if he were working. Second, he has less money than working women and the same as unemployed women. Thus, in both relative and absolute terms, his economic position in the courtship market deteriorates substantially. In South Wales – as in many areas – this is given a further twist by the fact that female labour is more in demand than male, so that young women are less likely to be unemployed than young men anyway.

There is thus the makings of a shift in the gendered balance of power with respect to courtship. Many unemployed young men are at a disadvantage with respect to securing a 'steady' girlfriend. Unemployed young women are, for a variety of reasons (local mores about drinking, the preferential admission policies of many night-clubs and discos, etc.) at less of a financial disadvantage. What is more, it is clear from our material, and this is once again in sharp contrast with Leonard's ethnography, that for many young women in Swansea and Port Talbot, finding a 'fella' is no longer the most important thing in their world.

It is much too early to speculate about whether or not orientations towards marriage, or marriage patterns themselves, will change in any marked or permanent fashion for these young people, particularly the young men. It is, however, possible to say something about the question of adulthood. In short, there is little support from this study for Willis's argument, referred to above, that long-term unemployment is barring young people from adulthood, problems with respect to courtship and marriage notwithstanding. Unemployed young people, despite all of the difficulties which they undoubtedly experience, continue to develop into adults. It is possible to say this with such confidence for at least four reasons.

In the first place, many attributes of adulthood are independent of either paid employment or marital status. These are the various thresholds of adulthood which are defined by the state and crossed at different ages. They include such things as criminal responsibility, sexual consent (which differs for heterosexuals and homosexuals by gender and between heterosexual and homosexual men), the conditional right to marry, the unconditional right to marry, medical consent, the right to vote, the right to enter full-time paid employment, if you can find it (which can also be expressed as the right not to attend full-time school), the right – given individual entitlement – to welfare benefits, and even the right to donate blood or organs for transplantation. And, of course, as one might expect, obligations are also involved: to register for National Insurance purposes, to pay income tax if in employment, or to attend if summoned for jury service, for example.

In this sense, therefore, adulthood is legally and administratively defined by the state and is bound up, in a weaker or stronger sense, with notions of citizenship and full membership in the polity. With the limited exceptions noted above, none of these dimensions of adulthood is gender-specific: they are universally bestowed aspects of citizenship, involving and invoking both rights and responsibilities. They are not all, however, automatically acquired: the responsibility for jury service, for example, depends upon the individual's inclusion on the electoral register. Nor do they all come together at one time in a sharply defined change of legal status. There is, instead, an incremental and gradual inclusion into adulthood, culminating for most people in Britain at the age of 18 with the right to vote.

Second, social security benefits, while not as symbolically powerful or economically substantial as a 'proper wage', allow young men and women more independence from their parents than they had whilst at school. It is a resource of their own, the management of which allows them the opportunity to exhibit – or not – a degree of adult responsibility. Claiming benefit is, in itself, an adult transaction between the individual and the state. Within the family of origin, benefit payments permit the giving in of 'lodge' money, even though it might only be a small amount. This is another adult transaction, an important indicator of the assumption of responsibility for oneself, recognised as such by both parents and their sons and daughters.

Third, the young people we looked at proceed into adulthood at least in part because their parents help them to do so. In all sorts of ways, mothers and fathers – particularly mothers – assist in this process: cajoling, bullying, supporting, constructively neglecting, pushing, whatever it takes, in fact. People *have* got to grow up. Most parents *want* their children to become adults. It is, in fact, a public testimony to their own success as parents in 'bringing them up'.

Finally, of course, it is not only parents who have a great deal invested in this process of growing up. Most young people *want* (eventually) to grow up. It is 'only natural'. The majority of young people, experiencing the complicated portmanteau of social, psychological and biological maturation which makes up the transition from youth to adulthood, have little option anyway.

The possibility of evading adulthood does not even bear thinking about. Within the bounds of socially defined 'normality' adulthood is more or less inevitable.

To sum up, while long-term unemployment does undoubtedly have specific effects upon young people's lives during their transition to adulthood, there seem to be no grounds for suggesting that it actually prevents them from becoming adults. Independent living and/or marriage and sexual partnership are but two facets of adulthood. It is the *right* to each, not their presence at any particular instance, which is most important. Willis's argument, therefore, is founded on too narrow a conception of adulthood, on the one hand, and a misunderstanding of the distinction between adult rights and responsibilities in general and the actualisation of those role requirements by particular individuals, on the other. Many social identities – and adulthood is one – do not require the fulfilment or activation of all of their constituent elements in order to be satisfactorily acquired or filled. Some of these elements may be central, some less so and some peripheral (Nadel, 1957, pp.31–5). Viewed from this perspective adulthood in British society is a robust, if inexactly defined, identity which, while certain aspects of it are likely to be threatened or curtailed by unemployment and economic hardship, cannot be undermined by circumstances which do not damage or destroy its central components. In the next section we will turn to a discussion of some of those central dimensions of adulthood.

When is an adult not an adult?

The answer to this question is – or so it appears – when he or she is classified as mentally handicapped. Perhaps putting it quite this bluntly prejudges the issue, but there is a need to examine critically the idea, implied towards the end of the previous section, that adulthood is somehow either inevitable or natural. It is neither, and the situation of people with a mental handicap provides us with a timely reminder of that fact.

What, in the first instance, is meant by 'mental handicap' or, in American usage, 'mental retardation'? There are three main kinds of conventional definition (Anderson, 1982, pp.25–8; Zigler and Hodapp, 1986, pp.4–10). The *medical* model emphasises physiological disorder or damage, typically of the brain and the central nervous system. It is sometimes known as the 'hole in the head' approach to mental handicap. The *psychological* model is concerned with impaired intellectual functioning as determined by standardised tests; by this token, mental handicap is typically held to mean an IQ score of less than seventy. Finally, there is a *behavioural* model, which relates to individuals' adequacy of performance in day-to-day, socially adaptive behaviours. This may also be measured using standardised tests. In the psychological and behavioural models, what is explicitly at issue is performative competence (Edgerton, 1967).

These are professional diagnostic models, used by doctors, psychologists, speech therapists and others. Not all professionals use all of these models and not all would agree with the application of particular models in particular cases. Although the medical and psychological models should not be dismissed as superseded, it is the behavioural model which is probably the most influential today. This is tied up with the shift from medical, institutional care to a social services based community care policy, as discussed later.

It is, however, important to remember that these diagnostic models of mental handicap are social constructs, varying with the clinical, social and historical context.[3] Although it occurs less often than it perhaps used to, for example, deaf people suffering from no other condition are still sometimes diagnosed as mentally handicapped (Sainsbury, 1986, p. 112). Nor is it too long since precocious sexuality, or overt sexuality in a person of apparently limited intellect, led to the label 'moral defective' and institutionalisation in a mental subnormality hospital (Marais and Marais, 1976, pp. 76–8). The distinction between mental illness and mental handicap is itself relatively recent.

But what of common-sense or folk models? For many centuries, various categories of the mentally handicapped were called 'idiots', 'imbeciles', 'cretins' or whatever by medical science. These descriptions passed into everyday language. Fear was one of the most important components of attitudes towards people with a mental handicap: fear of violence, fear of unbridled sexuality and lust, fear of unpredictable behaviour, fear of pollution through contact (Abbott and Sapsford, 1987, pp. 5–37). In many respects this is a model of the mentally handicapped as less than human, if not 'animals'. To judge from recent research, such notions remain a prominent aspect of the contemporary British popular model of mental handicap (Sinson, 1986). Sinson's research is particularly revealing with respect to the attitudes of her interviewees towards abortion and the Louise Brown case, where a father was tried for murdering his daughter (who had Down's syndrome). It is clearly not a crime, or less criminal, in the eyes of many, to kill someone with a mental handicap; abortion becomes more acceptable to those who oppose it normally if the foetus is shown by amniocentesis to be mentally handicapped (Sinson, 1986, pp.13–16). Support for such a conclusion comes from Shepperdson's research (1983) into parental attitudes towards the abortion and euthanasia of children with Down's syndrome, and similar views were expressed by supporters of the reforming Abortion Bill which successfully received its first reading in the British House of Commons in January 1988. Within the field of medical ethics, there is a well-articulated argument – which, of course, has its vociferous opponents – for the legal killing of some babies with a mental handicap (Kuhse and Singer, 1985).

Such views do not derive in any straightforward way from the image of the mentally handicapped as sub-human, however, although that is undoubtedly influential. The other important aspect of popular models of mental handicap may be characterised as the image of the 'eternal child' (Kurtz, 1977, p.10):

here one thinks of labels such as 'the feeble-minded' or 'the simple', evoking compassion, pity, and the quasi-parental role of the non-handicapped. This is a model with which many parents of mentally handicapped sons and daughters work, although there is also evidence that many other such parents are increasingly, albeit with misgivings and anxiety perhaps, advocating or accepting greater independence for their adolescent or adult offspring (Richardson and Ritchie, 1986). Religious beliefs may have a bearing here, particularly notions of spiritual innocence (Hoffman, 1961). This is also an area in which popular models and diagnostic models meet in the allocation of 'mental ages' to people with a mental handicap. With respect to diagnostic models, the influence of well-established popular images is obvious in the use of words such as 'sub-normal' (less than human) and 'retarded' (eternally children).

Policy models derive in part from both diagnostic and popular models. They may also, however, particularly with respect to the latter, be an attempt to modify such models. After many decades of remote institutional, almost penal and certainly custodial provision for the mentally handicapped, current policy initiatives stress 'community care' as the ideal (House of Commons, 1985; Jay, 1979). Without wishing to broach the issues involved by the care in the community policy, suffice it to say that it has generated a degree of controversy (e.g. Bulmer, 1987). Despite the community care programme, public attitudes do not appear to have shifted appreciably.

More radical than the community care model is the 'normalisation' approach, deriving originally from North America (Wolfensberger, 1972). This finds expression in the idea that 'each person has the right to a style of life that is normal within his or her own culture' (Zigler and Hodapp, 1986, p.214). This is an approach that has had some influence, certainly at the level of rhetoric, on policy in the United Kingdom concerning community care and de-institutionalisation, as in the first principle of the All Wales Strategy for the Development of Services for Mentally Handicapped People: 'mentally handicapped people should have a right to normal patterns of life within the community' (Welsh Office, 1983, p.1). It is recognised, however, that the achievement of such goals requires the provision of specialised and additional support and services.

Less specifically, policy is also reflected in the manner in which social services and health provision for people with a mental handicap are organised. There is, in particular, a clear differentiation between 'adult services' and 'children's services'. In large part, this may be symbolised by the transfer out of special educational establishments into day care provision, such as adult training centres, which typically occurs in the late teens. This is, however, an organisational divide which does not necessarily reflect any marked change in the attitudes of either families or staff towards the mentally handicapped young women and young men concerned.

So far, so good. The diagnostic models, with their reference to 'mental age' and 'retardation', and the popular model of 'the eternal child' explicitly deny the adulthood of people with a mental handicap. Current state provision and policy models – particularly the normalisation approach, the community care model being agnostic about the issue – appear to accord or allow them adult status. But what, however, of the models which are perhaps most significant in terms of facilitating (or not) the claim of mentally handicapped people to adult status, those which have a force in law?

Delineating the legal models is less than straightforward. In terms of statutory definitions, the only guidance comes from section 1(2) of the 1983 Mental Health Act, which defines 'mental impairment' and 'severe mental impairment' as combinations of degrees of diagnosed mental handicap with 'abnormally aggressive' or 'seriously irresponsible' behaviour. The latter may perhaps best be understood as whether a person with a mental handicap is perceived to be a danger to him or herself or to others. The Act is largely concerned with admission to, or detention in, psychiatric institutions, and the management of the property or affairs of those housed in such institutions. As such, it has little or no bearing upon the lives of most mentally handicapped people.[4] In so far as they are included within its definition of 'the disabled', people with a mental handicap are covered by the 1986 Disabled Persons (Services, Consultation and Representation) Act, according them certain rights of consultation and representation with respect to the services they receive. Other articles of statutory law which are relevant include the Road Traffic Act, 1960, which precludes the 'severely subnormal' from taking a driving test, and the Matrimonial Causes Act 1973, under which a marriage can be voided within a year from its pronunciation if either partner is diagnosed under the Mental Health Act as 'mentally impaired'.

It is in the common law, the law of case, precedent and judicial decision, that most of the legal model of mental handicap is to be found (Clarke, 1982, pp.44–6). It is also in common law that one can observe the coming together of diagnostic, policy and popular models within a unified framework of authorised and authoritative decision-making. A contract made by a mentally handicapped person may, for example, be cancelled if it can be shown that they did not understand what they were doing and the other party to the contract knew this.

Similarly, although universal suffrage is guaranteed by the Representation of the People Act 1949, the common law defines 'idiots' and those of 'unsound mind' as incapable of voting (this affects those categorised as 'severely mentally impaired'). There is a further problem for institutionalised, mentally handicapped people, who must be registered as voters in the constituency where they lived prior to admission. This in effect further bars many such people from voting. The reform of British local government finance planned at the time of writing (1988) – the community charge or 'poll tax' – has further implications in this respect. It is intended that the electoral register and the community charge register should be the same. In Scotland the issue has already been raised of who shall be diagnosed as sufficiently mentally handicapped to be exempt from the charge, and the register, and also, therefore, deprived of the vote. General practitioners will, it appears, be charged with this diagnosis (*Guardian*, 28 November 1987). Thus one of the most important dimensions of adulthood, the right to vote, is problematic for many mentally handicapped people.

Recent legal decisions have also highlighted important issues. In the previous section, on the impact of unemployment, it was apparent that areas of social life such as marriage, parenthood and sexual relations are central to the notion of adulthood. It is probably no coincidence that one of the most fraught areas in the debate about normalisation is sex and the mentally handicapped. It is also a very difficult issue for parents (Tapp, 1987, pp.13–15). One of the most prominent cases – certainly in terms of its media coverage – was that of 'Jeanette', a 17-year-old with Down's syndrome (*Guardian*, 19, 21 and 24 March 1987; *The Times*, 1 May 1987). Sunderland Borough Council, with the support of Jeanette's mother, applied for legal authority to sterilise Jeanette without her consent. Jeanette's eighteenth birthday was in May 1987 and the operation would then have required such consent. Following the case's passage though the Appeal Court and the House of Lords (at the behest of the Official Solicitor, in view of the gravity of the point of law involved), the case was decided in the council's favour. Jeanette was subsequently sterilised, still, one presumes, without her consent. In a more recent case, that of a 35-year-old woman with a mental handicap living in a hospital, who had formed an attachment to another patient, while sterilisation could not be specifically *authorised* because as the patient was over 18, the High Court declared that 'it was not unlawful to carry out a sterilisation operation on an adult ... who was incapable of consenting since the operation was in her best interests' (*Guardian*, 3 December 1988, Law Report). The legality of such an operation was subsequently confirmed by the Court of Appeal and the Law Lords, although the Appeal Court was explicit that this decision did not provide a general precedent. Similar subsequent cases would demand individual legal review (*Guardian*, 4 February and 5 May 1989).

The arguments in defence of decisions of this kind are basically of three kinds, although they are related. The first is concerned with the welfare of the girl or woman in question; in order to protect her from the physical and mental trauma of pregnancy and childbirth, some means has to be found of avoiding the consequences of her developing sexual awareness. Second, the individual is deemed to be incapable of understanding the relationship between sexual intercourse and conception. This was an argument for, in the words of *The Times* Law Report, depriving Jeanette 'of a basic human right, that of a woman to reproduce'. In this respect, Jeanette could not, it was argued, exercise informed choice. Third, bearing these arguments in mind, sterilisation was seen as the best or the only acceptable form of contraception; it is permanent and does not require regular administration.

Two other types of situation are also of interest. First, there is that of the woman with a mental handicap who is pregnant. In at least two such cases during 1987, the High Court authorised abortions in the absence of the woman's consent (*Guardian*, 28 May, 4 June 1987). Both women suffered from Down's syndrome and part of the argument for the decisions related to the likelihood of the children being similarly handicapped.

The second situation is different again, that of a child born to mentally handicapped parents, in this case the Morgans of Wolverhampton (*Guardian*, 3 and 15 July 1987). The pregnancy was unplanned; Mrs Morgan, a Roman Catholic, refused an abortion. The child was taken into care by the local Social Services Department. The parents were subsequently described as 'very confused and upset'.

There are at least three important themes to be drawn out from these cases which are relevant to this discussion. First, it must be emphasised that it is almost impossible to imagine most of the above happening, in a social democracy, to a person who was *not* mentally handicapped. A woman who, for reasons of physical infirmity or whatever, was considered incapable of bearing or caring for a child would not (could not?) be sterilised against her will. Similarly, a woman who *knew* – as a result, say, of amniocentesis – that the child she was carrying had a mental or other handicap, could not be compelled to have an abortion. It is difficult to imagine other circumstances under which a married couple's first child would be taken into care immediately after birth, without any opportunity being provided for them to demonstrate their ability to care for it satisfactorily.[5]

Second, this can be explained by the clarity with which it emerges from the court reports that, although they are regarded as biologically mature or chronologically adult, the individuals concerned are, in fact, regarded as non-adult in the intellectual, psychological or social senses of the word. At best, they are children. This is obvious both from the texts of the judgements and from the ubiquity and confidence with which they are assigned mental ages of 'three-and-a-half', 'five or six', or whatever. Here is the coming together of popular models – in the judicial application of canons of 'reasonableness' and 'common sense' – and diagnostic models with respect to professional judgements of 'mental age'. In defining adulthood in an essentialistic fashion, as naturally endowed competence or responsibility, the courts are effectively denying mentally handicapped adults some of the most important attributes of adulthood. The Morgans, for example, were permitted to marry but not to parent their child. Jeanette is to be allowed sexual activity but not to become pregnant.

The third point is that gender is also a factor to be taken into account here. It should, perhaps, not be surprising that, whilst sexuality is a general problem (or is seen to be) in this context, it is largely the *fertility* of women with a mental handicap which is considered problematic; the problem with men, however, is the perceived *threat* of their sexuality (as uncontrolled, or whatever). It is certainly the case that the transition into adulthood – if that is indeed what we can call it – of people with a mental handicap differs in this respect for men and women.

In closing this section, there are two more general points to be made. The first is about social change. One of the reasons for the legal decisions considered above is precisely that the nature of the status of adult people with a mental handicap has become an issue of concern and uncertainty. The community care approach and the influence of ideas such as normalisation have resulted in the need to explicitly (and legally) re-define the limits of the adulthood to which people with a mental handicap are to be admitted and the terms upon which they are to be accepted. The care in the community policy has had this effect because previously people with a mental handicap living in, for example, mental sub-normality hospitals were, in many senses, outside society. Living in total institutions (Goffman, 1968) they were in a social world where the effective legislators were doctors, psychologists, nurses and care staff. If a woman was pregnant then an abortion was simply done. Now, as the de-institutionalisation of people with a mental handicap proceeds apace, things are different. Hence the recourse to the courts for guidance and definition.

Normalisation has had an effect with respect both to its acceptance as a principle of policy and as an ideology of change and advocacy. Parents, professionals and pressure groups such as Mencap or the Campaign for Mental Handicap have begun a public debate about the nature of the 'normal life' which their sons and daughters and clients can expect, and the nature of their right to it. In the absence in Britain of a constitutional bill of rights, the latter is particularly problematic: the common law is the guardian of citizens' rights. Increasingly, people with a mental handicap are also raising their own expectations as a vista of increased possibilities opens up before them. The issue of their adulthood and what that might actually mean, at a level other than the rhetorical, has become contested.

It is not, however, simply the adulthood of people with a mental handicap which is at issue, and this is the second general point. It is also the nature of their humanity which is socially problematic. This is the heart of issues such as 'responsibility', 'consent' or whatever, and it is where popular models of the mentally handicapped as sub-human meet with notions of eternal childhood. Social change, with respect to institutional provision, policy and attitudes, has blurred the boundary between those labelled as mentally handicapped and the rest of society. Historically speaking, in western culture, this has always been a boundary between full humanity and something less, an ambiguous category of the half-human (or the half-animal).

At this point a comparative perspective may be useful. One of the organising frameworks of western culture is the mind-body dualism, with the human essence – the soul – conceived as 'lying behind the eyes' (metaphorically, not actually).[6] Hence the recognition of the biological maturity or adulthood of people with a mental handicap, but the problem in accepting their 'real' adulthood. And hence the importance attached to the issue in the first place. For all parties to the debate it is, one suspects, their own humanity and its nature which is the real point at issue.

The nature of adulthood

This chapter has discussed two apparently 'deviant' cases of the transition to adulthood in modern Britain in order to shed light upon the contours of the general or 'normal' model of adulthood. Several conclusions may be drawn in this respect. In no particular order of importance, these are as follows.

First, adulthood is a complex and multi-faceted social identity in modern British society. It is made up of informal and formal (i.e. legal or administrative) elements, some of which are more central than others. It is, what is more, a phase of the life course which has an imprecise boundary in terms of age. There is a cumulative process of transition from youth to adulthood. What was once clear at 21 (the 'key to the door') is now less clear at the age of 18.

Adulthood is also a role which partakes of the social, the psychological and the biological. It appears from the current situation of people with a mental handicap that the biological is much the least important of these. Looking at both of the cases in this chapter it is, however, equally clear that gender – another meeting point of the social and the biological – is influential in determining both the nature of adulthood and the process of becoming adult.

The mention of gender brings me to the final set of points. Not all social identities are as important, or as comprehensively apprehended and influential, as others. In this sense one might speak of a hierarchy of social identities or, more correctly, perhaps, hierarchies of social identity. In some contexts, for example, gender is more salient than adulthood (or other life-course categories) and vice versa. In other situations, of course, the two will combine, as in the hierarchy girl/woman, and so on. There is, however, one social identity which may have a claim to priority and overarching significance, that of the full member, the 'human'. This goes some way towards explaining the contrast between the robustness of adulthood for long-term unemployed young women and men and its apparent fragility and ambiguity for people with a mental handicap. The claim to adulthood is dependent upon the prior claim to full membership of the community of humanity: for the young unemployed that claim is secure, for people with a mental handicap it is not. To really be an adult, it seems, one must first be fully human.

© 1990 Richard Jenkins

Acknowledgements

This paper has benefited considerably from Pearl Jenkins's constructive criticism. In addition, I have found helpful the feedback received at the 1988

143

ASA Conference and the comments of Chris Harris, Susan Hutson and Billie Shepperdson.

Notes

1. In July 1987, 18–24 year olds made up a disproportionate 29.4 per cent of total unemployment in Britain (*Employment Gazette*, vol.95, no.9, September 1987, p.529).
2. This research was funded by the Joseph Rowntree Memorial Trust, whose support is gratefully acknowledged.
3. In saying this, I am not suggesting that the great majority of those people who are labelled 'mentally handicapped' do not have learning difficulties or intellectual disabilities of a greater or lesser degree of severity. The problems which they have of this kind are very real. However, the label *is* a label and serves merely to divide arbitrarily the continuum of human intellectual performance. It is also a broad and non-specific category, including within it many different syndromes or conditions and a myriad of intellectual circumstances; the precise aetiology of the bulk of mental handicaps remains a mystery (Zigler and Hodapp, 1986, pp.8–9).
4. The 1983 Mental Health Act is something of an improvement upon its predecessor of 1959, inasmuch as fewer people with a mental handicap fall within its terms of reference. Many professionals, however, feel that the inclusion of any mentally *handicapped* people in a statute dealing with mental *health* is inappropriate.
5. It cannot be emphasised strongly enough here that there are enough examples of mentally handicapped couples and single parents who, with appropriate support and provision, are successfully bringing up their children to make one sceptical about any claim that mentally handicapped people should not, by definition, be allowed to be parents.
6. I am grateful to my colleague John Parker for a discussion of this particular topic which has contributed to my thinking about the wider issues involved.

References

Abbott, P. and Sapsford, R. (1987) *Community Care for Mentally Handicapped Children*, Milton Keynes, Open University Press.

Anderson, D. (1982) *Social Work and Mental Handicap*, London, Macmillan.

Anderson, E. (1976) *A Place on the Corner*, Chicago, University of Chicago Press.

Aschenbrenner, J. (1975) *Lifelines: Black Families in Chicago*, New York, Holt, Rinehart & Winston.

Bostyn, A.-M. and Wight, D. (1987) 'Inside a community: values associated with money and time' in S. Fineman (ed.), *Unemployment: Personal and Social Consequences*, London, Tavistock.

Brake, M. (1980) *The Sociology of Youth Culture and Youth Subcultures*, London, Routledge & Kegan Paul.

Brown, P. (1987) *Schooling Ordinary Kids*, London, Tavistock.

Bulmer, M. (1987) *The Social Basis of Community Care*, London, Allen & Unwin.

Campbell, B. (1984) *The Road to Wigan Pier Revisited*, London, Virago.

Central Statistical Office (1986) *Key Facts 86*, London, HMSO.

Clarke, D. (1982) *Mentally Handicapped People*, London, Baillière Tindall.

Coffield, F. (1987) 'From the celebration to the marginalisation of youth' in G. Cohen (ed.), *Social Change and the Life Course*, London, Tavistock.

Coffield, F., Borrill, C. and Marshall, S. (1986) *Growing Up at the Margins*, Milton

Keynes, Open University Press.

Edgerton, R.B. (1967) *The Cloak of Competence: Stigma in the Lives of the Mentally Retarded*, Berkeley, University of California Press.

Frith, S. (1984) *The Sociology of Youth*, Ormskirk, Causeway Press.

Goffman, E. (1968) *Asylums*, Harmondsworth, Pelican.

Griffen, C. (1985) *Typical Girls? Young Women from School to the Job Market*, London, Routledge and Kegan Paul.

Hannerz, U. (1969) *Soulside*, New York, Columbia University Press.

Harris, C.C. (1983) *The Family and Industrial Society*, London, Allen & Unwin.

Hoffman, J.L. (1961) 'Catholicism, Medicine and Mental Retardation', *Practical Anthropology*, vol.2, pp.49–53.

House of Commons (1985) *Community Care with Special Reference To Adult Mentally Ill And Mentally Handicapped People*. Second report from the Social Services Committee, session 1984–5, London, HMSO.

Hutson, S. and Jenkins, R. (1987a) 'Coming of age in South Wales' in P. Brown and D.N. Ashton (eds), *Education, Unemployment and Labour Markets*, Brighton, Falmer.

Hutson, S. and Jenkins, R. (1987b) 'Family relationships and the unemployment of young people in Swansea' in M. White (ed.), *The Social World of the Young Unemployed*, London, Policy Studies Institute.

Hutson, S. and Jenkins, R. (1989) *Taking the Strain: Youth Unemployment, Families and the Transition to Adulthood*, Milton Keynes, Open University Press.

Jay, P. (1979) *Report of the Committee of Inquiry into Mental Handicap Nursing and Care*, Cmnd. 7468, London, HMSO.

Jenkins, R. (1982) *Hightown Rules: Growing up in a Belfast Housing Estate*, Leicester, National Youth Bureau.

Jenkins, R. (1983) *Lads, Citizens and Ordinary Kids: Working-class Youth Life-styles in Belfast*, London, Routledge and Kegan Paul.

Kuhse, H. and Singer, P. (1985) *Should the Baby Live? The Problem of Handicapped Infants*, Oxford, Oxford University Press.

Kurtz, R.A. (1977) *Social Aspects of Mental Retardation*, Lexington, Lexington Books.

Lees, S. (1986) *Losing Out: Sexuality and Adolescent Girls*, London, Hutchinson.

Leonard, D. (1980) *Sex and Generation: A Study of Courtship and Weddings*, London, Tavistock.

Liebow, E. (1967) *Tally's Corner*, Boston, Little Brown and Co.

McRobbie, A. and Nava, M. (eds) (1984) *Gender and Generation*, London, Macmillan.

Marais, E. and Marais, M. (1976) *Lives Worth Living*, London, Souvenir Press.

Nadel, S.F. (1957) *The Theory of Social Structure*, London, Cohen and West.

Rainwater, L. (1971) *Behind Ghetto Walls*, London, Allen Lane.

Richardson, A. and Ritchie, J. (1986) *Making the Break*, London, King Edward's Hospital Fund.

Sainsbury, S. (1986) *Deaf Worlds: A Study Of Integration, Segregation And Disability*, London, Hutchinson.

Shepperdson, B. (1983) 'Abortion and euthanasia of Down's syndrome children – the parents' view', *Journal of Medical Ethics*, vol.9. pp.152–7.

Sinson, J.C. (1986) *Attitudes to Down's Syndrome*, London, Mental Health Foundation.

Stack, C.B. (1974) *All Our Kin*, New York, Harper and Row.

Tapp, S. (1987) *Mentally Handicapped Young Adults at Home*, Social Work Monographs, Norwich, University of East Anglia.

Wallace, C. (1986) 'From girls and boys to women and men' in S. Walker and L. Barton (eds), *Youth, Unemployment and Schooling*, Milton Keynes, Open University Press.

Wallace, C. (1987a) 'From generation to generation' in P. Brown and D.N. Ashton (eds), *Education, Unemployment and Schooling*, Brighton, Falmer Press.

Wallace, C. (1987b) 'Between the family and the state: young people in transition' in M. White (ed.), *The Social World of the Young Unemployed*, London, Policy Studies Institute.

Wallace, C. (1987c) *For Richer, for Poorer: Growing Up in and out of Work*, London, Tavistock.

Welsh Office (1983) *All Wales Strategy for the Development of Services for Mentally Handicapped People*, Cardiff, Welsh Office.

Willis, P. (1977) *Learning to Labour*, Farnborough, Saxon House.

Willis, P. (1984) 'Youth unemployment: thinking the unthinkable', *Youth and Policy*, vol.2, no.4, pp.17–24, 33–6.

Wolfensberger, W. (1972) *Principles of Normalisation In Human Services*, Toronto, National Institute on Mental Retardation.

Youth Review Team (1985) *The Social Conditions of Young People in Wolverhampton in 1984*, Wolverhampton, Wolverhampton Borough Council.

Zigler, E. and Hodapp, R.M. (1986) *Understanding Mental Retardation*, Cambridge, Cambridge University Press.

Chapter ten

The social construction of parenthood in the People's Republic of China

Elisabeth Croll

For men and women, childbirth may well constitute the sharpest of discontinuities differentiating the phases of the life-course. As a rite of passage it
makes the transition from child to parent, from pupil to teacher and from one
generation to another. If 'once a parent, always a parent', it also marks the
beginning of one of the most continuing experiences of the life course. Yet in
the anthropological literature it seems that, within societies and cross-
culturally, notions of parenthood and the experience of parenting are much
under-studied especially when compared with the attention devoted to infancy, children, adolescence or youth, adulthood and the aged. Until very
recently, this was also the case in the People's Republic of China, but within
the past decade a number of socio-political and economic processes have
forced a rapid and radical reassessment of parenting incorporating the deconstruction and reconstruction of parenthood and its study. This chapter singles
out four of these processes for attention before analysing the reconstruction
of parenthood and the new social institutions for the schooling of parents.[1]

The crisis in socialisation

First and most importantly, for the first time since the Revolution in 1949
there has been a new investment in and sustained significance attached to the
socialisation of children by both state and the parent. Indeed from the beginning of the 1980s both dramatic economic reforms and family planning
policies have provoked something of a 'socialisation crisis'. The scope and
momentum of the recent reforms have abruptly telescoped and concentrated
radical economic, political and social changes into a few short years. The rapid
substitution of the self-conscious processes of modernisation, industrialisation and professionalisation since 1978 which followed the Maoist policies
and the Cultural Revolution (1966–76) required sharp reversals and transformations in the aims and procedures of most social processes. In terms of socialisation, the focus was not on the reproduction of 'revolutionary successors' or
'red suns' so much as on 'competent successors' equipped with expertise and
skills, and capable of achieving modernisation akin to that of the European

world. There is a sense in which rapid modernisation has required the resocialisation of all age groups in the acquisition of new skills and attitudes, but with the productivity of the next generation in mind, particular attention has been drawn for the first time to the quality of early pre-school education and a questioning of the past emphasis on docility, obedience and rote learning.[2]

The second process which has provoked a socialisation crisis is the near novel, universal and radical family planning policy which has transformed the size and structure of the family and intra-familial relations.[3] Although the single-child family policy first introduced in 1979 has passed through a number of nuanced phases in its implementation, it is sufficient here to note that there are upwards of thirty-five million 'single' children in China, and that this widespread phenomenon has had repercussions for intra-familial relations and particularly for parenting. First of all, child-bearing and child-rearing have for many couples become singular experiences, and as such, the value attached to those experiences has immediately and dramatically increased. For the first time, the state has separated child-specific from basic needs and encouraged parents to shift their interests from 'quantity' to the 'quality' of their only child. It is common to speak of the 4: 2: 1 ratio with the one child the focus of attention from four grandparents and two parents, and research into the allocation of time, energy, benefits, special foods and consumer items within households and in parental expectations suggests that the single child has emerged as the newest and most privileged of social categories.

However, research has also suggested that it is but a short step from privileged investment to indulgence, and professional practitioners have identified the single child as a 'problem' child and the single-child generation as the 'troublesome generation'. The adjectives most often applied by the media, parent, teacher and researcher alike to the single child are 'wilful', 'determined', 'selfish', 'assertive', 'aggressive', 'disobedient', 'lazy' and 'inconsiderate'. Indeed so out of control are they thought to be that they are often collectively referred to as 'little emperors' or 'little suns'. What is interesting about these semantic categorisations is that they generally suggest and signify a new relationship between the individual and the group or the self and significant others. What is at issue within the child-centred unit is the capacity of the young to negotiate their own needs and interests as individuals *vis-à-vis* those of the family group. Their emerging sense of self has interesting repercussions extending far beyond the subject at hand to embrace the role of the group, the collective unit and socialism, the norms of which have been reaffirmed in recent years by the state to counter new individualist, familial and entrepreneurial trends. In sum it is these two processes which form the rationale for the new interest of the state in, and its intervention in the socialisation of, infants and children and its simultaneous identification of the family as an appropriate unit or domain of socialisation.

The problem family

The new investment in, and significance attached to, the family or domestic group as a unit of socialisation follow thirty years of its marginalisation in this respect. A minimal passive role was assigned to domestic, family and kin groups as units of socialisation compared to the active all-inclusive roles assigned to the school, community and society.[4] To legitimise domestic socialisation and reduce the opposition between the influence of family and school, community and society, the family has been designated 'the first school' and, as such, a valid instrument for state intervention. Previously as a corollary of marginality, the family had been allowed considerable autonomy with little interference from outside agencies, but with the assignment of a central role to the domestic domain in socialisation, the state has appropriated a number of corrective intervening mechanisms. However if the family was a central unit of socialisation, it was also conceived of as a problem domain.

In the official rhetoric of the family, there has been an interesting recent move from a discourse or language of celebration based on a conflation of variables in slogan forms and on a reaffirmation of its marginality, if not demise, to the creation of a new language which incorporates and addresses problems. This new and official recognition or acknowledgement of 'family problems' has led to two new developments. First, in research, the family has become the focus of investigation in the search for the derivation of current social problems. Secondly, there has developed a new set of practitioners to apply the new mechanisms of correction and to advise on family problems among which it is parenting that has been identified as important.

There has thus been a new investment in and significance attached to parents as agents of socialisation. If the family is to be designated as the 'first school' then parents become the 'first teachers'. As for the family unit itself, the reassignment of agency in socialisation to parents follows a period in which parents had both been marginalised and periodically rejected as agents. Much of the new attention drawn to the importance of parents in socialisation derives from the current vogue for research into family problems which attributes much youth and adolescent deviancy to inadequacy of parenting.[5] Moreover, the prolific research on the single child has increasingly redefined its problems as the problems of the single child's parents. Indeed the generation of parents of the single child had grown up during the Cultural Revolution decade (1966–76) and because of their own disrupted education they are frequently and even officially referred to collectively as the 'lost generation'. They themselves were thus almost exclusively socialised for political roles that are no longer considered to be appropriate in a society which now values and rewards expertise, professionalism and educational skills. The modernisation programme itself has generally generated one of two responses among this parental age group. There is either a degree of cynicism and malaise, or more commonly in contrast an urgent need to educate and equip themselves for the new society and community. They have determined to reverse their own experience by compensating their own children. The desire of the single child to be indulged is matched by the desire of the parent to indulge.

For this generation of young adults placed betwixt and between the Revolution and the reforms, then, parenting is marked by a blurring and confusion of messages. Those based on indigenous and accumulated experience and transmitted by previous generations seem somewhat outmoded and there are few guidelines and models for the present and future. This has generated not only uncertainty or anxiety over appropriate methods of parenting, but also in turn an incapacity and a crisis of confidence in young parents which I myself observed at first hand in 1980.[6] Then, the sudden generation of new 'scientific' knowledge by professional practitioners had the immediate effect of generating ignorance among parents who were inclined, if the facilities were available, to hand their children almost entirely over to their professional care. For these reasons although parents in China have been newly designated as important agents of socialisation, they have also in turn become the objects of socialisation themselves.

Finally then in this larger multi-faceted process, there has been a new significance attached to the quality of parenting, and investment in and the training of 'quality' parents. The training programmes qualifying parents rest on the assumption that parenting skills can be acquired and learned. Interestingly, at the same time as the domestic unit has become the primary unit of socialisation, the very process of qualifying or training for parenting has been taken out of the domestic and reassigned to the public or, more appropriately, the social field or hybrid field lying between public and private.[7] That is, the state has appropriated the role of training and in so doing it has itself created 'the social' inhabited by new practitioners and new institutions. The establishment of a set of social practitioners entailed the creation of a new sphere of professional activity almost entirely devoted to the welfare and education of the family and in particular aimed at parents. Practitioners meet parents in hospitals, clinics, pre-school and school centres, in specially set aside consulting sessions in local parks and, most importantly of all, in new specialised institutions of the social: schools for parents. The aim of these 'schools' is to attract parent-pupils and produce new knowledge in the interests of constructing a new parenthood and increasing the quality of parenting. It is the novelty of these specialised institutions, the schools for parents, and their role in the social construction of parenthood which attracts the attention of the ethnographer.

Schools for parents

Schools for parents are variously sponsored by and attached to hospitals, neighbourhood administrations, enterprises, kindergartens and primary and middle schools.[8] The schools first set up in 1984 are both newly established and new types of government-sponsored institutions designed for learning adult personal intra-familial roles and relationships. To invest these institutions with a degree of designated importance and significance, the government has taken several initiatives. First, although what the sponsoring units have established are no more than a series of regular classes, albeit with additional attributes such as written assignments and in some cases even examinations for parents, these are collectively referred to as 'schools for parents' or *jiajiang xuexiao*. That is, the notion of 'school' has been imported to invest the classes with the heightened value that is associated with institutional permanence and educational professionalism. Although the classes for parents are sometimes held in the evenings, they are also frequently scheduled for late afternoons when arrangements have been made for units of employment to permit parents time off work without losing any wages. This is a device to validate the schools officially and equate them with productive and other socio-economic enterprises. Within the short time since their establishment, schools for parents have been commonly established in the cities, less frequently in the towns and so far their presence is unusual in the countryside although plans have been made for their spread throughout China.

The investigation outlined in this chapter was less concerned with the common indices by which the success of the schools might be assessed, such as their distribution and their density or attendance, the identification and measurement of their achievements in reducing infant and child mortality, or in improving parenting and child education and behaviour in the home, school and community. Rather this study was more concerned to ascertain the motivation of parents in attending the schools and their responses to its prescriptions by examining the messages of its curriculum, texts and role models in order to elicit the language and meanings of the codes and messages and their points of congruence and conflict with those inherited and previously practised. The official guidelines set down for the curriculum of these schools are very general, and interviews with the sponsors and founders of the schools suggest that a common set of goals underlies the official rhetoric for the founding of the schools. They include improving the physical, educational and emotional development of children; reducing the differentials between parents in their ability to nurture all-round development in their children; and helping parents to adjust to recent major changes in society (modernisation), the family (size and function) and schools (curriculum changes and teaching methods). For the teachers in the schools, mostly practitioners in the field of education and physical and psychological health in the employ of schools, hospitals or research institutes, the goals were more specific. They were mainly concerned with supplementing the kindergarten, school or hospital in its efforts to care for, teach and socialise the children. In particular many of the teachers felt that the rise in the numbers of single children and the differences in the types of behaviour permitted and encouraged by the home in contrast to school were such that their task of educating the children was made much more

151

difficult. They also hoped to increase contact and communication between parent and teacher, familiarising parents with their children's school and raising the status of and appreciation of the teacher's role in society. Most parents interviewed were highly motivated to attend these schools and, of the sixty or so interviewed in April 1987, the needs they identified most frequently could be roughly divided into three groups of twenty. There were those who were primarily motivated by a physical problem and in particular the food intake of their child which was sometimes linked to a concern with its rate of growth. There were also those who were perplexed as to how to cope with a particular behavioural pattern, usually to do with the will of the child, and in particular the claims expressed by the single child within the family. There was also a third category, who, while identifying no one single problem, were generally concerned with how to develop the intelligence and individual achievements of their child or 'create a dragon in a day'.

To meet the demands generated by sponsors, teachers and parents, schools devised their own curricula although the uniformity of their content reflects an official set of prescriptions. The topics commonly covered include the importance of family education in the multi-faceted socialisation process; changes in the kindergarten, primary and middle school curricula and teaching methods; the single child and family relations; health and nutrition; and child development and psychology with particular emphasis on behavioural incentives and sanctions. In compiling the lectures, most of the teachers in the parents' schools made use of the now considerable number of manuals, texts and specialist periodicals focusing on the physical and psychological development of the child. The origins of some of these texts were foreign, mainly the Soviet Union and Japan, and others have been produced within China. Many of the parents' schools have also compiled their own texts consisting of copies of the teachers' lectures, pertinent articles reproduced from newspapers, magazines, and manuals, and essays and reports written by parent-pupils themselves. The complexity and sophistication of the school texts for parents varied with the age of the child and with location so that the balance of the curriculum favoured health, hygiene and sanitation in parents' schools attached to nurseries, kindergartens and in rural areas, while the urban and higher-grade schools for parents favoured the psychological and intellectual development of children. The texts of all the visited schools however revealed a number of common messages transmitted to parents.

The establishment of new norms of parenthood required the deconstruction of past notions of parenthood, their reconstruction and in turn the recognition of new concepts of childhood. The language and content of the curricula incorporated all three of these prerequisites to 'quality' parenting. Childhood is now recognised anew as a more distinctive phenomenon distinguished by constituent age phases each with its own specific characteristics and developments. In contrast to inherited socialisation practices in which children were largely conceived of as junior adults with similar basic needs, now parents are encouraged to identify and separate out child-specific needs in the provisioning of nutritious foods and in health, educational and recreational prescriptions specific to the needs of the growing child. One of the largest growth areas in consumer goods has been in the supply of children's special foods, educational aids and recreational toys, and parents have been guided in their schools in the procurement and deployment of those appropriate to each age. The new messages of the curriculum have been endowed with the authority of science so that in both the definition of knowledge and in its application, nurturing is scientifically defined and practised. Thus 'parenting' is now denoted 'a science' and it should be the aim of the schools to produce 'a scientific parent'. Not to be a scientific parent is to prejudice a child's life chances and expectations. In this respect there has also been a redefinition of knowledge and ignorance, with knowledge born of experience or verbally inherited from previous generations substituted by knowledge born of the scientific child-rearing text or teaching of the practitioner. Grandmother, with her indigenous knowledge, has been replaced by the 'trained' nursery or kindergarten attendant as the preferred practitioner of child care.

A second and closely related trend is the elaboration of child-rearing practices beyond the physical and the acquisition of the most basic of literate and numerate skills. Traditionally and today, child education has been restricted by the almost exclusive emphasis on rote learning of texts. In the new schools, parents are encouraged to broaden their narrow expectations of children beyond the confines of character and number memorising after the example of the 'force-fed Peking duck' in order to attach new meanings to the concept of education to do with 'the imagination', 'free expression' and 'creativity'. Individual music, drawing, writing as modes of self-expression have been newly encouraged from pre-school and school age children in the cities. The nurturing of children's talents and creativity has drawn attention to the development of the individual, and in a society where the group has been accorded priority and resources are still scarce, there are newly competing claims by the child, the parents and the larger family unit. In the new child-centred household, parenthood is invested with the difficult task of redefining familial relationships and reconciling the frequently conflicting needs and demands of the individual and the group, although the texts do leave undefined the difficulties attendant upon the notion of the self and its relation to significant others in a society newly juxtaposing individual and group claims. These are some of the significant messages and meanings inherent within the texts which have drawn particular responses from the parent-pupils.

For the majority of the parent-pupils, or almost two-thirds of those interviewed, the most important lesson learned was of 'the special characteristics of the child' the clusters of which changed and varied with age – that is the concept of child development which is not only a physical but also a psychological process. The idea that a child might display certain behavioural characteristics or patterns at a certain age and that a child might be especially receptive to appropriate stimuli at a particular age had come as a revelation to most parents. They had tended to interpret negatively changes in a child's behaviour such as initiative, obstinacy or curiosity rather than understanding that these might be age-related and legitimate expressions of the growing separation and independence of the young child. The high expectations surrounding the achievement of the only child in the aftermath of the educational reforms emphasising privileged recruitment and achievement by results had encouraged many parents to negatively sanction the child who did not early memorise poems, characters and numbers. After the classes they referred to this phenomenon as 'force feeding the Peking duck' and said that they now appreciated better that to impose, force and punish too early would not yield the desired results. Moreover not only books but visual and verbal experiences of the natural, physical and emotional were also legitimate sources of knowledge. Positive, direct and indirect incentives encouraged the child to learn, share and contribute its best, in direct contrast to the deployment of the customary sanction of beating – a habit which most parents said they were learning to discard as a result of their acquisition of new knowledge and understanding after attending the schools. They were trying to understand the child's world from the child's point of view. The second most important category of lessons learned by parents had to do with the witting and unwitting privileging of the single child by parents and grandparents and the means by which children might be encouraged to relate to significant others by sharing and contributing to the running of the household. The third category of lessons most often cited was the acquisition of practical knowledge to do with health and nutrition.

Parenting and the institutionalised acquisition of 'quality' and 'scientific' attributes have been a self-conscious, interactive and reflexive process. In the schools, parents were invited to discuss and assess their own experience and that of other parents. A novel step is the formal recognition of parenting as an interactive process and the incorporation of children, as objects of parenting, into the very process of deconstruction and reconstruction of parenthood. Children's participation in both the selection of negative reference groups and role models for emulation is institutionalised, and they are encouraged to compare their own parents with those featured in the texts and to teach their own parents the recommended norms of parenthood.[9]

Finally an explicit trend is the endowment of the new messages with the authority of the state. The transmission of new values and norms to do with parenting by specialist practitioners and institutions marks a novel attempt by the Chinese government to regulate directly through the institution of the family. It is perhaps not a coincidence that as the economic independence and autonomy of the household has been increased as a result of the reforms, the government has sought other means to colonise or govern the family: mechanisms to do with socialisation which after decades of marginalisation have caused a new investment in and significance attached to the physical, educational and emotional development of children by family and parent at the behest of the state. Of all the phases in the life-cycle, parenting is now the focus of attention. Indeed in China over the past decade both new social, economic and political processes and family planning policies have created new demands on parents so that the continuing process of deconstruction and reconstruction of parenthood may be one of the most rapid and radical ever observed ethnographically. Ironically too, in China as elsewhere, the omission of parenting in any study of the life-course may lead to the exclusion of one of the most important if not the most taxing of the social factors contributing to the individual ageing process.

© 1990 Elisabeth Croll

Notes

1. This chapter is based on the study of documentary sources, observations from study visits to China over the past fifteen years and an intensive period of observation and interviewing on this subject in 1987.
2. Kessen, W. *Childhood in China*. Yale University Press, New Haven, 1975.
3. See Croll, E., Davin, D. and Karen, P. (eds). *China's One-child Family Policy*, Macmillan, London, 1985.
4. Croll, Elisabeth. *Chinese Woman Since Mao*. Zed Press, London, 1983.
5. Based on interviews with sociologists in China, 1984 and 1987.
6. For example where the facilities were available young mothers were likely to send their only child to a boarding kindergarten in their home village because they thought only 'professional courses' had the expertise to bring up children satisfactorily.
7. For a discussion of the social, see Donzelot, J. *The Policy of Families*. Hutchinson, London, 1979.
8. This section is entirely based on participation in parenting school programmes, interviews with sponsors, lecturers and parent-pupils, and collections of the texts in April 1987.
9. E.g. All China Women's Foundation. *Mommy, Daddy and Me; Chinese Kids Talk about their Parents*. New World Press, Beijing, China, 1986.

Chapter eleven

Old master, young master: retirement on Finnish farms

Ray Abrahams

It is a commonplace that humans are aware of ageing and mortality as their lot. This consciousness closely relates to our facility for language with its intrinsic qualities of abstraction and its formal recognition of time through tense and similar mechanisms. It is equally well known, however, that this universality of expressible human experience and imagination does not emerge in the same form everywhere. Formal groupings based on age and generation, for example, are quite rare, despite the widespread recognition of these principles of seniority in kinship systems. Similarly, interest in the relations between generations, as one ages and another starts to replace it, varies considerably from society to society. The existence of important property to be transmitted is clearly one of a number of significant variables in the situation.

These matters were sharply brought to my attention during work in eastern Finland. My own focus on inter-generational relations and succession was essentially academic, and it was therefore interesting to find a number of 'applied' Finnish studies of what farmers and academics alike there call *sukupolvenvaihdos* (lit. change of generation). One, published commercially, was available in the small bookshop which served the rural area where I was working. Others were produced by banks and agricultural research units, and there were also long newspaper articles on the subject.

The relations between the generations in the context of continuing connections between families and farm property has a long and complex history in this area. In addition to internal factors in the situation, it has been subject to a wide variety of important state and other external influences. Moreover, much more is involved than simply the transmission of wealth. A Finnish historian's comment on the medieval law is still highly relevant in this context. The law, he writes, was mainly interested in farms as property. 'But for the peasant farmer himself, keeping the farm under cultivation as the generations changed was often primarily a question of labour force' (Jutikkala, 1958, p.54). One might add that it also was a question of identity. Rural families and their individual members are often locally identified by reference to their farm, and farms themselves are often given family-derived names.

Internal factors in the family farm

The basic factors operating a family farm are well understood, and I outline them only briefly here. Because of their adaptability and the commitment of their members to each other and the farm, families have some advantages over other forms of farm labour force. Their members are usually willing to adjust to vicissitudes of seasonal and other shortages, bottlenecks and slack periods which seem typical of farming. The family farm is much more than a work place. It is also home, and as such it may serve as a base from which family members engage in other occupations in addition to farming, when conditions permit or demand this.

There are, however, also many problems. Despite some room for man-oeuvre as technology develops, farms are relatively static phenomena while families are fundamentally dynamic. Time and again one encounters the same basic difficulties. How can an ageing farmer and his wife ensure that the farm remains viable while also guaranteeing all their children a just share of the patrimony? What happens when the only available heirs are daughters, or where there is no heir at all, or at least none willing to take over? In addition, there are timing problems. For various reasons, post-mortem succession may not be the best strategy. Either it removes the matter from the participants' control, or it may tempt the junior generation to take it all too violently into their own hands as they tire of waiting to come into their own. Again, any wishes of the older generation to remain in charge must be balanced against increasing difficulties of coping with the physical and administrative work in-volved. Thus, there may be mutual advantages in pre-mortem transfer, and in any case it would be mistaken to see parents and children as purely self-centred and without sympathy for each other's problems.

In Finland, as elsewhere in northern Europe, a common solution to these difficulties has been inter-generational agreements whereby an heir takes over the farm from one or both living parents (Gaunt 1983, and Abrahams, forthcoming). Usually the heir in question is a son, but sometimes a daughter and her husband succeed. This last has happened typically when there are no sons, but it sometimes occurs when a son is unable or unwilling to take over. Nowadays such sons commonly have urban careers, but at times in the past the availability of new land made sons reluctant to wait for their fathers' farms when they could easily start new ones of their own. In some such cases it is reported that older farmers or their widows even entered into a contract with an unrelated person, who would run the farm and eventually inherit it (Kilpe-läinen et al., 1954, p.186). Today, a farmer who has no available successor will usually enter an agreement with the state to retire and close down the farm. Very many farms, and especially smaller, less attractive ones, have been closed in this way, as other sectors of the economy have developed and agriculture has been vigorously pruned.

In a recent extensive survey of Finnish farms to which the present holder had succeeded (Honkanen *et al.*, 1975), it was found that at least one parent was alive at time of transfer in 95 per cent of cases investigated, and both parents were alive in 60 per cent. Coupled with this, the use of wills has been rather rare. In the same survey it was found that only 3 per cent of intergenerational successions took place through wills, and this fits well with other Finnish data and with my own findings. Wills are not much used at all in Finland, and their main purpose – at least recently – has been to strengthen the lifetime rights of widows to the family home and other property (Aarnio, 1975).

The use of a written contract to effect the *inter vivos* transfer of a farm has a long history in Finland. The details of such contracts have varied but their general features have been much the same. The farm is transferred to a successor, usually a son, for a consideration. It appears that originally the farm only gradually changed hands, as the successor paid for it by providing the retiring owners with a pension in the form of food and shelter. This pattern seems to have been replaced about two centuries ago with one in which the transfer constituted a sale of the property to the successor, and arrangements were made at the same time to compensate other siblings. In addition to a payment to the retiring holder(s), various retirement services may be stipulated. The documents have been at times remarkably specific about the conditions of transfer, detailing for example the number of times a year that the retired couple should be taken to church, in addition to such other matters as their entitlement to particular amounts of food and forms of shelter, and to a decent funeral upon their death. I have discussed such documents elsewhere (Abrahams, forthcoming), and I simply note here that there are several reasons why such specificity should *not* be taken as a sign of poor relations and trust between parents and their children. Indeed, as I discuss later, there is reason to believe that there has been an element of fiction in many such documents.

Such arrangements represent, if not always literally, the wishes of the parties to the transfer. In a later section, I will discuss more fully what the practice of retirement involves, and also some of the elements of conflict as well as mutual interest in the transfer process. I want now, however, to consider some of the external factors which have been at work in such situations.

External influences

It is well known, though often forgotten, that familial systems of property holding and succession are of interest to a wider range of parties than those most immediately involved. Goody (1983) and others have pointed out how the history of wills in Europe is intimately connected with the history of the church and its interest in acquiring property. Similarly, there is evidence to suggest that systems of primogeniture are often the result of political influence upon peasant families from above (Goldschmidt and Kunkel, 1971).

In the history of Finnish farming families there are many instances of such wider interest and at times influence and interference. Family farms have been significant sources of food, labour and taxes for the state and other sections of the population, and because of this the size and structure of the groups resident upon them have attracted close political attention. The stability of society may also be at stake, and governmental efforts to provide land for discontented landless villagers in the early decades of the present century reflected this.

More recently, the 1960s and 1970s saw a serious running down of family farming, partly supported by deliberate policy, in favour of the developing urban industrial sector. Work in industry became more attractive as farming became more difficult, and an important contributing factor in this process was the mechanisation of the timber industry which removed a major source of off-farm income for many smaller farmers. The proportion of the work force engaged in agriculture has declined from about 50 per cent in the 1950s to around 11 per cent today, and this has been accompanied by the depopulation of many rural areas and even the collapse of many smaller rural communities (Abrahams, 1985, pp.44-6). Recent years have seen a variety of packages designed to tempt farmers into early retirement. Some are aimed at closing down the farms concerned while others are directed towards making succession by a son or other member of the younger generation more attractive. A main aim is to reduce the average age of farmers which has risen steadily since 1950 to its 1980 levels of about 55. Younger farmers have a reputation for greater openness to new ideas than their older counterparts, and the combination of early retirement and new blood is seen as a way of producing a trimmer, more efficient system. The early retirement schemes accompanied by farm closures offer farmers an attractive pension package, and those involving transfer to a suitable successor offer the incentive of cheap loans to help the successor buy the farm and pay off siblings. The schemes have been promoted through pamphlets, newspapers and local meetings. They have had considerable success, and I know of many farm owners who have felt they constitute an offer which it would be foolish to refuse.

Options and fictions

Despite the various constraints and influences I have discussed, it would be wrong to portray farmers and their successors as totally lacking in freedom for manoeuvre. The detailed arrangements which they make about the form of retirement and succession often involve considerable opportunity for choice and the expression of preference. Moreover, even in some of their most direct encounters with external forces and influences, farmers may be seen as taking advantage of things on offer rather than simply succumbing to pressure from them. Nor, as I have already hinted, is their behaviour in such contexts always what it seems.

One important area of choice is residential arrangements. As I have mentioned, the agreements between holder and successor commonly stipulate the former's right to shelter after transfer of the farm. Various arrangements are found. Occasionally, a retiring couple or individual may move into a flat in town, but many remain on the farm. There they may simply be given a room in the house, but usually they are provided with their own at least partially self-contained quarters when this is possible. There is also a growing tendency to build new accommodation on the farm for those retiring. An existing house may be extended, or sometimes new separate accommodation is provided. Such developments have been facilitated by new credit arrangements introduced in 1980. It is usually expected that the younger generation and their children will make good use of the new accommodation when the retired occupants die or become so infirm that they need to go to an old people's home or be hospitalised.

Such separate residential arrangements are usually best understood as mechanisms for avoiding conflict and maintaining good relations in the process. The former holders and their heirs may quite often get together, in the evening for example, and they may co-operate significantly in other ways as will be seen. Grandchildren particularly may form a vital link between them as they flit in and out of the two zones.

A commonly recurring issue, and one to which I will return later, is the problem posed by the presence of a young daughter-in-law in a house, and the transfer to her of authority for running it. The position of rural Finnish daughters-in-law has been notoriously difficult, and it seems very likely that more general strains in the relationship between daughter-in-law and mother-in-law are exacerbated by the issue of succession to the running of a farm and the farm household. Though there are many exceptions, husband's sisters too can be a source of discord if they remain on a farm or even when they simply return from time to time to visit. There is a risk that they will treat the place too familiarly as *their* home, so that the in-marrying sister-in-law may feel an outsider. In addition, the position of sons (and of course of in-marrying sons-in-law) is not without its problems. As elsewhere, fathers do not always age gracefully, and some widowed mothers seem to be as critical of their sons as of their sons' wives. The capacity for hard work and organisation of a now-dead father is recalled and invidiously compared with the son's behaviour, and this can create tension in a joint household even into the son's middle age.

Beyond all this, however, people generally seem conscious of the need to respect each other's freedom and the differences of taste and interest which are common between generations today. At some risk of oversimplification, it may be said that members of the older generation – at least in eastern Finland – tend much more to religious pietism than their juniors, and they are less interested in many modern technical developments such as cameras and hi-fi systems which attract the young. For some older people, any music other than church music seems to be suspect if not actually sinful, and although their tastes have recently been extending in some cases to classical and 'serious' modern music, they do not usually embrace the pop and jazz which younger people like. Again, younger people often find church matters dull and unattractive, and while they may peacefully tolerate a gathering at home of older neighbours for a session of hymn singing, it is not their ideal way of passing an evening. Another, partially related point is that rural younger people are in general better educated than their seniors, if only because they have had the benefit of more modern syllabuses. Many of them learn biology at school and take evolutionary theory for granted. The contrast between this and the fundamentalist 'creationism' of their parents can be one small extra element of discomfort between them.

I turn now to the question of what retirement may mean in practice, especially when the retiring individual, or couple, is relatively fit as often happens with an early transfer. There is variation on this issue, but my earlier point concerning property and labour generally applies here. Firstly, such a transfer clearly helps to guarantee the continuity of labour on the farm, and it may enhance its productivity as the successor responds to the incentives and advantages which ownership provides. At the same time, there is often a tendency for the radical change in legal property relations to be balanced by at least a short-term maintenance of the status quo in labour input. Many families continue their previous arrangements with little change for several years, and the technically retired parent(s) may still play a vital role in working the farm and, importantly, in planning and organisation. Health and good relations permitting, their handing over of these concerns to the younger generation often takes place gradually.

As in other contexts, a significant variable here is whether the succeeding son has married. This is a complex issue. Parents in rural Finland as elsewhere are keen to see their children marry. Partly this is simply a matter of wishing to see them follow a 'normal' life cycle, and there is also the wish for grandchildren. Again, a daughter-in-law should make a significant labour contribution, which should help to relieve the burden of the older generation as they age. Transfer of a farm to an unmarried son may also help to make him 'a better catch'. There is a shortage of young rural women these days, due partly to their desire to escape from agricultural drudgery, but it is also true that the idea of marrying a farm owner is likely to be more attractive than simply marrying a farmer's son whose prospects are uncertain.

But a son's marriage may be intimately related to the transfer of a farm in other ways. For a daughter-in-law is also a sort of wedge between him and his parents. She and the family they will found together provide him with concerns which give him a legitimate identity beyond his ties to parents and to siblings. If she arrives before a transfer, she may well accelerate its occurrence through exhortation, criticism and her very presence, and later she may push him faster than he might otherwise be tempted towards taking over the control of the farm in addition to its formal ownership. This is of course an old story, which goes well beyond the present ethnographic setting, but it is none the less an important way in which the life cycles of adjacent generations are tied up with each other, and it is especially significant in 'stem-family' type situations.

It is clear from my discussion that transfer of legal ownership is but one stage in a process of retirement, and that the pace and rhythm of this process are often subject to other influences such as health and the structure and inter-personal dynamics of the families concerned. In addition, there is the point I mentioned earlier that the process of legal transfer is not always absolutely what it seems. Two main types of transaction are important here. Firstly, there are the purchase and retirement agreements between holders and successors. Secondly, there are often related arrangements which deal with the rights of a successor's siblings. This usually involves the buying out of their shares in the property, but it may include the reservation of some limited rights for them in the farm and its amenities. Both inter- and intra-generational arrangements may be included in a single document. The need for both arises from the fact that a farmer's children all have equal rights of inheritance, but it is commonly thought desirable to keep the farm intact by passing it on to one successor while at the same time trying to do justice to the others.

Most of the documents of transfer which I myself have seen are relatively recent, and I give an outline of a modern one as an example. The document sets out the transfer of a farm from the farmer, O.K., and his wife to their son T. The document is from the early 1970s and it is formally laid out, signed and witnessed. It is entitled 'Document of Sale' (*kauppakir.ja*) and it begins as follows.

> By this document of sale I, the undersigned farmer O.K. with the agreement of my wife ... sell and transfer my farm holdings ... along with all buildings on them and other presently or future attached benefits and rights plus all movables, livestock, machinery and fittings to our son T. for a price formed as follows.

The document then specifies the price (70,000 marks) and its component parts, and it notes that just under a third of this is covered by the successor's taking on the repayment of loan debts. A further reduction of 3,000 marks for a brother, and 2,000 and 1,500 marks respectively for two sisters, is noted. This sum is to be paid to the siblings without interest as soon as a loan to cover this has been received or within a year, whichever is the shorter. The payment to the parents is to be further reduced by a sum of 9,000 marks. This is because the buyer is to provide his parents with dwelling space, lighting and heating on the farm during their lifetime, and he is to provide similar facilities for his two under-age sisters until they reach their majority. The remaining money (just over 30,000 marks) is to be paid to the parents within 18 months and without interest. Some further details, about tax liability, electricity and the absence of other agreements, are then specified and the document is signed by the parties and witnessed by a public notary who drew up the agreement.

In another case, from the 1960s and 1970s, a retiring farmer and his wife first sold their land to their daughter and her husband, and they later made a comparable arrangement concerning other property, including livestock and machinery, on the farm. In the document marking this second transaction the buyers are contracted to give the sellers subsistence for their lifetime, a dwelling with heating and lighting included, and cleaning when the sellers cannot do this for themselves. On their death buyers are to give them a decent funeral in accordance with local custom. The sellers are bound to use their state pensions for clothing, medical and other personal expenses, and the buyers are responsible for sharing in such expense only when the state pensions are insufficient or if medical insurance does not cover them. No payments are set out for the siblings of the succeeding daughter in this case.

My better understanding of documents involving the transfer of properties within families began when I was shown one dealing with a transfer in the 1960s of a different though related kind. In this case, land was being sold to the father, rather than vice versa, but the principles involved were of more general relevance. The mother of the children had died, and they had inherited a share. The document set out the terms of sale whereby the father reacquired rights of ownership in this. I spent some time translating the document which one of the children had been kind enough to show me, only to be told that 'of course no money actually changed hands'.

It appears that this document of sale was a fiction whose main purpose was to avoid liability to gift tax for the father. Spurred on to pursue the matter further with regard to transfers in the opposite direction, including the two cases outlined, I discovered that there were quite often fictional elements there also. I was told how parents and, perhaps less often, siblings had not insisted on receiving their legally contracted payments, and it appears that they never had envisaged otherwise. Indeed, a succeeding couple often could not have survived if they had had to make such payments. It seems that the willingness of siblings to forgo their due commonly depended on whether they had already established themselves elsewhere, and especially in an urban setting. Urban siblings are said often to appreciate the willingness of a successor to undertake the maintenance of the farm and the main responsibility for looking after the retired generation. More generally it began to emerge that a main function of such documents was to provide evidence entitling successors to cheap loans originally designed to ease the burden of such payments. Such loans could then be used for other purposes, e.g. developing the farm's buildings and equipment.

I am not sure how widespread such practice has been, but the need to treat farm transfer documents with caution is, it seems, by no means new, and the fictive element in them has taken diverse forms. In many cases, varying in detail from one area and period to another, the value placed on a farm in the records of transactions between close kin has been different from the going open market price for comparable farms. There are also historical cases in which onerous and detailed pension rights of parents were specified but were not in fact expected to be honoured by a succeeding child. Rather they seem to have been designed mainly as an encumbrance on the farm to be observed if the successor sold it to a stranger. There would be less reason to expect good will and commitment to the parents from a new owner, and in any case the aim was as much to discourage such a purchase as to protect against its consequences.

Such fictions clearly involve a degree of intra-familial connivance, albeit coupled with a certain element of caution, which provides an important counterbalance to the impression they might give at first glance. Superficially, the documents seem to show familial relations fully penetrated by the legalism and commercialism of the modern world, but it becomes clear that this is much more true in form than spirit. Family members have to adapt to such forms, just as they need to adapt to other strong external pressures, and it may sometimes, though by no means always, even be convenient to do so. They still none the less tend substantially to operate, when they can, according to their own longstanding and intrinsically ambivalent imperatives of mutual commit-ment tempered by diverging and at times conflicting interests.

The problem of farm closures

It is clear that an interlocking of the generations is to some degree a feature of life cycles anywhere, and in any socio-economic setting. But the point emer-ges with exceptional clarity, and in its own particular ways, in the farm family context. I have emphasised that the farm is a special multi-faceted institution. It is both property and a focus of labour, and it is also home, and in this latter context particularly it serves as a symbol of both family and individual identity. Who a person is, and what ageing and retirement mean to that person, are intimately linked into this framework. At the same time, the farm itself and its associated family are not the only sources of significant input into the situ-ation. As we have seen, the state and other wider social institutions play an important role in the lives of farmers and the continuity of farms, and such intervention has a long and varied history.

In presenting my material, I am conscious that I have mapped out only some of the main elements in the modern rural Finnish situation, and that I have said much more about retirement in the context of farm transfer than in that of closure. For the sake of completeness, and for the contrast which it partially provides, I turn now briefly to this latter issue.

Here, as in a situation of farm transfer, there is considerable variation. One woman, A.T., who closed down a good farm in her late fifties when her hus-band died, perhaps provides an archetypal case of a person able to make the best of such a situation. The period immediately after her bereavement was extremely hard for her, not simply because she and her husband had been exceptionally close, but also because many friends and neighbours seemed embarrassed to call. This phase has, however, passed. A married daughter, with a lively young son, now lives close to her, and she exchanges visits with her other children who live at a distance. She leads a full life, travelling widely both in Finland and abroad, and pursuing weaving and other craft work at which she is highly skilled. She has also made herself more mobile by learning to drive.

Despite some such examples, retirement on closed farms is often a great deal more depressing than when transfer is involved. As with A.T.'s farm, closure is common when one spouse becomes sick or dies, and no suitable successor is at hand. Finding a successor is especially difficult, however, in the many cases where farms are too small and too isolated to be attractive, and many old people remain on such holdings in the more remote settlements of North Karelia (Rannikko and Oksa, 1985). Loneliness and friendlessness are especially likely to hit those left behind in such circumstances. For them, the main issues in the social construction of retirement may arise less from the interaction between generations than from its absence. Moreover, even when, as sometimes happens, members of the younger generation remain on a closed-down farm, their presence tends to have a pathological quality. Often, such younger people are relatively poorly educated and trained, and many are unable to find jobs. The lack of opportunity to realise oneself in work which one has grown up to respect and see respected can, here as elsewhere, have a seriously depressing effect, and cases of alcoholism and petty crime are not uncommon in such circumstances. It seems too that the very sight of unused fields is quite depressing to retired farmers and farm wives, and some of them, whose farms are relatively well situated, prefer to rent their fields to others, rather than officially close down the farm.

Most closure cases have derived from the decline of farming in the 1960s and 1970s, when small farms in outlying regions became harder to maintain as viable units. There was mass migration to urban and industrial zones, and there was also some internal movement from the 'backwoods' into larger rural settlements in their vicinity. Some degree of stability has now been reached. There is a smaller number of more efficient farms, and rural depopulation through emigration has slowed down. Problems are, however, still in store even for some of the present generation of successor farmers on better farms. Over a third (38 per cent) of Finnish farmers under 40 years of age were unmarried in 1980 (Tauriainen, 1982, p.18), and the national farming newspaper, optimistically called *Maaseudun Tulevaisuus* ('The Future of the Countryside'), carries regular advertisements by 'hard-working, teetotal farmers' looking for a wife. This does not bode well for them when they come to plan their own retirement.

©1990 Ray Abrahams

References

Aarnio, A., 1975, *Jälkisäädköset* (Wills), Vammala.

Abrahams, R.G., 1985, 'Family, farm and wider society: the Finnish case', *Ethnos*, 50, I–II, 40–59.

—— forthcoming, 'Heating, lighting and a decent funeral', *Ethnos*.

Gaunt, D., 1983, 'The property and kin relations of retired farmers in northern and central Europe', in Wall, R., Laslett, P., and Robin, J. (eds), *Family Forms in Historic Europe*, Cambridge.

Goldschmidt, W. and Kunkel, E.J., 1971, 'The structure of the peasant family', *American Anthropologist*, 73, 5, 1058–76.

Goody, J., 1983, *The Development of the Family and Marriage in Europe*, Cambridge.

Honkanen, S., Komonen, A., Korkeaoja, J., Köppä, T., and Varmola, R., 'Sukupolvenvaihdoksen ongelma maatilataloudessa' (The problem of generation change in agriculture), *Publications of the Pellervo Society Marketing Research Institute*, No. 16.

Jutikkala, E., 1958, *Suomen talonpojan historia* (History of the Finnish peasantry), Helsinki.

Kilpeläinen, A.S., Hintikka, A.L., and Saloheimo, V.A., 1954, *Pielisjärven Historia* (History of Pielisjärvi), Kuopio.

Rannikko, P. and Oksa, J., 'The social consequences of the differentiation of agriculture and forestry', in J. Oksa (ed.), *Papers on social change in North Karelia*, Joensuu.

Tauriainen, J., 1982, 'Maaseudun väestökehityksen pääpiirteet 1950–1980' (The main features of the rural population 1950–80), in Vuorela, P., Kosonen, M., and Virtanen, P., *Suomalainen maaseutu* (The Finnish countryside), Helsinki.

Chapter twelve

Strategies for old age among the Berti of the Sudan

Ladislav Holy

Comparison of ageing in industrial and nonindustrial societies points to the differences in the status of the elderly as yet another characteristic of these two types of society. In the vast amount of social gerontological and sociological literature now available, the position of the elderly in industrial societies has been repeatedly characterised in terms of disengagement, isolation and rolelessness. Any roles that the elderly may perform are their own creation; there are no socially available ready-made roles which they can nonproblematically assume. Their low status is the inevitable consequence. It contrasts sharply with the status of the aged in many nonindustrial societies.

The status of the elderly in nonindustrial societies

With the exception of a few hunting and nomadic societies in which survival depends on the physical ability to move around in a harsh environment and which may in consequence resort to geronticide (see Glascock and Feinman 1981: 25–7 for rates), usually combined with infanticide, the nonindustrial societies emerge as distinctly old-age oriented. In particular, French anthropologists working in the Marxist tradition have stressed the ways in which elders exploit the juniors, especially in relation to control over women (Meillassoux 1964; Terray 1972, 1975), and societies in which this control is institutionalised in formal age grades have been characterised as gerontocracies (Spencer 1965). Even if such form of control may be an extreme case, the ascendancy of the old over the young through the control of property, politics or knowledge emerges as a general characteristic of nonindustrial societies from numerous ethnographic reports. Fortes generalises the situation by saying that 'the idea that one might fear or resent growing up or growing old does not evidently occur in traditional preliterate, preindustrial societies' (Fortes 1984: 119–20). As he puts it, 'old age is perceived as a stage in the maturational life cycle marked by declining physical and mental process but very often counterbalanced by high generational status' (Fortes 1984: 107).

The differences in the status of the elderly in nonindustrial and industrial societies relate to specific features that Goody sees as distinguishing these two types of society. The first is that 'nonindustrial societies are marked by economic systems where production is carried out by domestic groups' whereas in industrial societies the domestic group is for most part only a consuming group and production is separated from the domestic domain. In consequence, in nonindustrial societies, 'an individual is directly dependent upon his own senior generation for the acquisition of rights in the basic means of production' (Goody 1976: 117–18). Another critical feature of nonindustrial societies is that they are also societies without writing. This, according to Goody, results in the fact that

> in oral societies, the aged are always an important resource for information about the past and hence about tradition and the right way of doing things; they remain 'useful' not simply as repositories of family lore but as repositories of social life itself. This is particularly so of communicative acts that become relevant only at long intervals.
>
> (Goody 1976: 128)

It is particularly in this context that the role of the aged is crucial. The proper performance of central rites of society that occur only at long intervals is dependent on the past memories the old have of these events. As Goody says, 'their memories are other people's culture' (1976: 128; see also Amoss 1981). In industrial societies, with writing as the main form of communication and learning not confined to the familial context, the senior generation in one's own family or kin group cease to be the important reference points in one's personal system of orientation (Goody 1976: 128).

It may, however, be possible that the emergent image of the differences in the status of the elderly in industrial and nonindustrial societies is the result of comparing two quite disparate categories of the aged. The occurrence of certain kinds of physical and mental disabilities is inevitable in the final decades of the human life span (Beaubier 1980, Weiss 1981) and in consequence

> it is ... nearly universally true that societies divide the category of aged persons into two classes. The first consists of people who are no longer fully productive economically (and who must consequently depend on others for at least a portion of their livelihood) but who are still physically and mentally able to attend to their essential daily needs. The second consists of the totally dependent – people who require custodial care and supervision whether for physical or mental reasons.
>
> (Amoss and Harrell 1981: 3)

(See also Simmons 1960: 87; Maxwell and Silverman 1970: 40; Glascock and Feinman 1981: 22, 24, 26-7.) These two categories have recently been distinguished by gerontologists as the 'young old' and the 'old old'. The interest of social gerontologists and sociologists in ageing in Western societies has of course been triggered off by the perception of a practical problem arising from the emerging necessity of supporting the increased proportion of old people in the population and they have for the most part been concerned with the plight of the incompetent aged. The anthropologists, who have stressed the elders' control of knowledge and scarce resources, have for the most part been concerned with the category of the aged who are still mentally and, at least to some extent, physically competent (see Amoss and Harrell 1981: 4).

The control of property, ritual knowledge or exercise of political power by the elders is, of course, not an instrument of the dominance of the seniors over juniors, but of the dominance of older men, as even older women are excluded from exercising such control and power. This raises two questions. To what extent does the dominance of older men affect their position in advanced age when due to increasing physical and mental debility they are no longer able to exercise any effective control? To what extent does the situation of indigent women differ from that of the indigent men? To provide at least a partial answer on the basis of specific ethnography, this chapter discusses the main strategies through which the power which the elders exercise over their junior kin is employed to secure the necessary support for the indigent old among the Berti.

Elders and the old

Among the Berti, norms of age-appropriate behaviour are not the result of collective recognition of age-determined capabilities and limitations. The physical and mental abilities play different roles at different life stages and they are perceived by the Berti as determining an individual's status only in the early stages and towards the very end of his or her life course. The roles which people are expected to perform in their adulthood are determined more by the stage of the development of their household than by their physical and mental abilities. When children age and gradually reach adult status, their parents are usually still physically capable of carrying out all productive tasks. Nevertheless, they gradually diminish their active participation in economic activities in anticipation of the transfer of the household property to the children upon their marriage. The man and his wife feel by now that their own efforts need no longer be aimed at building up their own wealth but at securing the future welfare of their children. They gradually assume a managerial role in the household leaving the actual care of animals, the weeding of fields and the pursuit of other strenuous tasks, like drawing water from the well, to their adult children. The withdrawal of the parents from an active pursuit of various economic activities becomes even more pronounced after their daughter marries for the household then acquires the labour of her husband for a few years before the young couple establish their independent household.

In the case of men, their gradual withdrawal from productive activities is counterbalanced by their assumption of new roles in the public domain. A man's status as the head of his own household (*rājil be bētu* – man with a house; *rājil be 'iyālu* – man with children) is linked with his status as an elder (*ajwad* – a knowledgeable one). As such, he is personally notified about the meetings of elders to hear cases in the village and his attendance at such meetings is expected. His importance as an elder, however, increases only gradually over time. It is usually older men whose opinion carries more weight in the elders' meetings and on the whole it is the older men among the elders who contribute more significantly to the resolution of various disputes with which the elders are concerned. The man's status as an elder thus increases proportionately with the decrease of his direct involvement in production. Unlike men, women exercise no formal role in the public domain but a woman's gradual withdrawal from direct involvement in production is, nevertheless, also paralleled by her increased involvement in extra-domestic activities. Women with adult children are in charge of organising feasts that accompany major life crises rituals and public sacrifices, they visit ill relatives, attend funerals, assist during births or go to greet women who have given birth, etc. The Berti consider all these activities and all the activities in which men are involved as elders to be work in exactly the same sense in which various productive activities are work. The direct contribution of older men and women to production may have diminished but this certainly does not mean their retirement as their decreasing involvement in domestic work is accompanied by their increasing involvement in extra-domestic work. Disputes have to be settled immediately after they have arisen even if this means abandoning the weeding of fields or watering of livestock, and indispensable rituals have to be performed even at the peak of the agricultural season when they interfere with the necessary productive activities on which future livelihood depends. Ultimately, the age-based division of labour makes it possible to carry out both types of work simultaneously.

The household's wealth diminishes as the children marry. Part of the household's collection of fields is allocated to them to form the core of the land worked by their new households and both sons and daughters receive cattle upon their marriage; the parents keep for themselves only such animals as they alone can look after. When all the children have married and established their own households, their parents, who now remain alone in the household, have again to carry out by themselves all the productive tasks. The amount of land which they cultivate has, however, decreased and so has the size of the herd. Eventually, even the remaining animals may be farmed out to the married sons who look after them and treat them as part of their own herds. The ageing couple are now interested in maintaining rather than increasing their diminished wealth; they produce only for their own subsistence and no longer also for the market as they did when their household was expanding. By now they are most likely to be classified as old people. The man is addressed and referred to as *shāib* (old man) and the woman as *'ajūz* (old woman). There is no precise moment in one's life course at which one becomes *shāib* or *'ajūz*. The criteria by which these terms are judged appropriate are a combination of physical characteristics like white hair and deteriorating eyesight, personal demeanour like style of speech and walk, the physical activities in which one is or is no longer involved, like for example riding a camel (typically a young man's animal) or a donkey (typically an old man's animal), or the degree of ease with which one is able to carry them out, the stage of the development of one's own and one's children's households and the degree of respect enjoyed in the community. Nobody is considered to be *shāib* or *'ajūz* if none of their children has yet established an independent household; some people are, however, addressed and referred to as *shāib* (pl.) or *'ajāwiz* (pl.) after their first child has established his or her own household, whereas others start to be *shāib* or *'ajūz* only after their last child has done so.

A man reaches his highest standing in the public domain after he has become a 'big elder' (*shāib al-kabīr*). In every village a few men have this status. Although they are always old men, age alone is not the decisive qualification for this status. They have to be, above all, *jāid* (knowledgeable) of the Berti customs, even-tempered, skilful orators and they must have demonstrated these qualities frequently in many previous meetings in which they took part. Big elders are men who are well known outside their own villages and they are called upon to settle disputes between members of different villages which occur at wells or in the market places.

Old men and women face no problems in maintaining their independent household as long as they are physically able to supply it with water and firewood and as long as they are able to carry out the tasks connected with the production and processing of food. Their gradually declining physical ability affects in different degrees these various activities. The old couple are usually able to cultivate their field long after they have to give up other work, particularly the drawing of water from the well. Sowing and harvesting are not strenuous tasks and even old people are able to perform them long after weeding has become too much of a strain for them. But as they grow only for their own subsistence, their field is usually small and it can be weeded in a day by a group of neighbours and kinsmen mobilised through the offer of beer. Their inability to do the work themselves is recognised and in such circumstances they are not refused the help. Particularly if the man has the status of a big elder, the help of kin and neighbours is assured. Threshing, which is strenuous work for old people, is always done by work parties on a rota basis and a household of an elderly couple recruits the labour for the performance of this task in the same way as any other household.

Old men and women strive to maintain their own household even when their survival requires an ever increasing degree of support from others. The first job with which old people cease to be able to cope themselves is the drawing of water from the well and its transport to the village. For this task, they become gradually fully dependent on their married children living in their village, or their grandchildren. If there is not enough firewood in the vicinity of the village, they also gradually start to be dependent on their kin for its supply.

As their debility increases yet further, it also falls on their kin to sow and harvest their fields. The old are also supported in maintaining their pattern of consumption through the obligatory Islamic dues for the needy (*zakat*) which each household distributes after harvest; and the problem of their increasing dependence on kinsmen can be alleviated if one of their grandchildren moves to live permanently with them. This is quite a common arrangement.

The old men and women are able to sustain their independent households not only as long as the woman is able to cook and brew beer and the couple are able to perform at least some of the other tasks on which their livelihood depends, but also as long as they are able to cooperate in performing them according to the customary sexual division of labour. At their age, their cooperation is more likely to end through the death of one of them than through divorce. As Berti men marry women who are younger than themselves, marriage is more often terminated by the death of the husband than of the wife. A widow is able to manage her own household, albeit with the support of her kin, for as long as she is able to cook for herself. She has to give up living on her own only when she is no longer able to do that; she then has to move into the household of one of her children where she becomes fully dependent on the support of others. A man is in a different position if his wife dies. As he cannot cook his food or brew his beer, he is unable to maintain his own household and has to start living as a dependent in his son's or daughter's household. He hates this state of dependency, for if he is still able to do at least some light work, then he feels that he should work for himself and a woman who is under his control. This is preferable to helping others over whom he has no control and on whose support he depends. He hates it even more if he is a respected big elder. He became an elder in the first place because he was a man with his own house and he quite rightly feels that the fact that he no longer manages his own household adversely affects the cherished esteem he enjoys as a big elder. For this reason, a widower who thinks that he is not yet old enough to be fully dependent on others, usually marries a widow and moves to live with her. The old woman has no warden who may raise the issue of the bridewealth and the man makes his marriage legal by transferring a token payment to his wife. Both partners find their new marriage convenient. The man has again a wife whose duty it is to cook and brew beer for him and who brings a dish to the group of men with whom he takes his meals, making it possible for him to maintain his self-esteem as a man with his own house. The woman has a man to keep her company and to help with light tasks like sewing, tanning hides, making ropes, repairing leather bags, etc. These are the man's jobs which usually remain undone if she lives alone as the kin on whose support she depends do not consider them essential. She too thus gains the feeling of having once more a proper household. If a widower does not remarry or if a woman is no longer able to cook, the old have no other option than to spend the rest of their lives as dependants in their children's households.

The Berti wish to live long and to ensure long life is the explicitly stated purpose of many ritual actions. However, it is not simply long life as such that is desired but more especially the right kind of life.

Maintaining one's own household is for the Berti the most powerful symbolic expression of full adult status and the independence that goes with it. Before and after the span of adult life in one's own household, one is dependent on those in whose household one lives – the household of parents in childhood and early adulthood and the household of younger kin in old age. Although at the beginning and towards the end of one's life, one is dependent on different people and dependent on them in different ways, the reasons for the dependence of the young and the old are seen as similar by the Berti. None of them is able to cater for themselves, the physical abilities of both are impaired and, most importantly, both lack the proper faculties of reasoning necessary for the efficient execution of the daily activities on which life depends. Old people cannot manage on their own when they have become *kharfān* – a word which denotes the declining mental ability accompanying old age. The Berti explicitly compare those who have become *kharfān* with small children. The similarity between old age and childhood derives not only from the fact that the young and the indigent old lack the full mental and physical abilities of the adults and are dependent on their care but also that the development or loss of their abilities serve as markers of the end or beginning of these two stages of dependency.

The dependency of old age is detested and life in one's own household is clearly perceived as the ideal even in old age; the attempts of old people to maintain their independent households against all odds are a clear manifestation of this attitude. With increasing physical debility, they are, however, able to achieve the ideal only with the gradually increasing support of their children and their fate depends upon their wealth in offspring. Early marriage is a strategy for maximising offspring open to both sexes. Any additional strategy is, however, open only to men who aim at maximising offspring through remarriage following the divorce of a barren wife or through polygyny. The woman's strategy for maximising offspring is severely circumscribed as she depends solely on her own procreative abilities, but at the same time it is not of the same urgency to her as it is to a man for she can go on living on her own after the death of her husband. This possibility is not open to a man. Unless he remarries, he becomes dependent on the support of his children sooner than a woman does.

Support for the old

The Berti neither abandon their own household to live as dependants in the household of one of their children like the Fulani do (Stenning 1958), nor do they tie the children to themselves through maintaining control over property as many other peoples do (see, for example, Colson and Scudder 1981; Nason 1981). On the face of it, it seems that they opt for the worst possible solution:

while not accepting a fully dependent status upon the marriage of the last of their children, they nevertheless transfer their property to them, depriving themselves of the powerful means of securing the necessary support of these children.

The allocation of property to children upon marriage can, of course, be seen as a reward for their work for the parents. The expectation of this reward is, on the one hand, the incentive for the young to work, and, on the other hand, the price the elders have to pay for their own withdrawal from the most strenuous productive activities. But more importantly, it is the means of circumventing the rules of Koranic inheritance and a practice that makes possible the culturally asserted dominance of men over women which adherence to the Koranic laws of inheritance would, at least to a certain extent, subvert. Upon marriage, daughters acquire land and a few animals but most animals are allocated to sons; when the Berti depended for most of their cash on the sale of gum arabic, the gum gardens were allocated only to sons. A greater part of the property is thus allocated to men through its transmission *inter vivos* than would be the case if it was inherited according to the rules laid down in the Koran and, as a result, the man's control of his wife is facilitated through his ownership and unlimited control of much of the property on which his household depends. The early transfer of property to the children relieves also the possible tensions between generations. Its consequence is, however, that the care of the young for the old cannot be enforced, or even reinforced, through the control of property by the old. Neither can it be reinforced by the ritual services on which the young depend and which only the old can provide. The control of Islamic ritual knowledge is dependent on literacy and the learning acquired in childhood and early adulthood in Koranic schools. Although the process of learning that qualifies a man for the position of a religious leader (*faki*) is a prolonged one, it does not extend into old age and this position is by no means the prerogative of old age.

Goody points out that, in nonindustrial societies, 'the continued support of parents who have handed over authority, property, or both, depends upon more diffuse sanctions, often of a religious nature, the pietas of individuals, the judgement of the community, and beliefs in the supernatural' (Goody 1976: 120). The Berti, too, rely on the force of such diffuse sanctions and on the young recognising their indebtedness to the old not only for the care they took of their physical well being in early childhood but also for the property with which they endowed them later in life and which made possible their independent existence as adults. They are, however, also realistic enough to recognise that obligations need not necessarily be fulfilled simply because they are asserted as moral imperatives.

From the point of view of enforcing the fulfilment of these obligations, the most important aspect of the allocation of property to children upon their marriage, and of the father's duty to pay his son's bridewealth, is that it is directly linked with the parents' right to arrange children's marriages. In the

Berti case, the elders' control is not used to create political power by making young men dependent through the bestowal of daughters upon them; it is used to secure support in old age.

It is of course generally the case in nonindustrial societies that the support of the indigent aged is provided by their kin. What makes the Berti rather unusual, however, is the fact that the old rely on this support without having left themselves any effective means through which they could enforce the moral obligations of kinship should these not be spontaneously forthcoming. Under these circumstances, the main cultural strategy is aimed at ensuring that the old will have their younger kin near by, and as the feeling of responsibility for the old operates with differing strength in different kinship relationships, that the kin near by will be those who will view their care of the old as reciprocity for the elders' earlier efforts rather than unrequited support of dependants. Such care can be achieved if the marriages of children are properly arranged with these goals in mind.

The only marriage prohibitions which the Berti recognise are those stipulated by the Koran. According to their understanding of the Koranic proscription, a man must not marry his own mother, mother-in-law, lineal grandmothers, lineal granddaughters, direct and half-sisters, his own daughters and daughters of his brothers and sisters, and his direct paternal and maternal aunts. Marriage with any kinswoman beyond the prohibited range is allowed and is, in fact, preferred to marriages between strangers. When talking about the most desirable marriages, the Berti have always in mind the marriages between cousins. All first marriages are arranged by the parents and the support for the aged parents which any particular marriage is expected to yield is one of the main criteria for judging its desirability. This is clearly indicated by the fact that if a son is not happy with a wife that has been chosen for him, he will be told that this wife is for his father and that if he does not like her, he is free to choose any subsequent wives for himself according to his own wishes.

After all the children have established their own households, the viability of the parents' household depends to a great extent on the labour of the grandchildren. The ultimate authority over the children rests with the father who alone has the right to decide whether his child will be lent to either his or his wife's parents. Irrespective of who is the son's wife, his parents can acquire the labour of his child or children if he is prepared to assert his authority. His wife might, of course, object to having her children brought up outside her own household and the danger of any possible conflict between parents is reduced if the son is married to a kinswoman and thus at least one of his parents is also her close relative.

The daughter's marriage is of crucial importance from the point of view of acquiring the labour of her children. The ultimate authority over them rests with her husband who will, naturally, favour his own parents unless at least one of his wife's parents is also his own relative. Thus, while it is good but not essential for the parents to marry their son to a kinswoman if they want to acquire for themselves the labour of his child or children, it is essential for them to marry their daughter to a kinsman if they want to acquire the labour of her child. The parents' strategic considerations relate positively with the fact that they can assert more strongly their right to choose the daughter's husband than their right to choose the son's wife. It is rare for a man to be married without his prior knowledge or consent and his right to refuse a wife chosen for him by his father is usually recognised. On the other hand, a woman is quite often informed about her marriage only after the negotiations have been formally concluded. Her consent is not seen as necessary.

When considering the marriage of their children, the Berti do not aim merely at securing the labour of their grandchildren. One of their major considerations is to secure provision for their old age when they will no longer be able to produce and prepare their food and will depend entirely on the support of their children. The children can, however, provide the necessary support only if their spouses allow them to do so and only if they live nearby. Parents have thus to arrange the marriages of their children with this fact in mind. The strategic considerations of a man differ in this respect from those of his wife.

The Berti consider the support of his ageing father to be the son's moral obligation. But although a son can support his ageing father in many ways, for food and beer the father does not depend ultimately on his son but on his son's wife. The latter takes care of her father-in-law only because he is the father of her husband to whose authority she is bound. This is not the case if her husband's father is also either her 'father' (FB) or her *khāl* (MB). A man's marriage to either his FBD or his FZD is thus an outcome of his father's strategy to secure provision for his old age.

The Berti do not agree among themselves whether it is more advantageous for a man to rely on the help and support of his son or of his daughter. Although they all agree that it is a son's moral obligation to support his father in his old age, some argue that a man will be better looked after by his daughter. It is, after all, a woman who cooks and brews beer, they say, and if the father is looked after by his daughter, he can always be sure that he will not go hungry. A married woman is, however, under her husband's authority and if the latter objects to using his household's produce for supporting his father-in-law, his wife can support her father only in secret and she runs a perpetual danger of being accused by her husband of stealing. He will not object to his wife's behaviour if her father is at the same time also his 'father' or his *khāl*. A daughter's marriage to either her FBS or her FZS is thus possibly again an outcome of her father's strategy to secure provision for his old age. A woman's marriage to her FZS is, of course, a marriage with his MBD from the point of view of her husband. Most marriages which could be classified as MBD marriages following the usual practice of classifying cousin marriages from the man's point of view, are in fact better viewed as marriages of a woman to her FZS. As mentioned before, a man does not object to his wife supporting her father if the latter is also his FB or his *khāl*. In his strategic considerations a man's relationship to his future son-in-law is thus of utmost importance. Berti men differ in their respective evaluation of this relationship. A considerable number of them are of the opinion that a man will be better treated by his son-in-law if he is the latter's MB than if he is his FB. BS attachment to his FB derives from the normatively asserted solidarity of close agnates which is, however, perpetually threatened by the rivalry between them. Should the relationship between a man and his brother become strained, his effort to secure provision for his old age may to a great extent be frustrated if he married his daughter off to his brother's son. To avoid this danger, a considerable number of men prefer their daughter to be married to their sister's son. They argue that their sister's son will support them under all circumstances, not because of the normatively stipulated obligation on his part but because of his genuine love and affection for his MB.

If a woman tries to secure the help and support of her children in her old age, the marriage of her children to those of her brother and sister will be her aim in the same way as the marriage of his children to those of either his brother or sister is the man's main aim. A son's marriage to his MBD or MZD and the daughter's marriage to her MBS (FZD marriage from the latter's point of view) or her MZS can thus be an outcome of their mother's strategy to secure provision for her old age.

As a rule, a woman is much more concerned with the marriage of her daughter than with the marriage of her son for in her own economic activities she depends on the continuous support of her daughter more than she does on the support of her son. Furthermore, as virilocal residence is considered normal and ideal, it is expected that the son will build his household in the village of his parents irrespective of whom he marries and that his economic cooperation with his parents will thus not be completely interrupted. The daughter's economic cooperation can be completely lost if she resides virilocally. Under the prevailing conditions of virilocal residence, the daughter's marriage to any other cousin than her FBS is likely to take her away from her parents' village. The question of postmarital residence enters more strongly into consideration of the daughter's than the son's marriage. While on the one hand a woman certainly prefers her daughter to be married to her own kinsman, on the other hand she does not want her to leave her own village. Should her marriage to a matrilateral cousin take her away, her mother herself may prefer her to be married to her FBS who lives in the same village and will thus establish his own household there. The marriage of the daughter to her FBS can then be not only her father's preference but quite often also her mother's. On the other hand, the mother may be prepared to put up with her daughter moving out of her own village if the daughter marries her own kinsman. The latter will then not object to his wife visiting her mother frequently, for her mother is also his FZ or MZ. When the mother is no longer able to maintain her own household, she will be living among her own kinsmen when she moves into the household of her daughter.

When the Berti try to secure for themselves various future economic services by properly arranging their children's marriages, their marriage strategies are grounded in their knowledge that these services will be provided because they ensue from the normative obligations people have towards one another as kinsmen and from the love and affection which obtains among them. They would not be provided if the parties were related merely as affines for two reasons. Firstly, the affines are not normatively compelled to cooperate to the same extent as the kinsmen are and, secondly, the normative prescription of their conduct practically inhibits any effective provision of desirable services: for example, a daughter-in-law who is expected to avoid her father-in-law, as she is if the father of her husband is not her own kinsman, can hardly cater for him effectively, even if she wants to.

The marriages between kinsmen are thus preferable to those between strangers because they do not create new relations of affinity and all existing kinship relationships with their concomitant rights and obligations remain practically unaffected by them. Any time a relationship is that of both kinship and affinity, the Berti treat it consistently as a kinship one: kinship terms which were used before marriage continue to be used after it and the conduct appropriate for the two kinship roles continues basically to be in force, or at least it significantly modifies the conduct appropriate for the parallel affinal relationship. It is precisely because of this nullifying effect on the relations of affinity that marriages between kinsmen are preferred to those between strangers. In fact, the expectations of all the advantages ensuing from such marriages are predicated on the continuity of the previous behaviour of those who have been brought into a close affinal relationship.

For the Berti, the continuity of the previous behaviour is particularly important in the relationship between parents-in-law and children-in-law. This is most clearly shown in their evaluation of inter-generational marriages between kin, some of which are marriages with either the father's or the mother's classificatory sister but most of which are marriages with a classificatory daughter, i.e. marriages with the daughter of the first or more distant cousin. Unlike intra-generational marriages, such marriages are ambiguous. While some people maintain that they are good marriages because they are, after all, marriages between kin, others are of the opinion that it is not a good thing to marry one's 'daughter' or father's or mother's 'sister' and on the scale of desirability they do not rank such marriages any higher than those between strangers. The reasons for this lie in the nature of the relationship between the parents-in-law and children-in-law which such marriages create.

In an intra-generational marriage, the child-in-law is always a relative to whom the parents-in-law refer by the same kinship term as to their own child and over whom they hold similar rights. Consequently, the children-in-law have similar duties towards their parents-in-law as towards their own parents.

It is this close and at the same time asymmetrical relationship that guarantees the rendering of economic services which the parents try to secure for themselves through marrying their 'children' to one another. In inter-generational marriages, the children-in-law are either classificatory brothers or sisters (i.e. first or more distant cousins) or 'grandchildren'. In the first case, the relationship between parents-in-law and children-in-law is that of equality which inhibits the desirable unidirectional flow of services; moreover, it is a relationship of rivalry which crosses the first potential line of cleavage between collaterals, and in the degree of mutual solidarity implied in it, it is always superseded by the relationship between parents and children. A 'brother' or 'sister' always tends to support first of all his or her 'parents' and only after that his or her 'siblings'. In the second case, although the relationship between parents-in-law and children-in-law is an asymmetrical relationship of subordination and superordination, it is again a relationship which is superseded by the relationship between parents and children as far as the degree of mutual solidarity is concerned. While from the parents' point of view much can be gained economically through mutual marriages of their 'children', no special economic advantages ensue for them from marriages between kinsmen of different generations.

The Berti point out that when seeking their future support through the marriages of their children, the strategic considerations of both parents can differ and conflict with one another. They characterise the situation by saying that a man wants his child to be married to his own kin whereas a woman wants her child to be married to hers.

Although marriages are formally negotiated by men, marriage arrangements are rarely discussed among them. They are, however, the most popular topic of conversation among women. Any time they chat among themselves, their conversation invariably turns, after a few minutes, to the discussion of past marriages, undergoing marriage negotiations and possible future matches. In line with this general pattern, the father never talks with his children about their marriage; he is likely to bring up the issue of his son's marriage only when he informs him about the bride he has chosen for him or, more rarely, when he feels that the time has arrived for him to get married and mentions this to him. The mother, on the other hand, quite frequently discusses her son's prospective marriage with him and in the course of these conversations encourages him to marry either her brother's or her sister's daughter. While a daughter is fully under the father's authority and can be, and very often is, married not only against her will but without her consent or even prior knowledge, a son has more opportunity to express his own opinion about his marriage and in many cases wins his way. His own possible preference for his MBD to his FBD can often well be the result of his mother's influence.

Although the Berti are certainly correct in their observation that the marriage strategies of a man and his wife often differ, the possible conflict of interest is in many cases avoided because the marriages between close kinsmen contracted in previous generations link the spouses through a multiplicity of connections and consequently a son-in-law or daughter-in-law is often closely related to both his or her parents-in law. The formal marriage negotiations are conducted by men but women have a considerable degree of informal say in the marriage arrangements of their children, and some of them are very skilful in manipulating them according to their own wishes. The marriage strategies are not as much a matter of older men striving at allocating the marriageable women to themselves or a matter of the direct control of the juniors by the seniors, as a matter of controlling the marital destinies of their own children for their future benefit. What is being sought is the care for the elderly provided by women in their roles as wives, daughters and daughters-in-law. This concerns both men and women, and women pursue their own interests as much as men do even if they often have to resort to intrigue and subterfuge due to their subordinate position.

Age and cultural creativity

In so far as specific forms of the transmission of property, marriage arrangements, ritual activity or whatever, can be seen as serving the interests of the elders, the creation and re-creation of these particular cultural forms can also be seen as lying primarily in their hands. The control of the young by the old or the power of the old over the young connote thus an uneven contribution of different age categories to the reproduction of social relations and cultural practices. The relationship between age and this kind of cultural creativity is, however, more complex than the model of the aged as guardians and creators of cultural tradition would suggest; and, in fact, forms which clearly serve the interest of the aged need not be produced only by the aged themselves. In specifying certain marriage partners as the most desirable ones, in recognising a wife's barrenness as a valid ground for divorce and in institutionalising polygyny, Berti culture projects forward the issues that appear to its members to be salient in old age. If in its arrangements this culture can be seen as expressing the dominance of the seniors over juniors, this dominance itself is the expression of concerns with ageing.

Different forms of dominance of seniors often reported in ethnographic accounts appear to be other specific forms of cultural manifestation of this wider concern present in all societies. Age thus seems to affect cultural creativity not only in the sense that the contribution of the senior age categories to the process of cultural production surpasses that of the juniors. It affects it also in the sense that the contribution of those who are in the prime of their adulthood and far from old is motivated by the interest of the aged. It is their perception of their own position in the future rather than their contemporary interests that motivates the cultural engineering in which they are involved. It thus need not necessarily be old age as such but the vision of old age that can be usefully seen as enforcing specific cultural practices. Seen in this way, it is the experience of the fate of one's predecessors rather than one's own experience that motivates action. It appears to me to be a distinct weakness of a great deal of gerontological studies that they concentrate on the experiences of the old as generating their observable strategies or on their ability to negotiate their position as individuals. People do not simply behave in a certain way because they have reached a certain stage in their life course. They envisage the future stages in their life course on the basis of their experience of those preceding them and plan for their own future on the basis of this experience when they are in the position to do so. Norms are age related not only in the straightforward sense of 'a system of social expectations regarding age-appropriate behavior' with these expectations being 'internalised as the individual grows up and grows old, and as he moves from one age stratum to the next' (Neugarten and Datan 1973: 59). They are age related in a more complex way in the sense that it is appropriate to do something at a certain stage in the life course to ensure a desirable outcome at some future stage in one's life course. The perceived rolelessness, disengagement, withdrawal and isolation of the elderly in industrial societies appear to be functions of the youth orientation of these societies (Berger and Neuhaus 1970, Simmons 1961–5: 158, Clark and Anderson 1967). Nonindustrial societies are age oriented not only in the sense that the status of the elderly in them cannot be characterised in these terms, but also in the sense that much of their culture can be seen as geared towards the interest of the old rather than of the young.

©1990 Ladislav Holy

References

Amoss, P.T., 1981, Cultural centrality and prestige for the elderly: the Coast Salish case. In Fry: 47–63.

Amoss, P.T. and S. Harrell (eds), 1981, *Other ways of growing old: anthropological perspectives*. Stanford, Cal.: Stanford University Press.

Beaubier, J., 1980, Biological factors in aging. In C.L. Fry and contributors: *Aging in culture and society: comparative viewpoints and strategies*: 21–41. New York: Praeger.

Berger, P.L. and R.J. Newhaus, 1970, *Movement and revolutions*: Garden City, N.Y.: Penguin Books.

Clark, M. and B.G. Anderson, 1967, *Culture and aging: anthropological study of older Americans*: Springfield, Ill.: Charles Thomas.

Colson, E. and Scudder, T., 1981, Old age in Gwembe District, Zambia. In Amoss and Harrell: 125–53.

Fortes, M., 1984. Age, generation and social structure. In D.I. Kertzer and J. Keith (eds): *Age and anthropological theory*: 99–122. Ithaca, NY: Cornell University Press.

Fry, C.L. (ed.), 1981, *Dimensions: aging, culture and health*: New York: Praeger.

Glascock, A.P. and S.L. Feinman, 1981, Social asset or social burden: treatment of the aged in non-industrial societies. In Fry: 13–31.

Goody, J. 1976, Aging in nonindustrial societies. In H. Binstock and E. Shanas (eds):

Handbook of aging and the social sciences: 117–29. New York: Van Nostrand Reinhold Co.

Maxwell, R.J. and P. Silverman, 1970, Information and esteem: cultural considerations in the treatment of the aged. In R.J. Maxwell and W.H. Watson (eds): *Human aging and dying*. New York: St Martin's Press.

Meillassoux, C., 1964, *Anthropologie économique des Gouro de Côte d'Ivoire*. Paris: Mouton.

Nason, J.D., 1981, Respected elder or old person: aging in a Micronesian community. In Amoss and Harrell: 155–73.

Neugarten, B.L. and N. Datan, 1973, Sociological perspectives on the life cycle. In P.B. Baltes and K.W. Schaie (eds): *Life-span developmental psychology: personality and socialization*: 53–69. New York and London: Academic Press.

Simmons, L.W., 1960, Aging in pre-industrial societies. In C. Tibbits (ed.): *Handbook of social gerontology*. Chicago: University of Chicago Press.

Simmons, L.W., 1961–5, *Problems of over-aging*. Duke University Council on Gerontology. Proceedings of seminars 1961–5. Durham, NC: Regional Center for the Study of Aging.

Spencer, P., 1965, *The Samburu: the study of gerontocracy in a nomadic tribe*. London: Routledge and Kegan Paul.

Stenning, D.J., 1958, Household viability among the pastoral Fulani. In J. Goody (ed.): *The developmental cycle in domestic groups*: 92–119. Cambridge: Cambridge University Press.

Terray, E., 1972, *Marxism and primitive societies*. New York: Monthly Review Press.

Terray, E. 1975, Classes and class consciousness in the Abron kingdom of Ghana. In M. Bloch (ed.): *Marxist analyses and social anthropology*: 85–135. London: Malaby Press.

Weiss, K.M., 1981, Evolutionary perspectives on human aging. In Amoss and Harrell: 25–58.

Chapter thirteen

Dimensions of change: three studies of the construction of ageing

Haim Hazan

Functionalist concepts such as 'role', 'status', and 'social moblility' are of little analytical value in socio-gerontological discourse which focuses on 'roleless-ness',[1] status ambiguity,[2] 'no exit',[3] anomie[4] and career impasse.[5] From the point of view of the sociology of knowledge, such conceptual inadequacies reflect a lack of fit between raw data and the analytical tools,[6] an incongruity that stems from ethnocentric and, in our case, ageocentric[7] postulates inherent in the analyst's own phase of the life course. One might assume that by invoking anthropological relativism to handle such problems of judgement, the conceptual myopia which blurs our field of vision concerning ageing could be rectified. However, a cursory glance at the literature reveals a consistent failure to conceptualise ageing satisfactorily. Neither as a social construct, such as 'culture'[8] or 'age grades',[9] nor as an intersubjective[10] or subjective experience[11] has the phenomenon of ageing been transcended to suggest a coherent explanatory model. It is for this reason and the desire to avoid fuzzy concepts such as 'role exit',[12] 'deculturation',[13] 'myth'[14] and 'disengagement'[15] that this discussion may seem distant from any common connotation of ageing in modern society. Instead, we are presented with a transformation from a state of linearly oriented existence governed by progress in occupational careers and set family trajectories to a state of socially dependent sinecure-based existence.

This change in the scope of meaning and control with ageing might render some aspects of previous experience irrelevant. We shall argue that the collapse of temporal perspectives, the disarray of social space and the everyday challenge to routine modes of conceptualisation, induce a reconstitution of reality which could be interpreted as a complex strategy to encounter and rationalise otherwise uncontrollable, meaningless change. Unlike other liminal phases where social marginality is furnished and reconstructed by the surrounding society, the ambiguities of ageing constitute a normative vacuum which acquires meaning only through the behaviour adopted by its incumbents – the aged. It is, indeed, the social nature of this endeavour to generate a nascent, unguided patterning of change that this chapter seeks to explore. It is suggested that while the contours of unpredictable change derive from some general constraints inherent in the state of being old, the manner in which that change is managed is conditioned and shaped by a given social context. Thus the issue of human universals in ageing versus cultural diversity is resolved by integrating these two seeming opposites into one model.[16]

Three case studies are used to illustrate facets of this transformation. The first facet is the conversion of social space from an open-ended expanse of cultural classifications into a closed arena of fixed taxonomy. The second is the inversion of time from a set of linear trajectories into cycles of repetition and replication. The third is the transformation of cognitive systems from cumulative into non-cumulative critical modes of conceptualisation. At the heart of this schema is the proposition that old age lends itself to be understood in terms of structural changes in patterns and configurations of space, time and concepts, rather than in terms of content and context. The meaning of ageing, therefore, ought to be sought in the structure of change as much as in the dynamics of process.

Case 1   A residential home as a closed arena

The first case study[17] to be presented concerns a group of elderly residents in an Israeli home for the aged. Since the institution only catered for able-bodied and mentally alert elderly, the threat of being relocated to another care facility loomed ominously in the lives of most residents. Precarious and tenuous though their lives were, the tenacity of residents in the social environment they created seemed to reflect an unequivocal and unyielding system of human classification.

Notwithstanding the variations shown by different groups and individuals in the home, there was an accepted social hierarchy of the home population. At the top of the pyramid stood an elite strata of residents whose public record of extraordinary accomplishments on the national level placed them in the pantheon of cultural heroes and rendered their stature in the institution and outside it almost mythical. For them, enforced removal from the home was as inconceivable as running the institution without their active approval.

Indeed, on one occasion, residents associated with this group tried to impose their will on the management by proposing to set up their own disciplinary court to rule on cases of recalcitrant and incapacitated residents whose mere presence posed a threat to the very rigid social order established in the home.

This undesirable category constituted the lower echelon of the social hierarchy. Confused-looking, relatively immobile and unable to fend for themselves, they were stripped of their human guise through the use of such terms as 'vegetable', 'animals', and 'exhibits' to describe the kind of existence attributed to them.

Between these two extreme categories, the socially immortal and the socially dead, a whole range of locally constructed human types emerged.

There were, for example, those who stood on the verge of becoming non-human, that is functionally inept, and whose painstaking efforts to qualify as active and acceptable residents drove them to measures such as fabricating personal biographies and creating a façade of over-zealous action and exaggerated social interests. Thus, members of the much disdained institutional synagogue, whose prospects for survival in the home were slim, preoccupied themselves with numerous Talmudic study groups where no form of learning was pursued, nor was any relationship established between the hired teachers and their elderly students, not even eye contact. Their rabbi, who was abhorrent to the idea of being associated with his congregants, condensed his scholarly life history into a disjointed sequence of events relating to a-religious markers of socialist-Zionism. In a home run by the welfare division of Israel's largest trade union federation, 'The Histadrut', such revision of personal history adequately served the expectations of the local arena.

The rules of that arena were strict and prescribed. Performance of adequate functioning was imperative if one was to stay a resident there, and deviations were regarded as a breach of the code of immutability which governed institutional life. Cyclical, almost ritualistic patterns of behaviour were keenly observed and those who were deprived of mythical atemporal haloes, had to resort to adherence to habit, norm and cliché. Thus, individuals, by becoming part of a collectivity, experienced an unbridgeable discontinuity between their newly acquired identity as change-resisting elderly bound by and within the constraints of the home environment on the one hand, and their former careers and past involvements in an open-ended ever-changing world on the other. This gulf was narrowed by the shared set of cultural categories adopted by all residents. This was based on the context-free ethos of socialist-Zionism whose ideals were set as the only yardstick for a worthwhile existence. The unfulfilled vision of an egalitarian and just society was rationalised by declaiming the intrusion into Israel of 'contaminating elements' such as immigrants of oriental extraction and Western materialistic influence. The home, therefore, was perceived by its residents as one of the last citadels of socialist-Zionism in its purest form. Since external circumstances could not reflect this ideal, they were deplored, decried and to a great extent disregarded.

Case 2   The day-care centre and the inversion of time

Whereas internal divisions determined the perception of social space in the residential home, the second group of elderly to be discussed developed their temporal perspective against the backdrop of external boundaries within which change was controlled and time suspended.[18]

This concerned a day-care centre for elderly Jewish inhabitants of an impoverished London borough. As first or second generation immigrants from Eastern Europe, they had started the English phase of their life cycle in poverty, cultural alienation and socio-economic dependency on Jewish organisations. While many of their contemporaries elsewhere climbed up the social ladder, the residents of the borough remained with a low income and an increasing reliance on local and denominational welfare services. With tenuous family ties, sometimes severed from their more successful offspring, and outside the circle of the Jewish establishment in London, those attending the centre were culturally stigmatised, socially isolated and economically dependent.

The centre catered for some material needs in the form of hot meals, liaison with welfare services and direct financial aid. The 400 members also benefited from having a self-regulating venue for a variety of social activities such as discussion groups, shows, handicrafts, card playing and art work.

Members' modes of behaviour suggested a coherent set of attitudes towards the relative importance of past and future. The past was revised in the process of retrieval and selection. They would express a seemingly nostalgic recollection of events and impressions grounded in early childhood experiences in the East End of London. Embellished memories of a happy upbringing in close-knit families constituted the cherished section of the past. In contrast, occupational careers and socio-economic positions during adulthood were so completely obliterated that previous differentiations were not seen to have any bearing on social life in the present. However, certain events during this long period were considered as major landmarks on the path to the establishment of reality in the centre. Thus participation in anti-Fascist demonstrations in the early 1930s, service in the army, hospitalisation and membership in friendship clubs were all highlighted as elements of special value in a member's past experience. An analytical overview of those situations would reveal an entrenched state of egalitarianism and social immoblity placing the revised past alongside the present.

Forestalling alternatives to the centre included renouncing family affiliations, especially the possibility of co-residence with children. This was accompanied by the declaration of fraternity among the members, with kinship terminology employed to label these imputed relationships. Thus members often referred to themselves as 'brothers and sisters', while avoiding the use of hierarchical relations implied by differential kin terms such as fathers, mothers or uncles. It should be noted that the disavowal of familial bonds included also conjugal relationships, and hence married couples in the centre were discouraged from displaying their attachment publicly as were those who had developed intimate relationships with members of the opposite sex.

This cognitive arrest of change was allied to a mode of behaviour markedly different from the pre-centre way of life. Members were expected to be unequivocally convinced that a meaningful existence should be founded on principles of boundless care and unconditional help.

Revisions of the past and re-evaluation of former affiliations were invariably made in the light of the presence or absence of the element of help and care in those ties. The distant past, mainly East End childhood, was often contrasted to other and more recent centre situations in a manner suggesting that mutual aid and community care predominated early relationships, whereas disregard and desertion were the prominent features of later life. Furthermore, the onus of obtaining help and evoking concern in the East End had not been placed on the recipient, but had been inherent in the population's moral code and intrinsic attitudes. On the other hand, help in later years was considered to be merely a function of selfish interests, nepotism or patronising charity. Care was not rendered any longer on the merits of need, but rather on the basis of influence and pressure. In contrast the ethos of care developed in the centre advocated that the right to receive help should be unconditional and so should the right to render it. There was a widespread recognition in the centre that relationships should be constructed in a way that would allow almost everybody regardless of physical and mental limitation to partake in this dual status.

The relevance of this moral code to time perspectives rests with the structure of its practices rather than in its content. The interactional patterns of helping procedures developed in the centre involved the non-reciprocity of giving and receiving and, furthermore, participants were not classified as either 'helpers' or 'helped'. Hence, those who had something to spare – time, attention, advice or material objects – passed it on to an individual in need regardless of their personal relationship. Such pre-existing attachments as obtained in the centre, i.e. by virtue of marriage or life-long friendship, came under inexorable pressure to be undermined or even dissolved. Members disassociated their roles in the care system of the centre from any long- or short-term considerations, plans or memories, so much so that assistance was often offered to a previously unacquainted person who seemed to be in a situation which warranted help. Furthermore, a stark dichotomy of helpful versus helpless participants was avoided by the dual nature of the member's position in the centre, namely the constant interchange between being a helper and being helped. Even members who did not feel in need of any help were expected to play the role of recipient.

The lack of reciprocal relationships was probably the foundation for the formation of a present-bound society. This indicates a crucial transformation in the organisation of events and hence in the patterning of time as a static construction rather than as a linear progression. This basic configuration of shared reciprocity was also embodied into other aspects of centre life such as the similarity, both in structure and content, of the activities fostered by members. Thus, games such as chess and cards were devoid of their competitive nature because they were regarded as 'teaching situations'; so were personal achievements and expressions of creativity which were dismissed as insignificant and worthless. Daily activities such as dancing and singing recurred cyclically with very little novelty or innovation.

This state was furnished and reinforced by various acts of denial of death on the one hand, and by adhering to life-long daily habits on the other. Thus, continuity was selectively maintained only where the interconnectedness of timeless events could be sustained. Personally expressed as it was, this form of lateral continuity is socially charged. Again, the submergence of the individual into a collectivity facilitates the acquisition of a new identity capable of responding to current problems of surviving as an elderly person stripped of a past and robbed of a future.

Case 3 A self-help organisation and the transformation of the cognitive system

Unlike the apparently clearly defined social boundaries in the first and second cases, the third study concerns elderly people whose only common feature is their involvement in a self-help organisation, the University of the Third Age in Cambridge, England. This is a voluntary association with a membership of about 500 people who engage in a variety of learning and social activities. This institution provides a setting for study groups in a wide spectrum of subjects, initiates a host of cultural events and promotes social links among its participants. Although admission into the university is not deliberately selective, the actual membership typically are highly literate, socially and economically established students. Retired professionals and academicians constitute the main core of the organisation.

Knowledge, being the core object of the organisation, was not only disseminated, circulated and exchanged, but also produced and developed by its members. Through its active research committee, in the course of social gatherings and in the process of formal studying, concepts and conceptions, perspectives and approaches, underwent revision, reassessment and remoulding. It was not so much new contents, pieces of information and data that were accrued, but rather novel cognitive patterns and modes of experience. The underpinnings of this experience were the devices constructed to dismantle some life-long beliefs and principles whose relevance to the members' present living was no longer certain. In other words, members of the University of the Third Age learnt to 'unlearn'.

Evidence of this process was embedded in various actions, interactions and organisational activities. A few examples may help illuminate the argument.

A major research enterprise carried out by members of the research committee of the university concerned the image of the elderly on British television. Having systematically monitored television programmes the researchers reached some conclusions which defied common conceptions, popular and scholarly alike, of the image of the elderly in the visual media as unremittingly negative. Equipped with the potent research tool of reflexivity – self-awareness of their own condition – the members were able to develop a unique knowledge of themselves.

One could expect that such reflexivity would reveal personal histories as mirroring devices for present existence. This cannot be corroborated by the

material at hand. Attempts by members to review their lives among themselves by applying tape-recording techniques did not receive the support of
others, and nor did projects of reconstructing the local heritage through members' autobiographical accounts. Grim prospects of the future were fore-
stalled in very much the same way. Thus a complex research project into
funeral arrangements in Cambridge was abandoned when members were confronted with questions concerning attitudes towards death, and death
anxieties became unavoidable. Another study designed to extend the scope of
interest of the university into old-age homes was aborted because of lack of
enthusiasm and cooperation.

The most intriguing self-reflection and rearrangement of consciousness
appeared to have developed in a classroom situation. There the articulate exchange of views would reveal unexpected attitudes among persons whose
scope of general knowledge, impeccable mastery of the language and professional qualifications might have suggested an entirely different approach to
knowledge. Reading relevant literature was dismissed as superfluous – if not
misleading. Mediated accounts of reality such as essays and analytic material
were considered 'unnatural' and 'distorting'. Direct touch with personal experience was deemed to supersede illusory phenomena distorted by false concepts and feigned perspectives superimposed on reality.

Thus, as members maintained that reading about life was camouflaging it,
they insisted not only that they should refrain from reading, but also that they
should engage in a discourse relating to 'life itself' as they called it. This was
an uncritical and dispassionate rendering of events and views related to
general existential issues and not to personal histories. Family life, for
example, was not discussed within the context of inter-generational relationships, but rather as a mosaic of occurrences patterned by universal human dilemmas, such as the quest for freedom and identity on the one hand, and the
duty and social obligation towards one's kith and kin on the other.

Indeed, frequent debates on human nature and the values that should guide
it drew disjointedly on present concerns alongside historical, prehistorical
and even mythological references.

This last point of synchronising diachronic time suggests one of the processes of reconceptualisation developed by members of the University of the
Third Age. Other cognitive strategies of reconstituting reality included avoidance of intimacy, renunciation of love, criticism of the British socio-political
system and contempt for status symbols, particularly those conferred on academics and doctors. Evidently, an analogy between the restructuring of the
world of this affluent, highly educated and socially established group of elderly
and that of the destitute social outcasts of the London centre is called for. To
quote one of the members of the Cambridge group, 'we must take it from first
principles' and 'see life with a third age eye'. This 'third age eye' indicates, as
we have seen, the collapse of basic concepts of social space, social and personal time and coordinates of meaning.

Conclusion: understanding the experience of old age

At this point we part with description and return to the analysis. So far, no claim for formulating any rule or regularity has been made, for the three case studies do not readily suggest a theory or a conceptual framework for understanding ageing. Rather, it is comprehending the experience of old age that lies at the heart of our concern.

The main issue at stake, therefore, is the implications of these three perceived realities for the feasibility of comprehending ageing. For, if some elderly people renounce their past, submerge themselves in a collectivity, suspend change and undo life-long conceptions, the problem of linking our linear conceptions to the non-linear state at the core of our studies becomes almost inexorable. This evokes Fabian's exhortation that, unless a rapport in terms of space and time between researcher and field is established, a form of socio-academic exploitation of the 'other' – i.e. the aged – might unwittingly emerge (Fabian 1983).

This is not to say that sociology and anthropology are impoverished through concepts of structure rather than of process. On the contrary, from the Simmelian form to the Goffmanian frame[19] and, with the Turnerian concept of antistructure and communitas alongside Lévi-Strauss's 'cold' and 'hot' societies,[20] the idea of atemporality as a viable constituent in man's life has been accorded intellectual significance. The problem lies with the explanatory framework for this phenomenon.

As for accounting for cyclical structure, interpretations could be drawn from a variety of dimensions, the most amenable of which is the socio-cultural. Here personal plights and predicaments, resulting in arresting change and revising life-history, could be construed in terms of stifled opportunities and blocked mobility, on the one hand, and cultural images of progress, youth and success on the other. The analytic domain of understanding old age is imbued with age-based boundaries of stratification, age-propelled images and models of age group interaction and structure.[21] Resorting to this well-tried set of concepts can only furnish us with some idea as to the social configuration of ageing, and not to the existential nature of its experienced meaning. It is, indeed, the nexus between age-generated divisions and the wider context that provides the core of gerontological understanding.[22] For, it is the gulf between social organisation and an awareness of meaning with which it could be infused that confines the elderly to a sphere of existence where past relevances and future prospects no longer inform the present. Repetitive patterns in the form of habit, egalitarian, non-mutual relationships, and disengagement from past investments and future obligations supersede defunct modes of progress and impertinent career trajectories.

Evidently the strategies reflected in the activities of the three groups greatly differ from one another by virtue of their varied social contexts and cultural resources. Hence, the residents of the home drew on a shared national ethos, the participants of the centre deflected the mirror image of their non-caring environment while the members of the University for the Third Age employed the corpus of knowledge – concepts and information – that infused their pre-retirement lives. However, the underlying theme of the management of unpredictable change through collective identity, equality and reflexivity was common to all three groups and could be extrapolated to other phenomena where similar existential conditions prevail. Indeed, a re-examination of studies of the socio-cultural context of situations of transition would reveal that the suspension of time, egalitarianism[23] and the revision of past world-views are predominant social characteristics among the chronically ill,[24] prison inmates,[25] immigrants to a new country,[26] the unemployed[27] and religious converts.

Evidently transition invokes the construct of liminality as an interpretative device for such situations. However, our cases do not seem to lend themselves to such a paradigm. In the absence of a meaningful passage into a socially anticipated stage, the concept of liminality as a transitional phase is rendered irrelevant. Moreover, reversible though they might seem, the constructed worlds within the three enclaves were not antithetical to a given structured social order. Rather, the social reality in each of our cases represented a highly structured milieu diametrically opposite to an alternative chaotic experience. Hence, unacceptable social categories were replaced by an ideal ethos; asynchronised time was transformed into a static temporal perspective and a defunct conceptual frame of reference was superseded by an existentially germane scope of meanings. In short, uncontrollable change was regulated and formulated to fill the lacuna of the lack of socialisation to old age.[28] In this respect it is unpredictable change, not preordained transition, that shaped the three social contexts at hand, and it is probably the social impasse rather than the social passage that goaded these three otherwise very different groups of elderly persons to embark on their penultimate social venture in a very similar manner.

The understanding of that manner spells a twofold challenge for the anthropology of ageing: the anthropologist is not only faced with the need to reach for appropriate metaphors to express the uniqueness of the studied phenomenon, but also with a compelling example set by the elderly themselves to deconceptualise, recodify and ultimately reconstitute a lived-in reality. The issue at stake is, therefore, our capacity to articulate a plausible anthropological model which could account for and make sense of that world. The question of such feasibility is yet unanswered and is, arguably, unanswerable.

© 1990 Haim Hazan

Notes

1. A concept coined by Burgess (1950) to indicate the sociological quandary concern-

ing the social status of the aged.
2. Status ambiguity in the aged is an extensively discussed subject in the relevant literature. For a succinct review see Rosow (1976).
3. A concept developed by Marshall (1979) in reference to the symbolically imputed social impasse in the lives of the aged.
4. This core sociological concept is often employed to describe the basic condition of the state of ageing. See for example Fontana (1976).
5. Ageing as a 'life career' (Myerhoff and Simić 1978) is a conception underlying the theme of continuity throughout the life course.
6. An extensive discussion of the need for compatibility between analytic concepts and ethnographic data could be found in, for example, Fabian (1983).
7. A term based on the fusion between the anthropological concept of 'ethnocentrism' and the gerontological concept of 'ageism' (Butler 1969).
8. See, for example, Clark and Anderson (1967). The problem of the contradiction between cultural values and ageing is expounded by Anderson (1972).
9. The analytic nexus between age-categorisation and ageing is examined in various studies. For example, Riley, Johnson and Foner (1972); Kertzer and Keith (1984). It would seem that, in the absence of other sociological yardsticks, age has gained considerable salience in the understanding of ageing as a social phenomenon.
10. Research on intersubjective construction of ageing has focused mainly on age-homogenous settings. For a review of the literature see Keith (1980a).
11. An account of several subjective views of ageing could be found in Blythe (1979).
12. See Blau (1973).
13. See Anderson (1972).
14. Consider, for example, Myerhoff's usage of the concept of 'myth' to describe the sense of belonging among the aged, to an atemporal reality (Myerhoff 1978).
15. The theory of disengagement is formulated in Cumming and Henry (1961).
16. The dilemma of human universals in ageing versus human diversity in cross-cultural research is discussed in Cowgill (1972); Simić (1978); Amoss and Harrell (1981).
17. For more ethnographic material see Hazan (1980a).
18. For more ethnographic material see Hazan (1980b).
19. See Goffman (1974).
20. See Lévi-Strauss (1967).
21. For an account of the growing emphasis in the anthropology of ageing on the age factor, see for example, Keith (1980b).
22. For an attempt to interweave the experience of ageing and the concept of age borders see Myerhoff (1984).
23. For a discussion of the phenomenon of egalitarianism in hunter-gathering societies, see Woodburn (1981).
24. See, for example, Miller and Gwynne (1972); Musgrove (1977).
25. See, for example, Cohen and Taylor (1973).
26. The dissolution of old structure and the rearrangement of social order among new immigrants has been extensively studied in the context of Israeli society. It would appear that the adaptation to an unaccustomed way of life entailed the dismantling of social, temporal and cognitive frames. See, for example, Deshen and Shokeid (1974).
27. See, for example, Liebow (1967).
28. See Rosow (1974).

References

Amoss, P.T. and S. Harrell (eds), 1981, *Other Ways of Growing Old: anthropological perspectives*, Stanford, Cal.: Stanford Univeristy Press.

Anderson, B., 1972, 'The Process of Deculturation: its dynamics among United States aged', *Anthropological Quarterly*, 45 (4): 209–16.

Blau, Z.S., 1973, *Old Age in a Changing Society*, New York: New Viewpoints.

Blythe, R., 1979, *The View in Winter*, Harmondsworth: Penguin.

Burgess, E., 1950, 'Personal and Social Adjustment in Old Age', in Derber, M. (ed.), *The Aged and Society*, Champaign, Ill.: Industrial Relations Research Association.

Butler, R.H., 1969, 'Age-ism: another form of bigotry', *Gerontologist*, 9: 243–6.

Clark, M. and B. Anderson, 1967, *Culture and Aging: an anthropological study of older Americans*, Springfield,Ill.: C.C. Thomas.

Cohen, S. and L. Taylor, 1973, *Psychological Survival*, New York: Pantheon.

Cowgill, D.O., 1972, 'A Theory of Aging in Cross-Cultural Perspective', in Cowgill, D.O. and L.D. Holmes (eds), *Aging and Modernization*, New York: Appleton-Century-Crofts, 1–13.

Cumming, E. and W.E. Henry, 1961, *Growing Old: the process of disengagement*, New York: Basic Books.

Deshen, S., and M. Shokeid, 1974, *The Predicament of Homecoming*, Ithaca, NY: Cornell University Press.

Fabian, J., 1983, *Time and the Other: how anthropology makes its object*, New York: Columbia University Press.

Fontana, A., 1976, *The Last Frontier*, Beverly Hills, Cal.: Sage.

Goffman, I., 1974, *Frame Analysis*, New York: Harper.

Hazan, H., 1980a, 'Adjustment and Control in an Old Age Home', in Marx, E. (ed.), *A Composite Portrait of Israel*, London: Academic Press.

Hazan, H., 1980b, *The Limbo People: a study of the constitution of the time universe among the aged*, London: Routledge & Kegan Paul.

Keith, J., 1980a, 'Old Age and Community Creation', in Fry, C.L., *Aging in Culture and Society*, New York: Bergin.

Keith, J., 1980b, 'The Best is Yet to Be, Toward an Anthropology of Age', *Annual Review of Anthropology*, 9: 339–64.

Kertzer, D. and J. Keith (eds), 1984, *Age and Anthropological Theory*, Ithaca, NY: Cornell University Press.

Lévi-Strauss, C., 1967, *The Savage Mind*, Chicago: University of Chicago Press.

Liebow, E., 1967, *Tally's Corner*, Boston: Little Brown.

Marshall, V.W., 1979, 'No Exit: A symbolic interactionist perspective on aging', *International Journal of Aging and Human Development*, 9: 345–58.

Miller, E.J. and G.V. Gwynne, 1972, *A Life Apart*, London: Tavistock.

Musgrove, F., 1977, 'A Home for the Disabled: a change of tense', in Musgrove, F. (ed.), *Margins of the Mind*, London: Methuen.

Myerhoff, B., 1978, *Number Our Days*, New York: Dutton.

Myerhoff, B., 1984, 'Rites and Signs of Ripening: the interweaving of ritual, time and growing older', in Kertzer and Keith.

Myerhoff, B. and A. Simić (eds), 1978, *Life's Career Aging: cultural variations on growing older*, Beverly Hills, Cal.: Sage.

Riley, M.W., J. Johnson and A. Foner (eds), 1972, *Aging and Society,* volume three: *A Sociology of Age Stratification*, New York: Russell Sage.

Rosow, I., 1974, *Socialization to Old Age*, Berkeley: University of California Press.

Rosow, I., 1976, 'Status and Role Change Through the Life Span', in Binstock, R.H. and E. Shanas (eds), *Handbook of Aging and the Social Sciences*, New York: Van Nostrand Reinhold.

Simić, A., 1978, 'Introduction', in Myerhoff, and Simić.

Woodburn, J., 1981, 'Egalitarian Societies', *Man*, 17: 431–51.

Chapter fourteen

Clubs for *le troisième âge*: communitas or conflict

Judith Okely

Inevitably a cross-cultural perspective of the aged would be likely to question the homogeneity of the category aged. In this chapter I shall examine the lurking suggestion that the aged within a single locality are a homogeneous group. My area is within Normandy.[1] The question of homogeneity is heightened by the fact that some indigenous academics, for example in a recent geographical study of rural France, have confirmed the stereotype:

> Pensioners, and more generally the elderly, despite the apparent heterogeneity of their origins, are certainly one of the most homogenous social categories of the rural world. Their age, their modest circumstances, their relative isolation, their reticence in the face of the current development in ideas and customs, give them a certain sense of belonging to a specific social category. The success of the clubs for the third age in the rural milieu is the best proof of this.
>
> (Chapius 1986, p.192, my translation)

This chapter commences from an alternative perspective, namely the evidence of major economic and social divisions among the aged within a single rural locality, whether in France or, as in my comparative research, in England. An overall average of the aged's financial conditions does reveal relative deprivation compared to the younger employed (see Chapius 1986, pp. 150–1), but it conceals the internal contrasts among the rural aged. There are marked differences between their financial resources, type of accommodation, extent of autonomy and mobility, freedom from institutional control, and access to basic facilities such as shops and medical care. These inequalities have indeed been acknowledged by other French specialists in gerontology:

> Retirement entails a noticeable lowering of income, but one can no longer speak universally of a population in poverty ... between 1970 and 1978, the financial resources of the retired have increased more than those of the economically active ... the inequalities are far greater among social groups of the elderly than among the economically active. In effect, inequalities

have accumulated throughout the life course; certain individuals have been able to create a heritage which ensures them an income, while others have accumulated nothing, not even the rights to a pension.

(Levet-Gautrat 1985, pp. 44–5, my translation)

Far from clubs for the aged being proof of homogeneity, as asserted by Chapius, this research reveals that clubs for the third age become the arena for confronting differences. Their structure and activities sometimes reflect and reinforce these differences. In other instances clubs act to submerge differences during the specific period of their meetings.

Whereas I argue that the potential for homogeneity may be undermined by socio-economic divisions, none the less, the clubs were seen by many of their members as an arena where divisions ought to be submerged. The ideal of the majority was for a 'communitas' (Turner 1969), a community without class, where people were united by the common feature of age and shared locality, and where people came together without contrasts in wealth and privilege. Thus where Chapius suggests that the popularity of the clubs is proof of its members' inherent homogeneity, he is unwittingly presenting the members' ideals, rather than the members' actual position. The members had to strive for their ideal of communitas in every detail of their activities.

In one club, the ideal of communitas never achieved dominance; the club was under the control of individuals with quite different interests. In this instance the club was seen as a vehicle for prestige and achievement within the small market town and region and in terms which did not coincide with those of the majority of members. External criteria for success were linked for example to the club's performance in regional competitions. A club was assessed for its 'dynamism' by its ambitious outings, production and display of neatly finished handicrafts, group singing and dramatic presentations. All these activities required the refinement of specific skills within a relatively structured organisation. These activities were embraced by members of a certain educational level and were consistent with the ideals of a bourgeois culture, with which they already felt at home. Other members had no such aspirations, and in any case their non-literacy excluded them. The organisation of this club was captured by the relatively educated bourgeoisie who set the ideological tone. The mass of its members found the ideal of communitas thwarted, since the cultural interests and economic privileges of the elite were made entirely apparent. Other clubs were more able to achieve a notion of temporary communitas where there were no ambitions to perform in terms of 'high culture' and where the local bourgeoisie deferred to an egalitarian ideal when participating in the club. The struggle for communitas expressed itself in competing notions of culture, that of the dominated and that of the dominant.

The material emerges from both inside and outside several clubs in a rural locality. The latter was notable for its dairy production, cider apple orchards and mixed farming. Large landowners had traditionally sublet to small tenants. Other farmers, or *cultivateurs,* had acquired their own parcels of land. Although the common agricultural policy has in recent years precipitated the amalgamation of small farms and mechanisation, small-scale mixed dairy farming had coloured the life experience of the major proportion of the aged. The identity of the locality, whether stereotyped or real for the residents, old or young, included notions about *le petit paysan* or *petit cultivateur.* Long-term residents who had worked in commerce and other occupations in the small market town at the centre of the locality had also to relate to this image. Some of the antagonisms and conflicts, latent or manifest in the clubs, can be related to the biographical experience of the aged as semi-autonomous small farmers. Other members had engaged in petty commerce which served both the villages and the market town. There were retired railway and other workers, former domestic servants and outworkers, such as dressmakers. The locality had its share of retired public servants, teachers and those with considerable economic capital from land and commerce, who also had to confront the image of the *petit paysan* which competed with an alternative non-rural image for the locality. The small market town also had its history of cultural links with the metropolis.

I shall focus on three clubs. One, with predictably the largest membership, was situated in the market town of some four thousand inhabitants. For reasons of confidentiality I shall rename the town Bourg. Another club was situated in an adjacent locality, at a major railway junction and separated from Bourg by the tracks of a major national line and itself a separate municipality which I shall rename Jonction. The third club was in a village I shall rename Pastorale, which, like the surrounding hamlets, villages and Jonction, had a long-term economic and political relationship with Bourg the market town. The latter was once the major outlet for local agricultural produce – some sent to Paris – and a place of commerce. Like Jonction it is less than an hour from Paris by rail. It is the residence of the *haute* and *petite bourgeoisie* and is still the controlling municipality. The Bourg club for the aged had been initiated as early as 1976. Those in Jonction and Pastorale came later, since clubs for *le troisième âge* were given a new boost by subsidies under the Mitterand government in the early 1980s.

Membership of a specific club depended in part on the individual's current residence. Those in the Pastorale village club were usually at an early stage in their retirement, that is in their 60s and mid 70s. Later, they were likely to find themselves residents of the market town and potential members of its club. There was a pattern of micro migration from the surrounding hamlets and villages to Bourg – those who could no longer continue working their farms would give up their tenancies, sell them or pass them on to descendants. They usually tried to stay as long as possible in the outlying rural area. When the decision came, those with capital could acquire compact and independent housing in the centre of Bourg, conveniently within walking distance of all services, including domestic assistance. Others with the right contacts rented self-catering accommodation in Bourg. The unfortunate, frail and poor were moved to the town's crowded and spartan hospice. Some former rural inhabitants chose instead to move to the other side of the tracks, the adjacent Jonction, where rates and accommodation were cheaper. They mixed with retired railway and other workers in the Jonction club. This locality also attracted retired Parisian workers. Once, however, a certain frailty reduced their self-catering capacities or pressure was put on them by doctors or relatives to be institutionalised, the poorer elderly were moved to the hospice at Bourg. They were unable to attend the club at Bourg, if they were physically or psychologically institutionalised. The Bourg and Jonction clubs attracted both residents who had lived and worked in the place all their lives, and incoming migrants from the surrounding rural areas. The Bourg club could, like that at Jonction, also draw on retired Parisian incomers, who tended to be of a higher economic standing than those who selected Jonction. In addition, Bourg drew on some residents from the Electricity Board retirement home, who came from all over France.

Compared to the average small market town, Bourg had an unusual cultural identity. It once attracted wealthy Parisians by rail to its casino and curative thermal waters. Earlier, Corneille and royalty had visited the town, and memorials to these symbols of high culture and aristocracy were conspicuously displayed as statues and place names. Postcards, posters and blown-up photographs of the visiting *haute bourgeoisie* with carriages, the women in vast hats and elaborate dress were on sale in the town. They were described to me by both a shopowner and a civil servant as souvenirs of the 'real', 'true' or '*vraie*' Bourg, an identity which was fragile and needed to be reiterated. The casino now faces bankruptcy. Attempts to revive interest in the thermal waters have largely failed. Parisians and others now travel to the warmer south for their cures. None the less, the local municipality and others work hard to revitalise the cultural potential of its past, especially in the light of economic changes.

With the mechanisation of agriculture, decline in agricultural population, new quotas on dairy produce and a national wine industry which has undermined the mass production of cider, the area is faced with unemployment among the young and outmigration. Attempts have been made to exploit the alternative economic potential of tourism. Here the history, real or mythical, of Bourg is elaborated to put the town on the tourist map. The club for the aged has also been seen as a possible tourist resource, especially since the over 60s can be imported as tourists from the entire region. When the mayor purchased a miniature train as part of a deal for the renovation of the thermal centre, it was said there were difficulties in covering the cost. Eventually someone contacted clubs for the third age throughout Normandy and tours in the miniature train were arranged. In the summer the brightly painted *petit train* wends its way through the main streets bearing its elderly passengers.

A museum named after the club and established from municipal funding is also a convenient visiting place for coach day trips and is extremely profitable.

The museum displays wooden models of 'traditional rural' occupations hand crafted by a retired Parisian. The rural peasant past of the locality is thus tamed and captured within Bourg's urban culture, and in this context not seen to conflict with the town's more cultured bourgeois past. Similarly the *petit cultivateur* incomers, who had in their past maintained an ambivalent if scornful attitude to the Bourgerons, find themselves, after retirement migration, enclosed within its cultural idiom and power structure. Within the club, the only one specifically for the aged, their identity as former rural workers is minimised and implicitly denigrated. They cannot be so easily romanticised and framed as passive museum pieces, so the culture of their experience is denied. By contrast, the long-term aged residents who identify with the bourgeoisie and Bourg's cultural pretensions feel sympathetic to colluding in its illustrious past, and are rewarded for so doing within the club's meetings. Many of those born there were keen to emphasise their right to be called Bourgeron.

It might have been thought that, given its majority membership of rural incomers, the Bourg club would have offered the opportunity for some autonomy. Within its arena the members are not subject to the sanctions once held over them by employers or landlords. This after all is their 'free time' after retirement. Even if constrained by residential controls as tenants in rented accommodation or as residents of the hospice, on the surface it would seem that leisure time among many others in similar conditions would offer 'relaxation' from controls. This is indeed what was voiced as an ideal by members of other clubs criticising the Bourg club and by many Bourg members in guarded tones. But instead of fulfilling a notion of communitas, the members found themselves confronted by the cultural idiom which the club organisers wished to emulate and reproduce. A key aspect of that idiom includes the hierarchy of cultural refinement.

Within France, the emphasis on *culture* or *formation* (education) can be seen as part of its culture, in the widest sense. It contrasts with the denigration of culture, the arts and refinement in the English if not British dominant culture. Whereas the French emphasis on culture in the specific sense can be embraced by British visitors and refugees in France as a welcome relief from the cult of barbarianism among the British bourgeoisie, it should also be recognised as a means of separating the educated elite and bourgeoisie from both the proletariat and the rural peasantry. It becomes, in Bourdieu's words, 'cultural capital' (Bourdieu and Passeron 1977). Bourdieu has also plotted the differences of attitude towards culture among the French bourgeoisie (Bourdieu 1984). I shall be content here to point to more general cross-national contrasts. Defensiveness and sometimes hostility to cultural and literate refinement assume massive class overtones in France. By contrast, in England, if not Britain, the hatred of culture and bookish refinement is to a great extent also the prerogative of the dominant class, whether aristocrats or meritocratic politicians. The British urban or rural working classes would not see 'high culture' and advanced education in quite the same way as the French. In Britain more emphasis is placed on accent and delivery of speech than its content. In France, however, a mark of the bourgeoisie is the literary or artistic allusion and stylised choice of vocabulary. French politicians are useful indicators; from the right to the left, from Le Pen and Chirac to Mitterand, there is prestige to be obtained in references to 'great writers' and high culture. Among British politicians on the contrary, from Wilson to Thatcher, there is certainly no shame in cultural illiteracy beyond academic circles, indeed it is something to boast about. These broad generalisations about French and British traditions, something which anthropologists are reluctant to attempt, point to the specificity and significance of seemingly value-free leisure pursuits among clubs for the aged in France. Their responses to cultural activities at the micro level are reflections of a wider national ideology and history.

In the light of these observations, it follows that conflicts of interest and differing ideas about the clubs' activities did not necessarily divide along rural/urban, village/town biographies. The specific positions of individual members coincided to a great extent with their level of education, past occupation and financial standing, as well as cultural allegiance and individual aspirations. For example, a retired couple, who had sold their ample farm near Pastorale and purchased a house in Bourg, proved to be most prominent in the club's public performances, in ballroom dancing and in the choir. Although once heavily engaged in the manual labour of agriculture, they were more than literate and wished to refine themselves further. The club was used by them to consolidate pre-existing aspirations.

The club at Bourg was the earliest focus in my fieldwork and it took some time before any underlying conflicts were revealed to me. This was partly because my access had to be through the organisers at the top. The public image desired by the organisers was at first the most marked. Indeed it was a front page local newspaper report with photographs of its activities which consolidated my decision to choose that locality. The President, approaching 70, was a retired school teacher and a local councillor. She saw the club as an opportunity to counter the image of passivity and other stereotypes among the aged. Here also, it seemed, was a chance to educate, refine or train its members who had previously escaped the attentions of people such as herself. In fact the cultural pursuits of the club presumed already a minimum level of education. Literacy classes for the many non-literate *cultivateurs* who might have left school when 8 or 9 did not feature on the agenda, so that the most basic educational needs of its members were not a priority. The President bemoaned the fact that so many of her members and other clubs seemed happy to concentrate on dominoes and card games. The former is identified in France as the working-class game *par excellence* (Bourdieu 1984). She wanted to move them on in every sense of the word: to take cycle rides, to do formal ballroom dancing. In fact most of the poorer rural workers had once depended on bicycles. There was also enthusiasm for a choir and public poetry recitals. Women were encouraged to sew and crochet items in the club which were then donated to the annual Exhibition-Sale (Vente-Expo) thus raising funds for the club. Having once been a teacher of English, she made full use of her connections and arranged two trips to England, others to southern France or Paris. Slides of these visits were shown at the club's tenth anniversary celebrations and blown-up colour photos were displayed in the meeting hall. They were a triumph of achievement. English schoolgirls on a visit to learn French were invited to join the *mardi gras* gathering. A quarterly cyclo-styled magazine edited by her was circulated to all the clubs in the commune. Her enthusiasm and the commitment of the officers of the club were poignantly impressive.

It was only much later that I began to get a glimmer of a counter view from many of its members. This came mainly when it was learned that I was a friend and companion of the President of the club at Pastorale and that she was teaching me to hand-milk cows, thus dramatically breaking my image as intellectual and teacher. A former resident of Pastorale grabbed my hand at the Bourg club one day and said quietly, 'Since we heard that Mme A. at Pastorale had taken to you, we knew you were all right, that you would really understand us.' Thus it was only when I was seen to associate with the President and club from Pastorale that I could be given a major, but subordinate, perspective of the club members in Bourg. My attempts at hand milking, however amateur, questioned the divide between bourgeois refinement and manual labour, a divide which could be a clue to differences in the practices of each club.

My acquaintance with several clubs also confirmed a familiar anthropological observation that groups may define themselves partly through opposition to others. The clubs at Jonction and Pastorale more especially defined their values by affirming that they were not like the club at Bourg. They were both on the periphery of the dominant municipal centre. Self-definition was more fragmented at the Bourg club. Competing definitions emerged. The relative insignificance of Jonction and Pastorale in the dominant system was confirmed by the rarity of their mention by members at Bourg.

In order to reveal how clubs for the aged are not neutral gatherings for people who share a common chronological age and municipal locality, I shall give a detailed description of each.

Bourg

The name *Le Club de l'Âge d'Or* (the club of the golden age) already carried ambiguous meanings. On the one hand it could refer to old age as the fulfilment and pinnacle of life. On the other hand the golden age conjures up references to the golden age of the town now fallen on hard times. The word 'gold' emphasises material riches and also in this specific instance cultural capital. A prestigious national competition for the best singer of lieder songs held several times in Bourg was called Le Voix d'Or. In effect the club's name, while ostensibly intending to counter a negative stereotype of the aged as facing the lowest grade period in their lives, inadvertently conveys images of privilege and capital inaccessible to the majority of the aged.

The club meets weekly and without charge in the communal room of sheltered apartments owned by the municipality. A few have arrived in private cars, others, if not within walking distance, are brought in the partly subsidised bus. As with other clubs, the most visible activities appear to be dominoes and card playing. Men and women sit at tables of four. There is an atmosphere of control rather than ribaldry. In an adjoining room separated by glass doors are the women who crochet, knit and sew at one large table. For these women such handicrafts have rarely had more status than hobbies in the past. The town has in fact many former *couturiers* who made their living at home or in workshops making clothes and soft furnishings for the local bourgeoisie, their clients. One such *couturier* who had only attended the club a couple of times said with anger, 'I don't want to go there just to *sew*.' In contrast, a regular attender of the club who had married into a wealthy family and loosened ties with her humble small-farm relatives, first took up crocheting at the club as physiotherapy against progressive arthritis. She sits at the round table with the others.

Once these activities have been launched, a number extricate themselves for a rehearsal of the 'chorale'. This takes place in a small room off the main corridor. Self-selected members of the choir are presented with song sheets of both the words and music. Its participants have to be able to read both and so the non-literates, of which there are many in the club, are entirely excluded. The choir was initiated by the then newly appointed Director of the Electricity retirement home who offered his services to the President. Leather jacketed, bejeaned and with long curly hair until his promotion, he looked like a leftover from *les événements* of '68. Alongside the romantic songs about fields, flowers, Normandy and windmills were inserted a few revolutionary numbers emphasising comradeship. The conductor had a lively jokey manner, doing a self-parody of a schoolmaster reprimanding the males and females in turn. The singers loved it. The choir made modest appearances at the annual festival for St Cecilia in the main church, following on from the massed choir of the schools, the town brass band and the orchestra. The star professional performer at this concert was the previous year's winner of the Voix d'Or. Her prestigious curriculum vitae was read out and she was lavished with bouquets. In this setting the Club de l'Âge d'Or was made visible – a small frail group which held its own while musically unaccompanied. The public identity of the choir was confirmed by its 'uniform' at some public events. The women wore white blouses and long purple satin skirts. The men wore dinner jackets. Any radical tone conveyed by the occasional song was softened by the choice of attire. The conductor (who eluded all attempts to be interviewed) no doubt saw his initiative as radical and creative. The elderly were given a niche in the public cultural endeavours of Bourg. But as I learned, both from the clubs at Jonction and Pastorale and from the non-singers at Bourg, the choir was seen by many of the aged as something to be denigrated. Members from Jonction and Pastorale said 'We don't like the Bourg club; there's too much noise – all that singing.' It was seen merely as a means to increase the President's *gloire* or prestige. It confirmed the cultural exclusion of the majority, since participation required a minimum educational expertise. It served to refine the pre-existent interests and skills of the bourgeoisie, rather than drawing on those of the rural proletariat. On another level, unbeknown to that majority, the choir was judged by the President in terms of even higher cultural ideals which she was aware that the choir could never achieve. After I had been invited to participate in the choir, presumably because I was recognised as someone of a high cultural literacy, the President took me aside in the corridor and apologised abjectly for the choir's performances; 'You see the results come to zero, but one can't expect anything else.' She straddled several cultural ambitions, the niceties of which were irrelevant to the mass of working-class members.

The routines of the club were more perceptibly structured than in the other clubs. The domino and card players kept in their places, being every now and then asked to listen to an announcement by the President. A regular clique of women was delegated to take charge of the catering. First, sweets were handed out, one to each member who was then asked to take a card marked coffee, chocolate or tea. The different requests were counted up and the women re-emerged with a trolley of beverages and factory-made biscuits. The cost of the refreshments came from the membership fees and other funds. No one made food donations. The empty glasses or cups were collected up by the same women who spent the rest of the meeting washing up, drying and cleaning up. The President, Treasurer and other officers would check up on the work, but not participate.

The club was organised in a 'professional', hierarchical manner. The officers sought permanent assistants for the administrative and other duties. Collective contributions were not generally envisaged. As I came to know the members more intimately and heard also their opinions expressed to former neighbours from Pastorale, it became apparent that every activity which could be seen as a potential sign of success by external criteria was scornfully re-interpreted. The large sums of money raised by the Exhibition-Sale of the club's handiwork and raffled donations from local commerce, were said to have been used to enrich the President's personal bank account. The museum was dismissed as a waste of rates. The singing and dancing caused 'too much noise'. This could be taken to mean too much public noise and acclaim, rather than audible interference in the meetings. The club's organisation of holiday trips to Paris, the South of France or England, although part subsidised, were criticised because they drew attention to inequalities in wealth. Every applicant had to make some initial contribution, which the poor could not hope to do. The invitation to visiting English schoolgirls to join the *mardi gras* celebration was seen as an odd intrusion and merely a means to enhance the 'international' image of the hostess.

It has been suggested (in some early discussions with colleagues) that my findings are consistent with standard themes in club organisations – namely that the organisers are always the subject of criticism and that such conflicts are typical within any small group. I suggest that the *form* which the criticism of the organisation takes is relevant. Moreover, the relative lack of criticism of the officers at Jonction and Pastorale cannot then be explained. These clubs have a different ethos which also minimises the authority of the officers. The Bourg members expected a deferential role in their own officers, some of whom they would criticise for their display of authority. The members frequently referred favourably to the Vice President, a Parisian incomer, whom they considered less haughty. Whereas the President was accused of ignoring, or even humiliating, the *illettrés* and only shaking the hands of the *grands personalités*, the Parisian was valued for her equal treatment and friendliness towards all members, regardless of social and economic status. The preference for the Vice President as future President would be likely to be tempered upon promotion. For in private discussion she and her husband revealed an uncomprehending attitude towards the *petits cultivateurs* whom they considered 'mean' with their allegedly hoarded wealth. They criticised their dress and manner, which lacked style. As a recent incomer, the Parisian was obliged to show a deferential profile, but as organiser and mediator within the municipality and with her own cultural allegiance to the bourgeoisie, it is unlikely that a shift in individual personnel would radically alter the club ethos. To that extent the negative reactions among club members are explained by the club structure and context rather than by the individual personalities of the organisers, who are replaceable.

My contention is that the club's conflicts cannot be viewed out of its total context. The animosity within the Bourg club and outside it reflects the larger relation between the central municipality, with its dominant bourgeois cultural traditions, and the culturally marginalised majority, who came from the countryside.

The clubs at Jonction and Pastorale were able to resist such dominance. One explanation is their very political marginality. Since Jonction and Pastorale and their clubs for the aged represented so little, and were not exploitable for tourism, they were free from appropriation as political and cultural emblems. Any attempt to impose cultural refinements upon a diminishing rural or semi-proletarian population would seem irrelevant. Although in the past, Bourg depended both on the agricultural produce and political votes from the villages, it could now afford to ignore them as peripheral. The Bourg President was astonished at my interest and participation in the Pastorale club and urged me to look beyond this *tout petit pays*.

Another explanation for the relative autonomy of the clubs at Jonction and Pastorale lay in the residential continuity of the majority of members. The aged at Pastorale if not at Jonction were still 'at home'. Members at Bourg were more likely to be recent migrants. Uprooted from their past, they were now enclosed as uncertain residents of a place they previously visited only on market days. They were not well placed to challenge the hierarchy of cultural refinement which formerly they could comfortably ignore. The activities of clubs at Jonction and Pastorale reveal the differing ethos.

Jonction

Here also dominoes and cards were played at the weekly meetings. Despite the members' complaints that Bourg was too noisy, the exclamations and chatter during the games seemed louder. There was also a table for the women who sewed and crocheted. In this instance the President and Secretary joined in. They helped serve the refreshments which were administered with informality. As a regular practice bottles of wine, home-made cider or even champagne and sweet bread were donated by individuals from the village. The President would inform the members who were asked to clap in rhythm three times as thanks. The only division of labour was one based on sex rather than class. The washing up was not restricted to a set group – any woman could and did choose to volunteer, including the women officers.

Again, despite the complaint that the Bourg club had 'all that singing and dancing', Jonction had its own kinds. In this case there were no choirs who rehearsed with scripts in a separate room. After the table games and refreshments, a record player would be brought out. *Chansons* of the boulevard and music hall would be played. There was a microphone which members were encouraged to take. Individuals sang solos of popular songs from memory. They could be comic, sentimental or risqué. The absence of song sheets meant there was no threat to any non-literate, who in turn could feel free to sing. The listeners made informed commentary on the pitch and delivery of each performer. They were all potential experts in this culture with which they were familiar. They also were *qualified* to comment. In contrast to Bourg, there was no emphasis on any new acquisition of refinement. Some of the songs were what the true Bourgeron would call *vulgaire*. A favourite duet was between a man who sang of his desire for the woman partner to scratch his flea-bitten back. The actions were mimed to the shrieks of the spectators. Each song was followed by noisy applause. Instead of formal ballroom dancing practised by the few in special sessions at Bourg, someone would suggest a conga type dance to a particular record. Soon everyone in the room would form a twisting snake, each person putting their hands on the hips or shoulders of the person in front. Ideally no one was excluded, it was a communal movement which also resolved the numerical preponderance of females who normally would not have male dancing partners. If one individual looked comical lurching and twisting so could anyone else.

The name of this club at Jonction is the Club de la Joie de Vivre. Its exuberant 'vulgarity' lived up to its name. The officers were of a different social standing from the President at Bourg. The President at Jonction had formerly owned a haberdashery at Bourg which she sold at retirement and moved to Jonction. The Treasurer, a man, had graduated from being a humble farm hand who slept in the proprietor's stable to owning his own small farm near Pastorale. He sold up upon retirement and bought an expensively modernised Normandy cottage in the centre of Bourg. Despite such economic mobility, he avoided the club at Bourg and acquired a position of power at Jonction which would have been denied him in the Bourg cultural hierarchy. These officers had indeed relative economic capital in contrast to what Bourdieu (1984) has differentiated as cultural capital. Their greater economic wealth relative to many members at Jonction was not seen as a subject for discontent in the club. They had no programme of cultural refinement and education for the members and were seen to behave as equals. Any interest in municipal recognition at Jonction was related to subsidies and fund raising rather than to cultural displays such as a museum, poetry recitals and well rehearsed choirs. Even the annual sale of handicrafts made at the club was not presented as a separate exhibition and unique event as in Bourg, instead the club hired a street stall at Jonction's annual fête. The funds were donated towards holiday subsidies. In some instances the differing financial resources of the members were apparent in the ability to take club holidays. But the club ethos was such that the inequalities were not blamed on the club officers. The members were keen to describe to me and thus perpetually recreate their ethos of egalitarianism. When first meeting anyone, I was invariably volunteered statements such as: 'Here we're more friendly, more at ease, everyone is welcome. Not like the club at Bourg.' I never heard divisive criticisms about their own club. It seemed that within the club its members both wanted to and succeeded in creating a communitas where differences were minimised. Potential differences based on economic capital were modified by a unity of familiar cultural practices which affected the favoured form of singing, dancing, games, manners, food and even a view of the body. They amounted to a coherent system, but one which was opposed to that favoured by the dominant organisers at Bourg.

The egalitarian ethic did permit luxury and material riches, provided they were available to all and on their own terms. The apogee occurred in the club's annual banquet which started at 12 noon and for the strong of stomach ended around midnight. It had many of the characteristics of other banquets in the area except its time span and unmodified supply of traditional rural beverages – cider, calvados – *le trou Normand* – in addition to different aperitifs, wines and champagne. There was the customary *table d'honneur* with the officers and others. In contrast to the banquet at Bourg, the Jonction mayor only came in towards the end of the main courses. At the end of the official feast at 5.00 p.m., guests and those with other commitments left. The tables were

205

pushed back, the record player put on and the snake conga set in motion. Individual solos were sung. I thought it was over after the last plate was washed at 8.00 p.m. but saw the tables being re-set. Stay for just a little *souper* I was asked. This included veal, salad, vegetables, cheese. Every woman, not just the hired caterers, later washed up. The official timetable for the banquet and the hiring of the hall had been so subverted that at midnight the local gendarme arrived to see why the lights were still on. He was incorporated with the offer of a drink. At midnight and after twelve hours of *La Grande Bouffe* there were still some revellers.

The contrasts between the Jonction and Bourg clubs, their organisation, ethos and internal relations were most vividly portrayed in symbolic fashion in the celebrations for *mardi gras*.

The idea for the Bourg celebration came from one of the most active middle-class members. A wedding between Mlle Cochon (pig) and Monsieur Chameau (camel) was to be enacted. The bride, groom, mayor conducting the ceremony and accompanying relatives wore grotesque masks, several of pigs, and formal dress, e.g. black tie, dinner jacket, top hat, or evening gown with or without elaborate lace hat and coiffure. Mr Camel had a bulbous false nose and eye mask. They processed down the length of the hall while the massed membership sat as passive spectators around the edges of the hall. The central space was given over to the ceremony which reinforced the club's hierarchy. Those who participated in the procession had to provide their own attire. The majority dressed as members of the *haute bourgeoisie*, some from the turn of the century. One couple came in exotic silk mandarin costume, just one woman from the Electricity retirement home dressed in bulky black tights like a clown. She looked out of place. The mayor read an elaborate *discours* from a written scroll. The presumed humour depended on the paradox of animals and of different species being considered worthy to participate in a civilised formal ceremony. The scroll, like the costume, contrasted with the illiteracy and utilitarian dress of the masses. After the ranked procession, the mayor's speech and introduction of each partner's kin, the participants paired off for formal ballroom dancing. The event consolidated the hierarchy of bourgeois culture and *savoir-faire* and made fun of any animals who dared to cross cultural boundaries. Animals whose mating was sanctified by the mayor with due ceremony were the subject of a grotesque spectacle.

The ceremony not only mocked at animals in culture, but also at a hybrid union. This takes on a new significance in the light of increasing racism and anxiety at mixed ethnic marriages in France. Newspapers reported a growing number of marriages between Arab men and French women. The locality was not free of its racism. One farmer at Pastorale refused to sell milk to the children of an Arab father and French mother. The club President at Pastorale made a point of selling her milk to the children. 'Je ne suis pas raciste.' The hybrid union could be interpreted as a mixed ethnic one between an exotic Mr Camel/Arab and the Islamically tabooed Miss Piggy, a gluttonous European of dubious cultural refinement. The idea of the ceremony was gleaned by the mock mayor from a newspaper. Whether or not he and the Bourg club responded to any hidden connection between camels and exotic foreigners, the image of the pig mask was entirely familiar as farm animal, reared by so many of the *petits cultivateurs*. The pig of dubious cultural refinement could be seen by some as farm-bound peasant.

The Jonction club celebrated *mardi gras* in terms of a Tahitian utopia. The organisers and others made grass skirts for the women and coloured shirts for the men, and crêpe flower garlands for anyone who wished. So participation was not restricted to those who could provide the correct costume. Tahiti, according to a survey in *Paris-Match* of that year, was considered the most popular fantasy location among all the French respondents. In fact its utopian image has a long cultural history traceable back to Diderot. The South Seas island represented a land of abundance, warmth and leisure. There was no ranked procession by those in costume. There was no polished *discours* to be read out. The main display consisted of the 'Tahitians' all holding hands and moving in a circle, a symbol of egalitarianism, a movement without leaders. The only reservations against wearing the colourful costume were among some of the men who feared the flowers were effeminate. The Tahitian fantasy did indeed attempt to break down the demarcation of gender.

The previous year the theme at Jonction for *mardi gras* had been Arabia or *les petroliers* (oilmen). Sheikh like costumes were made for the men and veiled extravanganzas for the women. The numerical preponderance of women could be normalised as a harem with a minority of male sheikhs, although the costume makers said they had difficulty in persuading the men to dress up. The image from the photographs I was shown and the members' accounts was one of wealth and plenty, but available to all. In both years the Jonction club selected a fantasy land, an exotic place beyond France and so outside its hierarchical and cultural structure. What Turner (1969) has called 'anti-structure' where anything may be possible. The participants could invent these other cultures. Any member could assume the attire and become a sheikh or Tahitian. Since they were uniformly made by the club, private wealth and privileged access to a specific costume were not apparent. Once in the fantasy attire, the participants were subjects of shared fun rather than objects of ridicule.

At Bourg, however, participants had to provide their own costume and, with a few exceptions, the more dressy and ostentatious the better. Here the *haute bourgeoisie* came into their own. One woman wore a long black taffeta ball gown, another found an antique hat with ostrich feathers. Even if such clothing had been handed out to the rural peasantry or former shop assistants they would not have moved easily in this attire. The pig masks were the source of laughter not the chic clothing. An aged peasant woman dressed in taffeta ball gown would not have needed a pig's mask to be laughed at. The mock ceremony within the civilised order spoke clearly of structure and the dominant culture.

Pastorale

The club, like those of other relatively small villages, met monthly. All those villagers over 60 regularly attended, except one couple who resisted such 'modern developments', and two single women, one too frail and the other who it was said was forbidden by her daughter. The venue was again a municipal room, and eventually the newly completed community hall. People divided up into domino or card players. The playing continued virtually uninterrupted from just after 2.00 p.m. to 4.30 or 5.00. At the outset pleasantries and local information were exchanged and then the groups settled down to playing which, as in the other clubs, made a continuous thread of conversation impossible. Speech consisted of remarks related to the games, sometimes loud and excited. There was no sewing, no crochetwork.

The majority of the members had worked in agriculture; one couple had sold a relatively large farm and still owned two houses which they planned eventually to sell for one in Bourg. Two couples still retained working farms, others had retired but kept their hand in tending vegetable gardens and clearing their own wood for the winter stoves. A retired builder, a lorry driver, the widow of a factory worker and a retired nurse mixed with a former farm hand and a school cleaner. From April to November the club was also attended by the owners of the imposing sixteenth-century château on the hill. In the winter they retreated to their apartment near Rouen. When I was first told about the château dwellers it was important that I was also told that they attended the club 'like everyone else'. In fact the club was the only context where most of the other village inhabitants met with these representatives of the *haute bourgeoisie*. One retired farmer worked in their garden; the school cleaner also cleaned the château.

In Pastorale, despite the fact that the château dwellers owned and sublet a large farm and orchards, in the club context they met the members' ideal state of communitas, i.e. where the privileged and 'highly cultured', in the terms of the dominant society, deferred to the culture of the *petit cultivateur*. The madame of the château, 'the châtelaine', could, if she wanted, convey and communicate her own culture on her own territory. The President at Pastorale, knowing the madame spoke English, took me to meet her. I was served with champagne on the lawns, the same brand, she was proud to relate, that the Queen served at Prince Andrew's wedding. She quoted Shelley and Rupert Brooke, played her Bach records and at our last encounter gave me books by Charles Morgan and Saint-Exupéry. In the club her 'culture' was not seen as threatening because the participants played out what they could have in common.

Apart from the choice of games, another aspect of the club's constructed communitas was the shared meal. The money for this came in part from the club's subsidies. It was called a *collation* or snack, and consisted of charcuterie, cheese and Normandy apple tart, along with wine, home-made cider and calvados. Members took it in turns to donate dishes. Local produce was preferred. The wife of the wealthier farmer and Treasurer planned to buy a tart or *galette* and gâteaux from a Bourg *pâtisserie*. This was interpreted by the President as stepping out of line, of being extravagant both of any available subsidies and her own privilege. The President persuaded another woman to make a *galette* and at the meeting the Treasurer brought his wife's apologies for her absence. A mysterious *cousine* had arrived. Later this same woman was keen to keep up the front of this excuse to me. She did not want to be seen to be threatening the appearance of harmony.

After the *collation*, the men rearranged the chairs and all the women joined in the washing up. The number who helped, up to ten, was more than those who took responsibility for the catering at Bourg.

At Pastorale, just as at Bourg, the President set the tone. She had been selected by mutual agreement by the members. It had been decided to exclude the retired driver who had a despotic manner. 'If he'd been President no one would have come.' His unpopularity was confirmed during the building of the community hall when it was said he gave a stream of orders, while being unable to contribute his own labour. In fact the President was an extremely powerful personality but she represented egalitarian and frugal values. She was most articulate in contrasting the activities of the Bourg club with that at Pastorale. She was not intimidated by the *châtelaine*, who had no power over her and who had no interest in capturing the club's ethos. Similarly, the mayor of Pastorale, a wealthy businessman, treated the club as a group of potential allies in 'his' village. He deferred to the majority and used his political skills to argue for greater subsidies which the Mairie at Bourg had tried to deny the club. The President's insistence that the *châtelains* be treated like everyone else emerged in a dispute with the regional authorities who questioned whether they, as visibly wealthy, had the right to any subsidies for their food at the club. The President insisted on their 'rights'. If it had been ruled that subsidies depend on individual finances, the egalitarian ideal would be brought into question.

In the relationships both with the mayor and the *châtelains* it can be seen that, where the elderly residents were 'at home' in their locality and culture, the club was able to exist without appropriation by the local bourgeois elite. Any successful attempt at cultural refinement took place outside the club in a sacred and separate sphere. The mayor had his own musical interests and encouraged the formation of a small choir for the church where he assembled mainly the schoolchildren and willing adults. It was interpreted as an attempt to revive religious practice since the church no longer had a resident priest. Here the cultural refinement which came with the religious music was not seen as threatening in the way that the secular choir was at the Bourg club. Similarly at the Armistice dinner the Pastorale mayor had distributed song sheets after the meal. His wife and the *châtelains* made a few attempts at group singing, but the gesture was benevolently ignored by the majority.

209

The club at Pastorale was called Le Club des Amis. As at Jonction, considerable thought, I was informed, had gone into the choice of name. Both had resisted a suggestion of Le Club des Ainés which emphasised an external, possibly stigmatised, label. Both names carried aspects of communitas, an arena for joy and living (defying future death), or one without divisions.

Concluding remarks

Some key monographs on the aged by anthropologists (Myerhoff 1978; Hazan 1980) have studied groups of elderly people who have a common ethnic identity and where the implications of class differences are not the focus. Whereas there is considerable research in the social sciences on the aged in residential care, and an increasing amount now on gender, there is very little on class and the aged (Phillipson 1988).

This study of clubs in Normandy examines the ways in which participants confront differences in class and the forms which those differences take in terms of 'leisure activities' and definitions of culture. In his perceptive research into a North London Jewish day centre, Hazan notes the negative response among the majority of participants to 'innovation and creativity' which he links to such activities as art appreciation classes and rehearsed musical performances. The majority's preference for what he calls 'a rather limited selection of music hall and variety entertainment of the late 1920s and early 1930s' (Hazan 1980, p. 143) is seen as consistent with the club's preference for repetition although Hazan mentions 'improvisations and additions' in this music hall culture. I suggest that there are powerful class connotations to an apparent 'stifling' of 'creativity' whose cultural definition is value-loaded for its working-class members. Similarly the centre participants' interest in breaking down 'barriers of hierarchy' is analysed by Hazan in terms of internal dynamics of the institution. There are parallels with the Normandy clubs' ideal of communitas both in the resistance to hierarchy and in the vision of the centre or club as a place apart. Hazan outlines how the centre participants create a 'new constitution of time' where the future is obliterated and there is a radical break with the past. In my case study from Normandy I suggest that the ideal of communitas in the clubs is not so much an attempt by its working-class or peasant members to create a time-free zone, as one that is class-free, or rather free of the dominant bourgeoisie and its culture outside. Like those at the centre, the Normandy club members also seek an 'alternative viable social reality'. This, however, can be interpreted not so much as a defensive response to the time changes of ageing where there is no future 'achievement' and 'advance' (these are class specific ideals), but as a resistance to the divisions of the wider society within which the working relations of the retired have now changed.

After retirement, so called leisure and cultural pursuits may assume added importance. Those who remain in the smaller rural localities can to some extent resist cultural appropriation by the dominant elite. Those who have migrated to or who have always resided in the more powerful municipality of Bourg find resistance through communitas thwarted. The club for the aged has been incorporated into the bourgeois power structure and its cultural values. It is seen as a resource in the town's political and economic programme which includes the advancement of tourism. The club is encouraged to be visible in terms of specific activities and cultural artefacts which give the town a history and identity of bourgeois refinement. For example, the Club d'Or has produced a series of tapestries now hanging in the assembly room of the Mairie which mark prestigious moments in Bourg's history, e.g. the first performance of Corneille's play in the park, the king's visit in the eighteenth century and the visit by de Gaulle. Only one reference is to its agricultural, peasant connections. There is a pretty scene of peasant women selling flowers and poultry in the square. The tenth anniversary of the club was celebrated by poetry and songs delivered by selected members in satin and lace 'traditional' Normandy costume. The performers were those least likely to have been Normandy *petits cultivateurs*. Their equivalents were instead the spectators at this gathering in the glitteringly refurbished theatre. Thus the town's peasant associations are refined and transformed into the culture of folklore through the agency of the club.

The Jonction club had different cultural priorities. It did not condemn 'innovation and creativity' so long as these were not identified with the dominant structure and its high culture. The theme of oil rich Arabs recognised changes in the world economy and also belied Chapius' (p. 194 above) claim that the rural aged show 'reticence in the face of the current development in ideas and customs'. The choice of both Arabia and Tahiti offered alternative utopian possibilities of wealth and plenty, shared power or equality, most of which had been unavailable in the members' past and which were unavailable in the contemporary French class structure.

Ironically the fact that Tahiti as utopian idyll can be traced back to Diderot and the Enlightenment reveals a link between the leisure pursuits of Jonction and high culture. Diderot intended a critique of French culture which the club members re-enacted. They would, however, have been unimpressed by the cultural pedigree. But if presented as the enactment of a revered literary text, the Tahiti *mardi gras* might have appealed to the Bourg elite, especially if it were discovered that Diderot had once visited the town and drunk its curative waters.

To conclude, this chapter has shown how the elderly cannot be seen as a homogenous group in terms of age and locality, since there are other factors, notably social and economic divisions. Despite claims to the contrary, clubs may be the arena for conflict, and differentiation. Although the ideal for the majority of members was one of communitas where differences should be submerged, this was not achieved where the club was under the control of individuals with contrasting ambitions. The struggle for communitas expressed itself in competing notions of culture attached to games, singing, dancing, food and the celebration of *mardi gras*. In one club, the organisers established a hierarchy of cultural refinement. Other clubs drew on cultural practices consistent with the majority's history as small farmer/peasants or railway workers. Thus 'leisure' activities cannot be seen as culturally neutral.

© 1990 Judith Okely

Note

1. Fieldwork 1985–6 was financed by the ESRC and in 1987 by the Fuller Bequest.

References

Bourdieu, P. (1984) *Distinction: A Social Critique of the Judgement of Taste*, Routledge & Kegan Paul, London.

Bourdieu, P. and Passeron, J.C. (1977) *Reproduction in Education, Society and Culture*, Sage, Beverly Hills, Cal.

Chapius, R. with Brossard, T. (1986) *Les Ruraux Français*, Masson, Paris.

Hazan, H. (1980) *The Limbo People*, Routledge & Kegan Paul, London.

Levet-Gautrat, M. (1985) *A la Recherche du Troisième Âge*, Armand Colin, Paris.

Myerhoff, B. (1978) *Number Our Days*, Dutton, New York.

Phillipson, C. (1988) *Theories of Ageing*, Open University Workshop, London.

Turner, V.W. (1969) *The Ritual Process: Structure and Anti-structure*, Routledge & Kegan Paul, London.

Name index

Aarnio, A. 158
Abbott, P. 137
Abendstern, M. 27
Abrahams, R.G. 23, 26, 157, 159
Ahern, E. 108, 109
Aijmer, G. 109
Almagor, U. 11, 27
Almond, R. 47, 52, 55
Althusser, L. 117
Amoss, P.T. 5, 8, 12, 14, 26, 168, 169
Anderson, B.G. 181
Anderson, D. 136
Anderson, E. 132
Ariès, P. 20, 27
Armstrong, R.P. 123
Aschenbrenner, J. 132
Aspin, D. 104

Barth, F. 9, 11
Baxter, P.T.W. 11, 27
Beall, C.M. 1, 3
Beattie, J.H.M. 68
Beaubier, J. 3, 168
Belsey, C. 76
Berger, P.L. 181
Bernardi, B. 11
Bettelheim, B. 46, 48, 54
Black, M. 104
Blacking, J.A.R. 4, 19, 123, 125, 126,
    128, 129
Blurton Jones, N. 1
Bolinger, D. 103
Bostyn, A.M. 132
Bourdieu, P. 198, 199, 205
Brake, M. 131
Brown, J.K. 14
Brown, P. 131
Bulmer, M. 138

Burridge, K. 51

Cain, L.D. 15–16, 18, 21
Campbell, B. 132, 133
Cavan, R. 23
Chapius, R. 194, 195, 211
Charachidze, G. 97
Charsley, S.R. 11
Chodorow, N. 4
Chu Xi 104, 105, 107, 108, 110, 113
Clark, D.H. 46
Clark, M. 181
Clarke, D. 139
Coffield, F. 131, 132
Cohen, M. 106
Cohen, R. 7
Colson, E. 173
Cooper, D.E. 103, 104
Counts, A.C. 14, 23, 26
Counts, D.R. 14, 23, 26
Cowgill, D.O. 26
Croll, E.J. 21, 26
Culler, J. 76
Cumming, E. 24

Darwin, C.R. 5, 6
Datan, N. 16, 98, 181
Demos, J. 20, 27
Demos, V. 20, 27
Diderot, D. 211
Dilthey, W. 19, 22
Dolhinow, P. 3
Dore, R. 116
Dragadze, T. 16, 26, 89, 90, 91, 93, 94,
    97, 100
Durkheim, E. 25

Eagleton, T. 76

Subject index